Cleanroom Software Engineering

Technology and Process

Stacy J. Prowell

Carmen J. Trammell

Richard C. Linger

Jesse H. Poore

Addison-Wesley

An imprint of Addison Wesley Longman, Inc.

Reading, Massachusetts   Menlo Park, California
New York   Don Mills, Ontario   Wokingham, England
Amsterdam   Bonn   Sydney   Singapore   Tokyo
Madrid   San Juan   Paris   Milan

 Software Engineering Institute

The SEI Series in Software Engineering

The publisher offers discounts on this book when ordered in quantity for special sales. For more information, please contact:

Corporate, Government, and Special Sales
Addison Wesley Longman, Inc.
One Jacob Way
Reading, Massachusetts 01867
(781) 944-3700

Library of Congress Cataloging-in-Publication Data

Cleanroom software engineering : technology and process / Stacy Prowell
   . . . [et al.].
      p.   cm.
   Includes bibliographical references and index.
   ISBN 0-201-85480-5
   1. Software engineering. I. Prowell, Stacy.
QA76.758.C535   1998
005.1—dc21   98–38520
                                                  CIP

Portions of the following publications are used in this book with the permission of CMU/SEI:
Linger, R.C. and Trammell, C.J., Cleanroom Software Engineering Reference Model Version 1.0, CMU/SEI-96-TR-022.
Linger, R.C., Paulk, M.C., and Trammell, C.J., Cleanroom Software Engineering Implementation of the Capability Maturity Model[SM] for Software, CMU/SEI-96-TR-023.
®CMM is registered in the U.S. Patent and Trademark Office.
[SM]Capability Maturity Model is a service mark of Carnegie Mellon University.

ISBN 0-201-85480-5
Text printed on recycled and acid-free paper.
1 2 3 4 5 6 7 8 9 10—MA—0302010099
First printing, February 1999.

This book is dedicated to the founder of Cleanroom software engineering,

Dr. Harlan D. Mills (1919–1996),

whose insights into the mathematical foundations of software
have had a profound and enduring impact on countless students,
practitioners, managers, organizations,
and the entire software engineering profession.

—STACY J. PROWELL,

CARMEN J. TRAMMELL,

RICHARD C. LINGER,

JESSE H. POORE,

1999

Contents

Preface

This book is about Cleanroom software engineering technology and management. It provides an overview of Cleanroom for application to software engineering projects, and a road map for software management, development, and testing as disciplined engineering practices. It serves as an introduction for those who are new to Cleanroom software engineering and as a reference guide for the growing practitioner community.

The book is organized into three parts as follows:

1. *Part I: Cleanroom Software Engineering Fundamentals* is a presentation of Cleanroom theory and engineering practice. The principal Cleanroom practices are described: incremental development under statistical quality control; function-based specification, development, and verification; and statistical testing based on usage models. The Cleanroom Reference Model (CRM) is introduced as a framework for an overall Cleanroom engineering process. A small example, the security alarm, is used in Part I to illustrate practices and work products.

2. *Part II: The Cleanroom Software Engineering Reference Model* provides a process model that can be adopted, tailored, and elaborated by a software engineering organization. The CRM is expressed in 14 Cleanroom processes and 20 work products. Each process is defined in terms of an augmented ETVX (Entry, Tasks, Verification, Exit) model. The CRM is a guide for Cleanroom project performance and process improvement. Chapter 11 relates the CRM to the Key Process Areas of the Capability Maturity Model for Software.

3. *Part III: A Case Study in Cleanroom Software Engineering* presents a large example, the satellite control system, that includes key technical

work products produced in a Cleanroom project: a box structure specification and design, a usage model and usage model analysis.

In many situations, Cleanroom technologies can be applied without special tools. For example, box structure specifications and designs can be recorded using conventional word processors and templates. It is often the case, however, that tools can simplify and improve Cleanroom practice, and help enable scale-up to larger systems. Accordingly, the principal examples in this book are augmented with output from Cleanroom tools to provide additional analysis and insight.

This book is intended to give managers and technical practitioners an understanding of Cleanroom technologies, and to provide an overall process framework for managing Cleanroom projects. Part I describes the underlying theory and the methods of practice, and is recommended for all readers. Part II defines Cleanroom processes and may be used as both a reference and as a guide for management activities. The large case study in Part III will help readers to understand what is produced in a Cleanroom project and to envision how Cleanroom can be applied to their own projects.

We also recommend this book for both undergraduate and graduate students in computer science and software engineering programs. It is important for students to understand the value and necessity for intellectual control in large-scale software engineering, and the importance of the technologies and processes used to achieve it. Of special importance for students is an appreciation of the incremental development life cycle, methods for precise specification, design, and verification, and application of usage-based testing to certify software.

Acknowledgments

The authors thank Ingrid Biery, Laura Prados, and Kirk Sayre for their valuable assistance in the verification of various work products presented herein.

We also thank Helen Goldstein, our editor at Addison-Wesley, for her patience and support in working with us to produce this book.

Introduction

Our Software Society

From its modest beginnings some 50 years ago, computer software has become a critical element of modern society, with global reach and impact on virtually every aspect of human endeavor. Software technology is a principal enabling agent in business, industry, government, and defense, and permeates products and services of all kinds. Every day, trillions of tasks are performed by software, ranging from personal computer applications to large-scale, worldwide networked systems of astonishing complexity. Economic sectors such as manufacturing, banking and financial services, communications, health care, energy, transportation, and education, as well as national defense and government, rely on software for the conduct of daily operations. It is no exaggeration to say that the progress of modern society is dependent totally and irrevocably on software.

As a result, software has become a pivotal component in the global economy. The computer hardware industry relies on software to bring its machines to life, and industries and services of all kinds depend on software to increase productivity and unleash the creativity of millions of workers. Software is a profound agent of change, enabling reengineering of corporations and jobs on an unprecedented scale. It is driving deep structural changes in the global economy through automation and augmentation of mental tasks, much as the industrial revolution in the past century transformed society through automation of physical tasks. In short, software has become a critical resource—vital to well-being and competitiveness.

With the increasing societal dependence on software has come increasing risks of software failure. The vast majority of software today is handcrafted by artisans using craft-based techniques that cannot produce consistent results. These techniques have little in common with the rigorous, theory-based processes characteristic of other engineering disciplines. As a result, software failure is a common occurrence, often with substantial societal and economic consequences. Many software projects simply collapse under the weight of unmastered complexity and never result in usable systems at all.

Software development is a task that challenges the limits of human understanding and control. There is, however, a substantial body of science and engineering knowledge that points the way to disciplined processes for software engineering. This body of science and engineering knowledge is the foundation for Cleanroom software engineering.

Cleanroom Software Engineering

Cleanroom is a theory-based, team-oriented process for the economic production of high-quality software. Cleanroom is theory based because sound theoretical foundations are essential to any engineering discipline, and no amount of good management can substitute for their absence. Cleanroom is team oriented because software is developed by people, and theory must be reduced to practical application to harness human creativity and cooperation. Cleanroom deals with economic production of software because real-world business constraints and resource limitations must be satisfied in software engineering. Finally, Cleanroom deals with production of high-quality software because high quality improves manageability, reduces risks and costs, satisfies customers, and provides a competitive advantage.

Development and Demonstration

The theoretical foundations of Cleanroom were established in the late 1970s and early 1980s, when Harlan Mills, an accomplished mathematician and IBM Fellow, related fundamental ideas in mathematics, statistics, and engineering to software. Influenced by Edsger Dijkstra on structured programming, Nicholas Wirth on stepwise refinement, and David Parnas on modular design, Mills defined the scientific foundations for an engineering approach to software.

Two fundamental insights drove Mills' work: first, that programs are rules for mathematical functions and second, that potential program executions are infinite populations requiring statistical sampling for quality certification. The first insight opened all of function theory to software development and led to the technologies of box structure specification and design, function–theoretic correctness verification, and incremental development. The second insight opened all of statistical theory to software testing and led to the technology of statistical usage testing and quality certification.

Mills' ideas were refined and demonstrated in collaborations with colleagues Alan Currit, Michael Dyer, Alan Hevner, Richard Linger, Bernard Witt, and others in IBM's Federal Systems Division. *Structured Programming: Theory and Practice* (by Linger, Mills, and Witt), published in 1979 by Addison-Wesley, introduced function–theoretic methods for software specification, design, verification, and reengineering. *Principles of Information Systems Analysis and Design* (by Mills, Linger, and Hevner; Academic Press, Inc., 1986) introduced box structure methods for system specification, design, and verification, and introduced incremental development for project management. In 1987 these ideas were integrated under the masthead *Cleanroom*—a term borrowed from the semiconductor industry to reflect an emphasis on defect prevention rather than defect removal. "Cleanroom Software Engineering" (by Mills, Dyer, and Linger) was published in the May 1987 issue of *IEEE Software.*

The first Cleanroom software project was managed by Richard Linger of IBM in the mid 1980s. The COBOL Structuring Facility project developed a commercial software reengineering product that exhibited remarkable levels of quality and reliability in customer use, and provided an initial validation of the Cleanroom process.

Validation and Practice

In 1990 Richard Linger established the IBM Cleanroom Software Technology Center, where further improvements in Cleanroom methods, automation, and technology transfer were achieved. In the early 1990s a mass storage control unit adapter developed using Cleanroom was introduced by IBM. Thousands of units were sold, and after an extended life the product was retired in 1997 without a single field failure reported against the Cleanroom microcode. The development was led by Mike Brewer, and included Paul Fisher, Dave Fuhrer, Karl Nielson, and other team members. Certification testing was led by Joe Ryan and Mike Houghtaling. Today, the testing laboratory in IBM's Storage Systems Division is arguably the world leader in the practice of statistical usage testing of software.

In the late 1980s and early 1990s the highly regarded Software Engineering Laboratory (SEL) at the National Aeronautics and Space Administration (NASA) Goddard Space Flight Center (GSFC) conducted a series of Cleanroom experiments under the guidance of Vic Basili, Scott Green, Rose Pajerski, Jon Valett, and others. The SEL series of Cleanroom experiments are considered by some to be the single most complete research study conducted to date in the field of software engineering. Four ground-control software systems of increasing size were developed using Cleanroom engineering, with results showing consistent improvement in quality and productivity over the already impressive NASA GSFC baseline.

During the formative period of the US Department of Defense (DoD) ARPA STARS Program (Software Technology for Adaptable, Reliable Systems) in the mid 1980s, Cleanroom was selected as a key technology for development and commercialization by STARS leaders, including Dave Ceely, Dick Drake, Bill Ett, Joe Greene, John Foreman, Jim Moore, and others. The company Dr. Mills founded with Arnie Beckhardt to advance Cleanroom—Software Engineering Technology, Inc. (SET)—was selected as the STARS vehicle for commercializing Cleanroom technology. Significant advances in Cleanroom methods and tools were made by SET under STARS support.

At the same time, Dr. Mills was consulting with L.M. Ericsson AB in Europe on the use of Cleanroom in their establishment of a company called Q-Labs that would transfer new software engineering technologies from the research laboratories of the world into Ericsson. Q-Labs and SET were business partners from the early days of both companies, and the two enterprises were merged into Q-Labs in 1998.

In the early 1990s the US Army Picatinny Arsenal conducted a Cleanroom project during which a 20:1 return on investment in Cleanroom technology introduction was realized. In 1996 the DoD Data and Analysis Center for Software reported a substantial cost and quality advantage for Cleanroom in a comparative analysis of software methods. Other organizations with historical data on software productivity and quality have conducted large projects using Cleanroom and have published the results in the open literature. Cleanroom practices have produced dramatic improvements in software project outcomes in IBM, Ericsson, NASA, the DoD, and many other organizations. The data on Cleanroom are in, and they consistently show that substantial improvement in software team performance is possible under Cleanroom discipline.

The Software Engineering Institute (SEI) at Carnegie Mellon University has provided substantial national leadership for improvement in software engineering practice. The SEI Capability Maturity Model for Software (CMM) has become an accepted and widespread management model for improving software engineering practices. In 1996 the SEI completed a project to define a Cleanroom Reference Model and map the engineering technologies of Cleanroom into the management processes of the CMM. The principal finding of this work was that Cleanroom and the CMM are compatible and mutually supporting. This work was disseminated in two SEI technical reports: *Cleanroom Software Engineering Reference Model* (by Linger and Trammell 1996), and *Cleanroom Software Engineering Implementation of the Capability Maturity Model (CMM) for Software* (by Linger, Paulk, and Trammell 1996). The Cleanroom Software Engineering Reference Model is incorporated in this book with the permission of Carnegie Mellon University.

Cleanroom technology has been taught by Mills and his colleagues Vic Basili, Alan Hevner, Richard Linger, Jesse Poore, Dieter Rombach, Shirley Becker, Richard Cobb, Michael Deck, Chuck Engle, Philip Hausler, Ara Kouchakdjian, John Martin, Dave Pearson, Mark Pleszkoch, Stacy Prowell, Steve Rosen, Kirk Sayre, Alan Spangler, Carmen Trammell, Gwen Walton, and

James Whittaker in university and industrial courses throughout the world. Numerous others have contributed to advances in practice through extensive field application, including Mike Brewer, John Gibson, Mike Houghtaling, David Kelly, Jenny Morales, Rob Oshana, Jason Selvidge, Wayne Sherer, and Tom Swain. Each of these persons has contributed to the maturation of Cleanroom as a true engineering discipline for software.

Continuing Evolution

The evolution of an engineering discipline is based on its grounding in science. Refinements in practice flow from following first principles to derive practices and from the thread of connections between bodies of science. Refinements and advances in Cleanroom practice have occurred in exactly this manner, and are ongoing.

A major stream of research to refine the Cleanroom specification method has come to fruition and is incorporated in this book. Mills' use of function theory, inspiring David Parnas' work on sequence (trace) analysis and domain partitioning, in turn inspiring Hailong Mao's work on canonical sequence histories, have all paved the way for Stacy Prowell and Jesse Poore's definition of sequence-based specification that is presented in this book.

In a separate stream of research, Gwen Walton and Jesse Poore have connected Markov chain-based usage models to optimization methods in operations research. Their work on a constraint-based approach to usage modeling holds great promise for increasing control and value in Cleanroom statistical testing practice.

Other work is in progress to harness decision theory, advanced statistical designs, modeling and simulation, and other relevant areas of theory and engineering practice. Continuing improvements to Cleanroom software engineering are certain to follow.

PART I

Cleanroom Software Engineering Fundamentals

1

Cleanroom Overview

1.1 Economic Production of High-Quality Software

Cleanroom software engineering is the practical application of mathematical and statistical science to produce high-quality software in an economical manner. The Cleanroom name was borrowed from the hardware cleanrooms of the semiconductor industry, where defect prevention rather than defect removal is pursued through rigorous engineering processes. The emphasis in Cleanroom is on development of software that is correct by design, followed by certification of software quality in testing. Cleanroom methods are rooted in science, and constitute an engineering process that can be applied to achieve productivity in software development and reliability in software performance. Cleanroom software engineering is designed to achieve two critical goals: a manageable development process and no failures in use.

1.1.1 Manageable Development

Cleanroom methods enable managers and technical teams to maintain intellectual control of software development projects. Intellectual control requires that at each step in development, the status of work in progress is absolutely clear. It requires that work products accumulate into the final product in a predictable way during development, and that the integrity of the product is maintained throughout its life. Intellectual control requires teamwork based on well-defined engineering processes. It results in managing complexity, reducing risks, avoiding rework, and meeting business objectives for schedule and budget performance.

Intellectual control depends on the technologies employed by development teams. Inadequate technologies and processes can result in perplexing and frustrating muddles in software development, where nothing works and no one is to blame, and no amount of good management seems to set things straight. Cleanroom provides methods for precise specification and design, correctness verification, usage testing, and measurement of software quality and reliability. Cleanroom is rooted in theoretical foundations that help guarantee the critical properties of work products that are essential for project manageability and success: mathematical completeness and consistency, verifiable correctness, and traceability among work products.

1.1.2   No Failures in Use

The contemporary attitude toward software failures is to regard them as inevitable. Postproduction defect correction is an institutionalized and accepted process in many software organizations, involving substantial operations that drain productivity and profitability. The tangible costs of software failures—tracking problems, finding and correcting defects, distributing fixes, and so on—are not quantified in most organizations, and are far greater than most people imagine. The intangible costs of software failures in diminished customer confidence and loyalty are difficult to quantify, but obviously drive the total cost even higher.

Most software failures are avoidable. Software failures are the result of ineffective specification and development practices that permit introduction and survival of defects, and testing practices that permit defects to remain undetected, only to be discovered in field use. In Cleanroom, development teams use rigorous specification, design, and verification practices, coupled with testing practices that provide valid measures of development performance in approaching the goal of zero defects. The payoff is improved manageability, reduced rework, and sharp reductions in direct and opportunity costs of defect correction over the market lifetime of products.

1.2 Cleanroom Foundations

Cleanroom theoretical foundations are drawn from mathematics. Harlan Mills identified the appropriate science base for software development with his insight that a computer program implements a mathematical function. His early papers, such as "Mathematical Foundations for Structured Programming," "The New Math of Computer Programming," and "How to Write Correct Programs and Know It," explained that software development is based in mathematical function theory. Similarly, Mills identified the appropriate science base for software testing with his insights about its statistical nature; in other words, software testing amounts to sampling from a usually infinite population of possible uses. His early papers, such as "On the Statistical Validation of Computer Programs," enabled the application of statistical science to software certification. Mills' recognition of the scientific foundations for software has enabled Cleanroom software engineering to evolve as a true engineering discipline for software. The reader who would like firsthand exposure to Mills' foundational ideas may be interested in the 1988 publication of these and other early papers in book form in *Software Productivity* (published by Dorset House).

1.2.1   Function Theory

Cleanroom development methods are based on mathematical function theory. A function defines a mapping from a domain set to a range set. Each element in the domain is mapped to exactly one element in the range. A deterministic program likewise defines a mapping from a domain set (with elements that are every possible input sequence for the program) to a range set (with elements that are the corresponding outputs). The specification for a program is thus the specification of a function, describing the intended mapping from the program's domain (or input sequences) to its range (or output space).

A well-defined function exhibits properties of completeness, consistency, and correctness. Because the specification for a program describes an intended function, the specification should also be complete, consistent, and correct.

- Mathematical *completeness* requires that each element of the domain be mapped to at least one element of the range. That is, every possible input history must be defined and associated with an output.
- Mathematical *consistency* requires that each domain element be mapped to at most one value in the range. That is, every input history must be mapped to only one output.
- *Correctness* of specifications against requirements is a matter of judgment by domain experts. Given a correct specification, however, the correctness of a design with respect to its specification is verifiable using reasoning based on function theory.

The application of mathematical function theory to software development as presented by Linger, Mills, and Witt (1979) was recast as the box structure method for Cleanroom software development by Mills, Linger, and Hevner (1986), in which three functional forms of black box, state box, and clear box were treated explicitly.

1.2.2   Statistical Theory

Cleanroom testing methods are based on statistical science. Statistical testing methods have enjoyed decades of extensive and successful application in engineering. In situations when it is economically or technically infeasible to test all items in a large population, statistical sampling methods are used instead. If the statistics reveal that quality goals are not being met, the production process can be adjusted as necessary. This feedback loop from product measurement to production process is well understood, widely applied, and supported by a substantial body of statistical theory. How can it be applied to software? In manufacturing, the statistics lie in physical variation of items produced; in processes (like package delivery), the statistics lie in deviations from prescribed handling. Where are the statistics in software?

In software, the population to be sampled is the set of all possible scenarios of use. Each element of the population represents a possible execution of the system. The statistics lie in measuring the ability of the system to carry out correctly a sample of these executions. Because this population is infinite, exhaustive testing is impossible, and statistical methods must be used to obtain valid inferences regarding system performance for the entire population. No testing process, no matter how extensive, can sample more than a minute fraction of possible input sequences. All software testing is really sampling from an infinite population.

In Cleanroom, statistical testing supports both product measurement (results of a single development process cycle) and process measurement (results across multiple development process cycles). Cleanroom employs the iterative process of incremental development, which permits the consistency of performance to be measured and improved.

1.2.3   Cleanroom Team Operations

Cleanroom teams perform three principal operations—namely, system specification, development, and certification. Teams are generally small, often on the order of three to eight people, to minimize coordination and to simplify communication. A team member is designated as the team leader. Tasks are assigned and agreed to within a team according to overall team responsibilities and schedule priorities. For small-scale projects, a single team may be sufficient. In this case, all members of the team may perform specification, development, and certification activities at various phases during system development. For medium-scale projects, a team-of-teams approach may be necessary. An initial team is formed, typically comprised of the most experienced people, to specify and define an architecture for the system, to develop and certify an initial increment or two, and to create specifications for subsystems. These team members can then serve as leaders for new teams formed to develop and certify the subsystems. The initial team can always be reconstituted as necessary, for a day or a month or more, to deal with changes in user requirements or development strategies at the system level. For large-scale systems, the team-of-teams approach is required, perhaps with specializations such as specification teams, development teams, and certification teams. Thus, three initial teams might be formed: one to specify a system, one to develop its initial increments, and one to certify the increments. Members of these teams can then lead new specialized teams at the subsystem level. Whatever the organization, all team members require education in Cleanroom technologies. Education can be augmented with on-the-job training under the guidance of experienced team leaders.

Reviews are a crucial part of Cleanroom team operations. Every work product is subject to repeated team review as it is developed from initial concept to final form. Two types of reviews are employed. The first type is called a *development review*. Development reviews focus on technical strategies, better ideas, and team education and communication. For example, a team member may convene a development review for an initial program design strategy summarized in a page or two. The discussion at this point is on strategies for control and data structures, algorithm trade-offs, and so on. The best ideas are then incorporated, perhaps leading to a five-page elaboration for the next development review. Initial development reviews can be short, often on the order of a half hour or so, and may gradually increase in duration as work products evolve. A given work product may go through many development reviews. Efficiencies are gained and time is saved through cumulative knowledge transfer at successive reviews, so that evolving work products become increasingly familiar to team members as the reviews progress. Final work products produced by a team member ultimately incorporate the best ideas of all team members.

Simplification of all work products is an explicit objective in team reviews. The first idea is almost never the best idea, and a key goal of reviews is to develop better ideas in specification, design, and certification. For example, a better idea found early may result in a 1,000-line design instead of a 5,000-line design. It is far easier to verify (and maintain) 1,000 lines than 5,000, and redesign for simplicity and better ideas is almost always an efficient strategy. Simplification often results from identification and reuse of systematic structures, the verification of which can be done once and for all.

The second type of review is called a *verification review*. These reviews focus on correctness and completeness of work products through a formal verification process. These verifications are usually carried out through verbal assertions, with the designer articulating the reasoning required to show that function-based correctness conditions are met. Every condition is checked by the team in turn, with unanimous agreement required. Any changes required must be reverified at a subsequent review. A work product is regarded as correct and complete when no changes are necessary as a result of a verification review. At this point, the entire team assumes ownership of the work product, and any subsequent errors are the responsibility of the team. Verification reviews gain efficiency through the previous knowledge transfer that occurred during development reviews, whereby every participant becomes familiar with the structure and content of the work product being verified. In addition, reused patterns of specification and design can often be employed, with substantial portions of their verifications likewise reusable.

1.3 Cleanroom Technologies

Cleanroom software engineering is characterized by three principal technologies: incremental development under statistical process control; function-based specification, design, and verification; and statistical testing and software certification. These technologies can be used separately or together, and can be introduced in any order to improve software practice.

1.3.1 Incremental Development under Statistical Process Control

Incremental development is based on the engineering principle of controlled iteration in product development. Rather than a single pass through the development process, incremental development involves a series of smaller, cumulative development passes. Each pass (increment) is cumulative, involving all work in previous increments plus some new work. Incremental development is essential to the ability of the development team to maintain intellectual control of a project. Team members thus focus on only a portion of the work at any given time rather than trying to keep all things in mind at once.

An incremental development plan organizes a Cleanroom project into an orderly sequence of development cycles, with some amount of end user function developed in each cycle. The evolving product can be demonstrated to the customer at the end of each increment. With such concrete visibility into a project, the customer can reconfirm or clarify requirements in an informed way, minimizing surprises for either party at the project's completion.

The driver in increment planning is the system architecture. In a mature product line, a reference architecture may dictate the high-level structure and interfaces so that increments are devoted to reusing, modifying, or developing components with a known place in the architecture. In new developments, the top-level architecture will either precede the first increment or be the focus of the first increment, and subsequent increments elaborate stubs (placeholders) in the architecture. In a legacy system, the increment plan may dovetail with a reengineering plan, enabling changes that improve rather than destabilize the system over time. In a maintenance environment, fixes and enhancements are treated as a continuation of incremental development, using the same process discipline that would be applied in new development.

Given a system architecture, numerous factors remain as considerations in increment planning. In an embedded system, coordination with the hardware development schedule may be a factor. In a graphical user interface (GUI) system, the first increment is often devoted to prototyping the user interface, arguably the most volatile aspect of requirements. Because scaffolding is avoided in incremental development, allocation of development tasks across increments nearly always involves some consideration of functional dependencies: A file must be parsed, for example, before its individual tokens can be used for other purposes. Risk, complexity, novelty, reuse, and usage frequency are other factors that may affect increment planning. If possible, the greatest areas of uncertainty are addressed in early increments so that impact on the schedule is understood sooner rather than later.

In addition to the benefits of intellectual control, customer feedback, and risk management, incremental development enables the project team to employ statistical process control. Product quality is measured at the end of each increment and is compared with the team's quality goals. The deviation between actual results and goals is used to determine whether the development process is under control. A minor deviation confirms that the project is on track, whereas an unacceptable deviation occasions a careful performance review. If problems are identified, the team can make process changes to improve performance in the next increment.

1.3.2 Function-Based Specification, Design, and Verification

Cleanroom employs development methods that are both theoretically sound and highly practical. Specification begins with an external view (called the *black box*), is transformed into a state machine view (called the *state box),* and is fully developed into a procedure (called the *clear box).* These distinct but behaviorally equivalent forms are known collectively as *box structures.* Box structures are object based and support key software engineering principles of information hiding and separation of concerns.

A *black box* specification defines the required external behavior of a system or system component in terms of a mapping from the stimulus history (input) to its correct response (output). Only the external behavior is defined; no descriptions of internal state or implementation details are necessary or included. A black box focuses exclusively on defining the user view of a system or system part, where the user may be a person, hardware unit, or another program. Figure 1.1 depicts a conceptual view of a black box. *SH* represents the stimulus history and *R* represents the corresponding response.

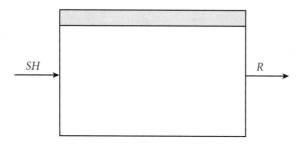

Figure 1.1   Conceptual view of a black box

A stimulus sequence is a series of individual inputs that might be presented to the system. A single stimulus may originate with a human user (e.g., a key press or a mouse click), a hardware component (e.g., a clock pulse or a signal from a sensor), or another software component (e.g., the operating system or a database). A series of these stimuli forms a unique stimulus sequence, which must be mapped to a single response. The black box consists of the stimulus list, the response list, and a stimulus history to response mapping rule for all possible histories of use. A black box is a state-free, procedure-free representation of a function, and the mapping must be complete, consistent, and traceably correct.

The *state box* specification, derived from the black box, is the first step toward implementation. The state box defines the elements of stimulus history that must be stored as state data to achieve the external behavior specified by the black box. A state box defines the required behavior of a system or system part as a mapping (transition) from the current stimulus and old state to the corresponding response and new state. After state data have been defined, it is no longer necessary to consider the stimulus history. Figure 1.2 depicts a conceptual view of a state box.

The state box describes only the response and state update of a system or system component. Procedural implementation details are neither necessary

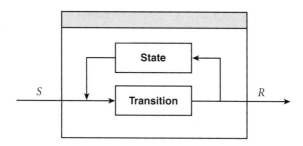

Figure 1.2   Conceptual view of a state box

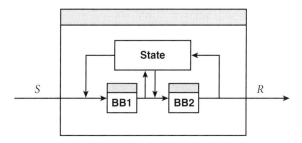

Figure 1.3 Conceptual view of a clear box

nor included. As with the black box, the state box must be complete, consistent, and traceably correct.

A *clear box* specification implements the corresponding state box in procedures that carry out the state box mapping rule, and may introduce new black boxes to represent major operations. The procedure must be sufficient to perform necessary state updates and to create required responses. Figure 1.3 depicts a conceptual view of a clear box, shown as a sequence *control structure*. Alternation (branching), iteration (looping), and concurrent control structures can appear in clear boxes as well. Any new black boxes introduced are subsequently refined into state and clear boxes.

As with the black box and the state box, the clear box must be complete, consistent, and traceably correct. Clear boxes can be defined in design languages or in the target language for a system.

1.3.3 Correctness Verification

In box structure specification and design, a black box is defined to record required behavior, then a state box is refined from the black box to define required state data, and finally a clear box is refined from the state box to define required processing. Each box structure is subject to correctness verification in development team reviews. The team verifies the correctness of each refinement step with respect to the previous step using reasoning based on function theory. In other words, the development team confirms that the stimulus–response mapping defined in one step is preserved in each subsequent step.

For example, in clear box procedure verification, a function–theoretic Correctness Theorem defines conditions to be met for achieving correct programs (Linger, Mills, and Witt 1979). These *correctness conditions* are verified in mental and verbal proofs of correctness in development team verification reviews. Clear box procedures can contain an infinite number of paths that cannot all be checked by path-based inspections or software testing. However, the Correctness Theorem is based on verifying individual control structures rather than tracing paths. Because procedures contain a finite number of control structures, the Correctness Theorem reduces verification to a finite number of checks, and permits all software logic to be verified completely in all possible circumstances of use.

All Cleanroom-developed software is subject to function–theoretic correctness verification by the development team prior to release to the certification test team. A practical and powerful process, verification permits development teams to verify completely the correctness of software with respect to specifications. The verification step is remarkably effective in eliminating defects, and is a major factor in the quality improvements achieved by Cleanroom teams.

1.3.4   Statistical Testing and Software Certification

Cleanroom testing methods are grounded in the fundamental statistical principle that sampling must be used when a population is too large for exhaustive study. A *usage model* is developed to represent the (usually infinite) population of all possible system uses, and test cases are generated from the usage model. Because the test cases are a random sample of the population, valid statistical inferences can be made about expected operational performance of the system.

A usage model represents all possible events in system use and their probabilities of occurrence. Usage models can be conveniently expressed in a number of forms, including Markov models and formal grammars. In the Markov approach, a usage model consists of a set of usage states connected by transition arcs that represent possible stimuli to the system under test, with a probability value associated with each arc. The probability represents the likelihood of choosing a specific transition arc from a given usage state. Test cases are generated by traversing the model from start state to end state, randomly selecting stimuli to include in the test case based on the transition probabilities. Figure 1.4 depicts the look and feel of a usage model. The arcs represent stimuli and the nodes represent usage states. The arcs are labeled with stimuli and probabilities of occurrence.

Usage models are reusable project assets capable of generating any number of test cases. In practice, a number of usage models may be developed to test a system, and various probability distributions may be employed with a given model. For example, many systems provide infrequently used functions with high consequences of failure, such as functions to shut down the reactor in a nuclear power plant. Such functions are typically associated with low probabilities of execution in models of normal usage. Models of safety-critical usage, hazardous usage, malicious usage, or other special usage circumstances are developed when required for focused testing on high-consequence functions. Statistical usage testing can be readily combined with other forms of testing.

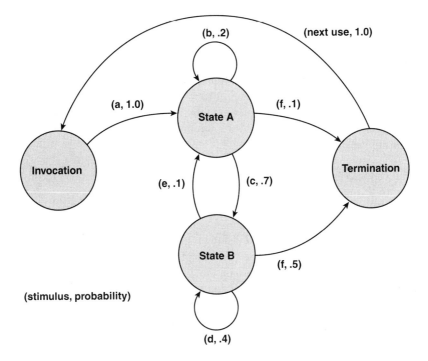

Figure 1.4 A simple usage model

1.4 The Cleanroom Process

The Cleanroom Reference Model (CRM), developed by the Software Engineering Institute (Linger and Trammell 1996), defines a set of integrated processes and work products for Cleanroom project performance. The CRM process flow is depicted in Figure 1.5. The CRM is composed of 14 individual processes for software management, specification, development, and certification:

- The management processes are Project Planning, Project Management, Performance Improvement, and Engineering Change.
- The specification processes are Requirements Analysis, Function Specification, Usage Specification, Architecture Specification, and Increment Planning.
- The development processes are Software Reengineering, Increment Design, and Correctness Verification.
- The certification processes are Usage Modeling and Test Planning, and Statistical Testing and Certification.

The four management processes shown at the top of Figure 1.5 affect all other processes. During the Project Planning process, the team tailors the Cleanroom process for the project environment, and creates and maintains software development plans. These plans are used during the Project Management process for managing and controlling incremental development and certification. The Performance Improvement process is used to assess project performance continually and to identify and to implement improvements. The Engineering Change process provides configuration management and engineering discipline for all change activity.

The Architecture Specification process likewise spans the life cycle and defines architectural structures and strategies. Aspects of a project from requirements to low-level design may be affected by architecture.

The Requirements Analysis process is used to create an initial definition of customer requirements. This definition is then expressed in precise terms in the Function Specification process (producing a specification of external behavior) and the Usage Specification process (producing a specification of users, usage environments, and patterns of use of the software system). The Increment Planning process allocates specified software functions to a series of increments, and schedules their development and certification within the structure of the overall project schedule.

The development and certification processes are shown on the right side of Figure 1.5 in "stacked" boxes, which represent successive increments. The

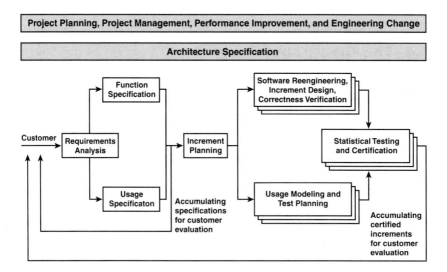

Figure 1.5   Cleanroom Reference Model

Software Reengineering process prepares existing software for use in an increment. The Increment Design and Correctness Verification processes are employed to develop the design and code for an increment, and to verify their correctness. The Usage Modeling and Test Planning process is conducted in parallel with development activity in each increment, and produces test cases generated from usage models. The Statistical Testing and Certification process is employed to assess an increment's fitness for use. On completion of each increment, the customer evaluates the executing system and provides feedback for requirements validation. As shown by the feedback loop from the completed increment to the beginning of the process, high-level specification processes may be revisited prior to each increment to incorporate clarifications to requirements resulting from customer evaluation of an increment.

1.5 Relationship of Cleanroom to Other Practices

Many of the best software engineering practices currently in use are strongly supported by the Cleanroom process.

1.5.1 Object Orientation

Cleanroom processes provide manageability and technical rigor for object-oriented development (Ett and Trammell 1995). Objects are essentially state machines with encapsulated data and a set of services. A Cleanroom component is defined in a black box view (an object's external behavior), a state box view (an object's encapsulated data), and a clear box view (services that process external requests and access encapsulated data). A Cleanroom component is an object in the most technical sense. Cleanroom box structures can help produce complete, consistent, and correct specification of object behavior. Moreover, box structures help define and manage data and control flow among objects.

In Cleanroom, mathematical formalisms underlie specification, design, correctness verification, and certification testing. These mature formalisms can add rigor and predictability to comparatively heuristic object-oriented approaches. Cleanroom is a process for application engineering rather than domain engineering. The common strength of object-oriented methods is their pursuit of abstractions and relationships that are characteristic of applications in a domain. Cleanroom application engineering can be complemented by object-oriented domain analysis.

1.5.2   Software Reuse

Successful reuse of software components requires precise definition of component functional semantics, and certification of component quality and reliability for particular usage environments. Without this knowledge, reuse can be an unpredictable and risky undertaking.

Cleanroom black box specifications can be used to define component semantics in all possible circumstances of use. If the scope of intended reuse is narrower than the scope of the component (e.g., reduced variable range), a specification of reduced scope can be developed by restricting the domain of the black box function. A "wrapper" (a component to contain the reused component) may be created to enforce preconditions for component invocation.

More often, the fitness of an existing component for reuse is assessed through execution experiments. Cleanroom certification through statistical usage-based testing can provide measures of component quality and reliability for given environments of use. Statistical testing allows assessment of component reliability at specified levels of confidence for specified usage conditions.

A quantitative approach to reuse analysis has been advanced by Poore, Mills, and Mutchler (1993) in connection with Cleanroom reliability planning. With this approach, component reliabilities and transition probabilities in the top-level design are established. A quantitative analysis of the top-level component network is performed, yielding information about the upper bound on system reliability given the reliability of components. The results of this analysis may be used to evaluate the viability of component reuse.

1.5.3   Software Architectures

Among the many definitions of software architecture, one theme is constant: An architecture defines primary system components and their connections. Cleanroom provides a process for precise definition of the functional semantics of an architecture—what the components are and what kind of connections they have.

The high-level internal design issues in the Cleanroom state box and clear box concern primary system components and their connections: Primary data objects are invented in state box design, and primary operations on data objects are invented in clear box design. The final, high-level clear box design embodies major elements of the system architecture.

Cleanroom specification and design involves systematic exploration of a system's solution space. The black box to state box relationship is one to many. A set of objects must be chosen. The state box to clear box relationship is also one to many. A set of object operations must be chosen. Classifications of design patterns are emerging from the evolving field of software architectures, and the Cleanroom practitioner's design choices during box structure system design will be facilitated as design patterns are cataloged.

In short, Cleanroom systems have always had explicit architectures, but they have been unnamed (other than "system top-level clear box"). The naming and characterization of design patterns that is occurring in the study of software architectures will expedite the evaluation of design choices in Cleanroom projects as it will in software projects in general.

1.5.4   Inspections and Reviews

Cleanroom correctness verification permits additional technical rigor and precision in inspections and reviews. Beyond local checklists that may be used, a Cleanroom review of design and code artifacts employs reasoning based on function theory: A program (the code) implements a function (the specification). The purpose of a Cleanroom review is to verify that the correctness of the function specification has been preserved in the implementation. Code is never reviewed in a vacuum; it is always reviewed against the function specification it implements.

Cleanroom specification and design produce artifacts with built-in traceability. Peer review is employed at each step in box structure specification and design. Every work product is reviewed; every team member is responsible for the correctness of every work product. Ultimate successes are regarded as team successes, and failures as team failures. The combination of technically sound practices and team accountability for correctness results in an extremely effective approach to defect prevention.

1.5.5   Software Testing Methods

Cleanroom testing based on usage models produces statistically valid inferences about expected operational performance of a given version of the software. Cleanroom usage models can be configured for other testing objectives as well, such as maximizing coverage or emphasizing critical functions. Usage models provide a scientific basis for model coverage testing, random testing, importance testing, partition testing, and other forms of testing.

Crafted testing can be used within a Cleanroom process as well. There are compelling reasons for creating special test cases that can remove uncertainty about how the system will perform under specific circumstances. Additionally, code coverage tools that run in the background may be used as a complement to usage testing. Regression testing, structural (white box) testing, and other traditional testing approaches are compatible with Cleanroom.

1.6 Cleanroom Project Experience

First demonstrated in the IBM Federal Systems Division in the early 1980s, Cleanroom methods have now been used in industry and government software organizations around the world. The award-winning National Aeronautics and Space Administration Software Engineering Laboratory (SEL) at the Goddard Space Flight Center conducted a well-documented series of Cleanroom projects, concluding that Cleanroom results improved on the SEL baseline. The US Army Picatinny Arsenal demonstrated a return on investment in Cleanroom technology of more than 20:1 over a five-year period. Ongoing research and technology transfer by the University of Tennessee has produced a stream of advances in Cleanroom methods that have extended Mills' original ideas, with powerful connections to related areas of science.

The effectiveness of the Cleanroom process has been demonstrated in projects from embedded software systems for computer hardware and telephone switches to software language and computer-aided software engineering tool products. Published accounts of Cleanroom projects by AT&T, Ericsson, IBM, Texas Instruments, the US Army, the US Navy, and others are listed in the reading list at the end of this chapter.

Organizations have reported significant gains in productivity and quality, as well as additional benefits in improved development team morale and confidence. In an era when software projects are notoriously unpredictable, Cleanroom organizations are exhibiting not just control but steady improvement.

1.7 References

W.H. Ett and C.J. Trammell. "A Guide to Integration of Object-Oriented Methods and Cleanroom Software Engineering." 1995. URL: http://source.asset.com/start/loral/cleanroom/guide.html.

R.C. Linger, H.D. Mills, and B.I. Witt. *Structured Programming: Theory and Practice*. Reading, MA: Addison-Wesley, 1979.

R.C. Linger and C.J. Trammell. *Cleanroom Software Engineering Reference Model*. Pittsburgh, PA: Software Engineering Institute, Carnegie Mellon University, 1996.

H.D. Mills, R.C. Linger, and A.R. Hevner. *Principles of Information Systems Analysis and Design*. Orlando, FL: Academic Press, 1986.

H.D. Mills. *Software Productivity*. New York: Dorset House, 1988.

J.H. Poore, H.D. Mills, and D. Mutchler. "Planning and Certifying Software System Reliability." *IEEE Software* vol. 10 (January 1993): 88–99.

1.8 Suggested Reading

K. Agrawal and J.A. Whittaker. "Experiences in Applying Statistical Testing to a Real-Time, Embedded Software System," in *Proceedings of the Pacific Northwest Software Quality Conference,* Pacific Northwest Software Quality Conference (Portland OR: October 1993), 154–170.

Air Force Space and Warning Systems Center and the DoD Software Technology for Adaptable, Reliable Systems (STARS) Program. "Demonstration project on a product-line approach to the development and evolution of software systems in two command and control (C2) systems." 1996. URL: http://www.asset.com/stars/loral/pubs/exprpt96/main.htm.

V.R. Basili, et al. "SEL's Software Process-Improvement Program." *IEEE Software* vol.12 (November 1995): 83–87.

V.R. Basili and S.E. Green. "Software Process Evolution in the SEL." *IEEE Software* vol. 11 (July 1994): 58–66.

M. Brewer, P. Fisher, D. Fuhrer, K. Nielsen, and J.H. Poore. "The Application of Cleanroom Software Engineering to the Development of Embedded Control System Software," in *Proceedings of the 2nd European Industrial Symposium on Cleanroom Software Engineering,* Lund, Sweden: Q-Labs, (March 1995) paper #12.

M. Donnelly, B. Everett, J. Musa, and G. Wilson. "Best Current Practice of SRE," in *Handbook of Software Reliability Engineering,* ed. M.R. Lyu (New York: McGraw-Hill, 1995), 219–254.

P.A. Hausler, R.C. Linger, and C.J. Trammell. "Adopting Cleanroom Software Engineering with a Phased Approach." *IBM Systems Journal* vol. 3, no. 1 (1994): 89–109.

D. Kelly and R. Oshana. "Integrating Cleanroom Software Methods into an SEI Level 4–5 Program," *Crosstalk* vol. 9 (November 1996): 16–22.

R.C. Linger and H.D. Mills. "A Case Study in Cleanroom Software Engineering: The IBM COBOL Structuring Facility," in *Proceedings of the 12th Annual International Computer Software and Applications Conference (COMPSAC '88),* (Los Alamitos, CA: IEEE Computer Society Press, 1988), 10–17.

R.C. Linger. "Cleanroom Process Model." *IEEE Software* vol. 11 (March 1994): 50–58.

H.D. Mills, M. Dyer, and R.C. Linger. "Cleanroom Software Engineering." *IEEE Software* vol. 4 (September 1987): 19–24.

R. Oshana. "Quality Software via a Cleanroom Methodology." *Embedded Systems Journal* vol. 9 (September 1996): 36–52.

R. Oshana. "Software Testing with Statistical Usage-Based Models." *Embedded Systems Journal* vol. 10 (January 1997): 40–55.

D.L. Parnas. "On the Criteria To Be Used in Decomposing Systems into Modules." *Communications of the ACM* vol. 15, 12 (December 1972): 1053–1058.

R.W. Selby, V.R. Basili, and F.T. Baker. "Cleanroom Software Development: An Empirical Evaluation." *IEEE Transactions on Software Engineering* vol. SE-13 (September 1987): 1027–1037.

S.W. Sherer, A. Kouchakdjian, and P.G. Arnold. "Experience Using Cleanroom Software Engineering." *IEEE Software* vol. 13 (March 1996): 69–76.

A.M. Stavely. *Toward Zero-Defect Programming*. Reading, MA: Addison-Wesley, 1999.

L.G. Tann. "OS32: A Cleanroom Success Story," in *Proceedings of the 1st European Industrial Symposium on Cleanroom Software Engineering* (Lund, Sweden: Q-Labs, 1993), paper #5.

C.J. Trammell, L.H. Binder, and C.E. Galbraith. "The Automated Production Control Documentation System: A Case Study in Cleanroom Software Engineering." *ACM Transactions on Software Engineering and Management* vol. 1 (January 1992): 81–94.

J.A. Whittaker and K. Agrawal. "A Case Study in Software Reliability Measurement," in *Proceedings of the Seventh International Software Quality Week* (San Francisco, CA: Software Research, Inc. 1995).

2

Cleanroom Management
by Incremental Development

Incremental development under statistical quality control is the Cleanroom
approach to establishing and maintaining management control of a software
project. Incremental development was proposed by Mills in the early 1970s, but
did not gain prominence until the late 1980s when Cleanroom articles and field
reports by Mills and associates began to appear. In his influential commentary
on software practice, "No Silver Bullet: Essence and Accidents of Software
Engineering," Fred Brooks described the profound effects of the incremental
development approach.

> Some years ago Harlan Mills proposed that any software system should be
> grown by incremental development [Mills 1971]. That is, the system should
> first be made to run, even if it does nothing useful except call the proper set of
> dummy subprograms. Then, bit by bit, it should be fleshed out, with the sub-
> programs in turn being developed—into actions or calls to empty stubs in the
> level below.
>
> I have seen most dramatic results since I began urging this technique.
> Nothing in the past decade has so radically changed my own practice, or its
> effectiveness. The approach necessitates top-down design, for it is a top-down
> growing of the software. It allows easy backtracking. It lends itself to early
> prototypes. Each added function and new provision for more complex data or
> circumstances grows organically out of what is already there.
>
> The morale effects are startling. Enthusiasm jumps when there is a run-
> ning system, even a simple one. Efforts redouble when the first picture from a
> new graphics software system appears on the screen, even if it is only a rectan-
> gle. One always has, at every stage in the process, a working system. I find that
> teams can *grow* much more complex entities . . . than they can *build*. (Brooks
> 1987, p. 18)

Brooks' observations have been borne out in industrial practice. Incremental development enables early and continual quality assessment and user

feedback, and facilitates process improvements as development progresses. The incremental approach avoids risks inherent in component integration late in the development cycle. Incremental development also permits systematic incorporation of requirements changes throughout the development cycle.

The technical basis for incremental development is the property of referential transparency. In the context of software development, this property requires that a specification and its implementation define the same mathematical function. When this property holds, a design can be shown to be correct with respect to its specification. The key ideas in incremental development are summarized in the following section.

2.1 Benefits of Incremental Development

Large software systems are organized collections of parts. The way a system is composed from parts has a critical impact on project success. Incremental development is a top-down approach to development in which a software system is developed and tested as a succession of cumulative subsets of function. A minimal system is developed in the first increment, and function is added in each successive increment until the system is complete. This controlled growth of a software system benefits customers, managers, and technical staff alike.

2.1.1 Visibility into Progress

With incremental development, each increment implements one or more end user functions. Each increment contains all previously developed functionality plus some new function; the system is "grown" in cumulative increments. At the end of the first increment, for example, one can be confident that 20% of the system is 100% complete, rather than speculating that 100% of the system is 20% complete.

2.1.2 Intellectual Control

Incremental development enables intellectual control over system development through referential transparency. This property—substitution of equals for equals—is satisfied when subspecifications for functions to be implemented in later increments are embedded in the procedural logic of the current increment. When referential transparency holds, a system part can be implemented from its subspecification with no need for backtracking. There is no rework of previous increments. This strategy enables correctness verification of each increment within a complete system context.

2.1.3 Incremental System Integration

Cleanroom incremental development permits continual integration of referentially transparent user–function increments over the entire development life cycle. Because the design of each increment is based on a verified subspecification and a tested interface in a prior increment, deep design and interface errors are rare. The system evolves in well-defined increments throughout the development process. Testing and certification activities begin early in the development cycle.

2.1.4 Continual Quality Feedback through Statistical Process Control

Incremental development as practiced in Cleanroom provides a basis for statistical process control. Each Cleanroom increment is a complete cycle of the process, involving specification, development, and verification of new user function plus testing of all work completed to date. As is typical in statistical process control, measures of performance in each iteration of the process are compared with performance targets to determine whether or not the process is "in control" (i.e., occurring as expected).

Typically, a Cleanroom team uses measures of product performance in testing as a gauge of process control. Measures such as errors per 1,000 lines of code, mean time to failure (MTTF), or reliability and confidence are commonly used. Other measures of process control might relate to management issues rather than product quality. Schedule conformance, budget conformance, conformance to the staffing plan, and so forth, all compare actual performance with performance goals in the increment. The standards against which Cleanroom increments are measured represent the specific level of process control a team requires to continue a project as planned. If standards are not met, the team can examine performance data from the increment to identify problems, adjust project plans if necessary, and modify the software development process to prevent recurrence of the problems identified. For example, if testing of an increment reveals that the process is "out of control" (i.e., quality standards are not being met), testing ceases and developers return to the design stage. If the process is in control, work on the next increment can continue.

Statistical process control (SPC) is a mature engineering practice affording well-developed techniques for data collection and analysis. A wealth of methods and tool support is available to those who wish to pursue advanced practice. Rudimentary practice of SPC, however, requires little investment or effort, and can result in substantial payoffs. The essential events in any application of statistical process control are simple: Measure performance in each process cycle, compare actual performance with predefined performance targets, identify the causes of unacceptable deviation, and address causes through process changes intended to improve future performance.

For example, if a Cleanroom team customarily produces a product that exhibits three or fewer failures per 1,000 lines of code in testing, then an increment exhibiting five failures per 1,000 lines is likely to represent an unacceptable deviation. On investigation, the team may discover that the failures were caused by errors that were in fact found during verification, but that the code was not reverified to confirm the correctness of changes. From this analysis, the team realizes that verification should not be regarded as complete until all changes to erroneous code have been verified to be correct. The team modifies the verification process accordingly, determined to prevent failures caused by incorrect fixes in future increments. In this way, feedback produced in each increment is used to improve the process in the next increment.

The strength in SPC lies in the ongoing examination of actual versus planned performance, identifying the causes of unacceptable deviations, and making specific process changes to regain or improve control. A Cleanroom team practices these fundamentals, and goes further. Each Cleanroom increment is tested against expectations of perfection. Any failure is regarded as unacceptable. Errors causing failures are analyzed carefully for what they reveal about the development process. What was the source of the error? Why was the error missed in team review? How can the process be improved so that similar errors are not made in the future? Cleanroom teams genuinely strive for perfection, and SPC is the engineering discipline for gauging and advancing the team's efforts.

2.1.5 Continual Functional Feedback through Customer Use

Incremental development enables early and continual feedback by customers on the executing functionality of an evolving system, to permit changes if necessary. Because the increments execute in a system environment and represent subsets of user function, early increments can be exercised by users for feedback on system functionality and usability. Such feedback helps avoid developing the wrong system and builds user acceptance of the eventual product.

2.1.6 Accommodation of Change

Incremental development allows systematic accommodation of inevitable changes in system requirements and the project environment. At the completion of each increment, the impact of accumulated changes in system requirements can be assessed in terms of current specifications and increment designs. If changes are isolated to future increments, they can often be incorporated within the existing incremental development plan, with possible adjustments to schedules and resources. If changes affect completed increments, modified system development can begin from the top down, usually with substantial (often total) reuse of code from existing increments, with adjustments to schedules and resources as required.

2.1.7 Schedule and Resource Management

Project resources can be allocated in a controlled manner through incremental development. The available schedule is a factor in determining the number of increments to be developed and their size. With a short schedule, a small number of increments will help maintain sufficient intervals between increment deliveries to the certification team to permit an orderly testing process. However, this places a greater burden on the development teams to design and implement larger, more complex increments. Schedule and complexity trade-offs can be reflected in the incremental development plan. In addition, feedback from successive increments provides management with objective measures of process and product performance to permit accommodation of shortfalls or windfalls in development and testing.

2.2 Theoretical Foundations of Incremental Development

Incremental development as practiced in the Cleanroom process is based on the principle of referential transparency. Referential transparency means that the only thing that matters about an expression is its value, and any subexpression can be replaced by any other that is equal in value. Referential transparency implies that the relevant lower level details of an entity are abstracted rather than omitted in a particular system of higher level description, so that the higher level description contains everything needed to understand the entity when placed in a larger context. The concept of referential transparency has been applied in a wide range of areas, such as computer science, linguistics, mathematics, and logic.

2.2.1 Referential Transparency in Arithmetic

Referential transparency is the property that guarantees that evaluation of lengthy arithmetic expressions one term at a time will produce the right answer. For example, in the expression $(6 + 2) \times (5 - 3)$, because $6 + 2 = 8$, the expression is equivalent to $8 \times (5 - 3)$, and because $5 - 3 = 2$, it is also equivalent to 8×2. Finally, because $8 \times 2 = 16$, it is equivalent to 16. Referential transparency guarantees that one can replace $(6 + 2)$ by 8 unconditionally; without worrying, for example, about whether the result will go on to be multiplied by

(5 − 3), or subtracted from 17, or whatever. Referential transparency is established once and for all in the formal logic of arithmetic.

Note that because of referential transparency, each step, properly done, progresses toward the correct answer. Thus, in this three-step problem we can say with confidence that after the first step is finished, the solution is one-third complete; that is, previous steps need not be revisited to complete subsequent steps. In addition, because each step has no side effects on other steps, terms at the same level can be evaluated in any order. Thus, the property has analogs to important software concepts of abstraction, specification, progress toward solution, and absence of side effects.

2.2.2   Referential Transparency in Software

The basis for incremental development in software lies in the view of programs and program parts as rules for mathematical functions (Linger, Mills, and Witt 1979). This view regards program development as a top-down refinement of functions (specifications) into control structures and subfunctions (subspecifications). Such refinement may result in object-based or functional decompositions, or a combination of the two. For example, a given function (specification) f could be refined into any of the following

do $f1$; $f2$ enddo	Sequence
if p then $f1$ else $f2$ endif	Alternation
while p do $f1$ enddo	Iteration

where $f1$ and $f2$ represent subfunctions (subspecifications) for further refinement. The successive function refinements must maintain functional equivalence for correctness verification at each step. For example, in the previous sequence refinement, the composition of subfunctions $f1$ and $f2$ must be equivalent in net effect on data to the original function f. Referential transparency requires that any function (f, $f1$, or $f2$) specify completely the required net effect of processing at the point it appears in the design, and no further information or reference to other design parts be required for its independent refinement.

Because of referential transparency, the verification of any refinement step can be conducted independently of any other refinement step. This means that the system architecture can be verified in early increments, before most of the system components have been written, and that the architecture need not be reverified in later increments. Note, however, that the specifications of system components enter into the architecture verification, and in fact provide the precise interface documentation required to guarantee that the system as a whole will perform as required when coding is complete.

An illustration of function refinement with referential transparency at the programming level is shown in Figure 2.1. The two-step refinement on the right side of the figure maintains function equivalence at each step. First, the initial specification *f* is refined into loop initialization code *g* and subspecification *k*, where *k* completely specifies interfaces and the required net effect of processing at that point in the design. Next, subspecification *k* is refined into an iteration in a second step. These expansion steps are referentially transparent, and represent possible increment definitions. In this case, the first increment would contain the loop initialization code represented by *g*, with the subspecification *k* defined and connected in the sequence for verification against *f*, but stubbed off in the code. A crucial point is that the sequence of code *g* followed by subspecification *k* is functionally equivalent to the original specification *f*. The second increment would refine *k* into the `whiledo` iteration, which is functionally equivalent to *k*. Other design strategies, such as the one given on the left side of Figure 2.1, would violate referential transparency and forfeit intellectual control of top-down design. The difference between these approaches may seem minor in this simple example, but if *g* and *k* represent 50,000 lines of code (KLOC) and 500 KLOC respectively, with a complex interface between them, referentially transparent increments could mean the difference between success and failure of the project.

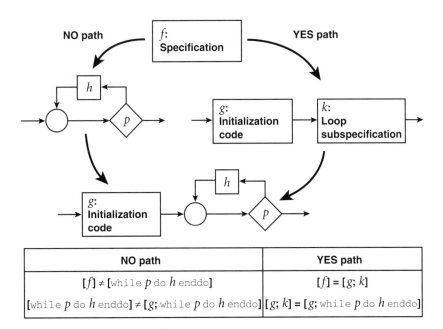

NO path	YES path
$[f] \neq [$while p do h enddo$]$	$[f] = [g;\ k]$
$[$while p do h enddo$] \neq [g;$ while p do h enddo$]$	$[g;\ k] = [g;$ while p do h enddo$]$

Figure 2.1　An illustration of referential transparency in refinement

2.3 Increment Planning in Practice

The overall objective of and constraint on incremental development is to grow a system with each new increment as an elaboration of the functions implemented in prior increments. That is, new functions in an increment should "plug in" to the previous increment at predefined points in its structure and should satisfy the subspecifications associated with the processing requirements at those points. This process of function allocation is the practical application of referential transparency to incremental development planning. Thus, logical allocation of functions to increments based on relationships among functions and intrinsic functional dependencies will predominate in the definition of increment content. In a database system, for example, functions to add data would typically precede functions to delete data. In a statistical system, functions to collect and enter data would ordinarily precede functions to analyze data and report results.

Within the framework of functional dependencies exhibited by a system, increment planning is also influenced by a wide range of management and technical factors in a project. These factors are discussed in the following pages.

2.3.1   Customer Needs

The customer may wish to place certain system functions into operational use prior to system completion. Such functions are likely candidates for early increments.

2.3.2   Clarification of Requirements

The common motivation behind iterative development methods is the fact that requirements can rarely be established with certainty at the outset of a project. With incremental development, customers provide feedback on an evolving system by direct operation of user-executable increments. The relative clarity of requirements may influence an increment plan in two ways. Volatile requirements may be implemented in an early increment so they can be clarified. Alternatively, unstable requirements may be planned for later implementation, when questions affecting the requirements have been settled. If the user interface is not well established, for example, it is an ideal candidate for an early increment. (Some would say that the user interface is invariably the most volatile aspect of the system and should always be implemented in the first increment.) On the other hand, requirements to be settled by concurrent research (e.g., performance benchmarking) might be scheduled for a later increment, after research results are known.

2.3.3 Operational Usage Probabilities

A functional usage distribution is developed as part of a top-level Cleanroom specification. Expected usage probabilities of system functions are established from historical data and estimates provided by customers. System functions with high expected usage probabilities will receive the greatest exposure in the field and may therefore benefit from the greatest exposure to testing. Because increments are cumulative, the functions developed in early increments will be tested every time a new increment enters the testing process. System functions expected to receive the greatest operational usage by customers, therefore, are candidates for early increments. Some functions expected to receive low usage may even be regarded as optional, and may be scheduled for development in the final increment if time permits.

2.3.4 Reliability Management

Increasingly, customers are specifying formal software reliability requirements. Poore, Mills, and Mutchler (1993) described an approach to increment planning based on reliability requirements for subsystems in a high-level design. Given a total system reliability requirement and transitional probabilities between subsystems, the reliability requirement for each subsystem may be calculated. Subsystems with the highest reliability requirements will have the greatest impact on total system reliability, and may be candidates for early increments.

2.3.5 Systems Engineering

Controlled iteration is a key engineering principle in hardware development. The minimal machine is often constructed in the first iteration and then enhanced in subsequent iterations until the complete machine has been built. Incremental development of software is entirely compatible with this standard approach to hardware development. Machines with embedded software must be developed as a coordinated effort between hardware and software engineers, and incremental development is an ideal framework for this coordination. A machine must be powered on, for example, before it can be used. The software for system start-up, therefore, would likely be among the functions implemented in the first increment of an embedded software project.

2.3.6 Technical Challenges

Novel or particularly complex components may pose a risk to the schedule or even the viability of a project. If such work is scheduled for an early increment, the experience obtained will either lend support to existing plans or suggest revisions. If aspects of a project are not novel or complex in absolute terms, but are indeed novel or complex relative to the experience of the team, an early gauge of team performance and schedule feasibility is still desirable.

2.3.7 Leveraging Reuse

The Cleanroom process emphasizes economy of effort through reuse of components across projects, and identifies opportunities to develop "common services" for use in multiple places within a system. When existing components are identified as potentially reusable, the development team must evaluate the relative effort required to tailor them for use in the new system versus development of new components from scratch. If the evaluation is in favor of reuse, the team may want to include the components in an early increment to validate their expected performance. New common services may be desirable candidates for an early increment as well. Because common services are used in multiple places in a system, they may have a greater impact on system reliability relative to other single-instance components. Because existing objects may be reusable components, the rationale for object development in an incremental development plan follows the rationale for reusable components in general.

2.4 Incremental Development in Practice

An illustration of an application developed under incremental development is presented in Figure 2.2. The successive increments in Figure 2.2 represent an unfolding of the "stacked" increments in the CRM work flow diagram in Figure 1.5.

The incremental development plan in Figure 2.2 divides the project into four increments with reuse of existing components in several increments. The top-level architecture is established during increment 1. Three lower level subsystems are defined, and one is implemented. The implemented subsystem includes a reused component. Stubs are used for the subsystems that will be implemented during later increments. The stubs are not merely placeholders; they include an interface specification and function specification so the relationship between implemented functions and stubbed functions is well defined. On completion, increment 1 is evaluated by the user. As a consequence of user feedback, a component in increment 1 is slated for change during increment 2.

A second subsystem is implemented during increment 2, replacing a stub in increment 1. Another preexisting component is used in increment 2, and modified to accommodate one additional function. The additional function is specified in increment 2, but is not slated for implementation until the final increment.

Implementation of the third subsystem begins during increment 3. The third subsystem includes one new component, one reused component, and one stub. User evaluation of increment 3 results in a change to one component during increment 4.

Increment 4, like all preceding increments, is the accumulation of all work so far, plus some new work. During increment 4, all remaining stubs are implemented. As the final increment, increment 4 represents the completed system.

The treatment of stubbed parts of the system is critical to the integrity of the design. Correctness verification of each increment requires that specifications for later increments appear in the procedural logic at their proper points of execution. The completeness of the design in each increment ensures the smooth integration of new work as development progresses.

Figure 2.3 shows the incremental development portion of the schedule for the project. After top-level specification, an incremental development plan is established. Both the specification and the incremental development plan are subject to revision after each increment based on development experience, quality measures, and customer feedback. After each increment is fully specified, designed, and verified, it is submitted for independent certification testing. The measures of quality in certification testing (e.g., MTTF, reliability, errors per KLOC) are gauges of development process control. If measured quality meets established standards, development proceeds. If not, problems are assessed and action is taken to improve the development process.

After increment 1 is submitted for certification testing, development of increment 2 begins based on its embedded specification in increment 1. If more than one development team is available, parallel development of increment 3 may also begin.

Incremental development affords customer feedback on the evolving system, intellectual control of the technical work, and management control of the

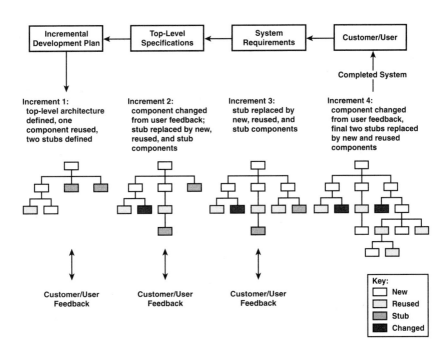

Figure 2.2   An example of incremental development and feedback

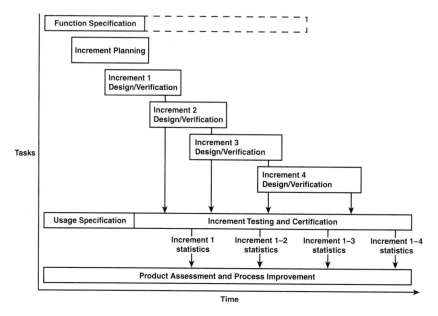

Figure 2.3 A sample increment construction plan

schedule and budget. User feedback on each increment is a gauge of whether the right system is being built, and quality measures in each increment are a gauge of whether the system is being built right. Product quality and process control are both supported.

2.5 References

F.P. Brooks. "No Silver Bullet: Essence and Accidents of Software Engineering." *Computer* vol. 20, no. 4 (April 1987): 10–19.

R.C. Linger, H.D. Mills, and B.I. Witt. *Structured Programming: Theory and Practice*. Reading, MA: Addison-Wesley, 1979.

H.D. Mills. "Top-Down Programming in Large Systems." In *Debugging Techniques in Large Systems*. ed. R. Ruskin, Englewood Cliffs, NJ: Prentice Hall, 1971.

J.H. Poore, H.D. Mills, and D. Mutchler. "Planning and Certifying Software System Reliability." *IEEE Software* vol. 10, no. 1 (January 1993): 88–99.

3

Cleanroom Software Specification

A fundamental change in the way computer programs were written occurred in the 1970s. Prior to that time, the absence of engineering foundations for program development, coupled with the increasing demand for large programs, had led to growing use of arbitrary control logic, with a complexity that defied human understanding. This complexity was addressed by the theory and practice of structured programming. Programs of any complexity whatsoever could be designed by nesting and sequencing just three fundamental control structures—namely, sequence (`do`), alternation (`ifthenelse`), and iteration (`whiledo`)—again and again in a hierarchical structure. Structured programming was an engineering process that benefited not only developers, but managers as well. In particular, managers of large software projects found that work could be structured and measured through top-down development in a systematic way.

Software system development, however, requires more than systematic control flow. Today's large-scale systems involve massive amounts of data and operations to store, retrieve, transmit, and process data on an enterprise-wide basis. In the absence of engineering foundations for system development, these operations can accumulate into data complexities with a similar loss of intellectual control. This chapter describes three system structures for specification and design—black box, state box, and clear box—known collectively as *box structures* (Mills 1988; Mills, Linger, and Hevner 1986, 1987). These structures embody important concepts of data encapsulation and information hiding. Box structures are developed in a stepwise refinement and verification process that integrates both system control and data operations. Systems can be developed by nesting and sequencing these structures again and again in a provable way. As a result, both developers and project managers benefit from improved intellectual control of software development projects.

3.1 Box Structures for Cleanroom Specification and Design

Box structures are descriptions of functions that exhibit properties essential for effective system specification and design. Figure 3.1 depicts the three box structures of black box, state box, and clear box. These structures exhibit identical external behavior but increasing internal visibility. A black box specifies the external behavior of a system or system component. A state box refinement of a black box specifies state data required to achieve the black box behavior. A clear box refinement of a state box specifies procedure designs required to achieve the state box behavior, and may reuse existing black boxes or introduce new black boxes for subsequent refinement. (Clear boxes are composed of program control structures. A sequence structure is shown in Figure 3.1) Each

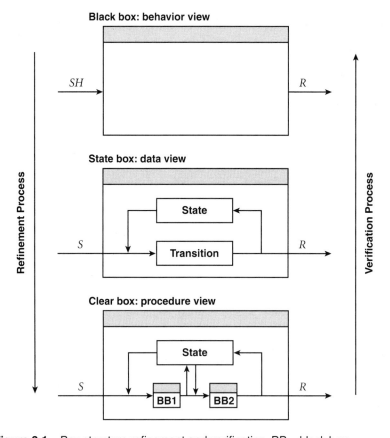

Figure 3.1   Box structure refinement and verification. BB = black box.

refinement is verified against the previous step. Box structures thus separate three aspects of system development (specification of behavior, data, and procedures) yet relate them in a coherent process of refinement and verification.

3.1.1 Black Box Behavior

The black box specification of a system or system component defines its required external behavior. A system accepts a stimulus, *S*, as input from its environment and produces a response, *R*, as output to its environment. The response depends not only on the current stimulus, but also on the history of stimuli received so far. For example, consider the external behavior of a hand calculator. Suppose a computation is in progress, and a current stimulus of 5 is entered on the keypad. If the history of stimuli when the 5 is entered is, say, C718 (C for clear), then the response is 7185; that is, the calculator will shift the current digit display one place to the left and insert the 5 in the units position. However, suppose instead that the history of stimuli is C718+. In this case, based on a different stimulus history, the calculator will begin a new digit string with 5 in the units position. Thus, the response of a system is uniquely determined by the current stimulus and the history of stimuli received up to that point.

Systems and their constituent components can be viewed in terms of their behavior. For example, a workstation accepts stimuli from keystrokes and mouse clicks, and produces corresponding responses that may change the content of current windows or display new windows. The user experiences only the stimulus–response behavior, and may have no knowledge of internal operations in the workstation itself, or in other machines to which it may be linked in a communications network, all of which support the behavior experienced.

The mathematical semantics of black box behavior is a function written as

stimulus history → response

or simply

$$SH \rightarrow R$$

where *SH* is the complete stimulus history, including the current stimulus.

A black box definition is state free and procedure free. It defines externally visible behavior experienced by users solely in terms of history of use. As such, a black box focuses on the user view in addressing questions of system behavior, and does not require decisions on state and procedure design. A black box specification defines required behavior in all possible circumstances of use. That is, the correct responses for all possible combinations of current stimuli and stimulus histories are defined in a black box specification. Black box specifications have three principal uses in Cleanroom projects, all of which are critical to effective system development:

1. For system owners and users, black boxes define required behavior for analysis and agreement prior to committing resources to development and testing.

2. For system developers, black boxes define required behavior to be designed and implemented.

3. For system testers, black boxes define required behavior to be validated during testing.

Black boxes can be defined in a tabular format, with columns organized by stimulus, condition on history, and response. The tables can be specified in any appropriate form—from natural language to set theory. Consider the informal black box definition depicted in Table 3.1. This low-level black box specifies a sales forecasting system based on a simple 12-month running average, which might be used to forecast sales for thousands of items in an inventory control system. The sales forecasting system accepts stimuli composed of a monthly sales value for a particular product, and produces appropriate responses. Black box rule 1 specifies correct behavior for fewer than 12 months of sales values for a product. Rule 2 specifies correct behavior when at least 12 months of sales values are available. The table expresses behavior in an informal manner and distinguishes important entities in angle brackets for later refinement and definition. Such a table might be developed in the early stages of system specification for discussion and analysis with users to reach a consensus on required behavior before committing resources to a more precise specification. For example, discussions of rule 1 could lead to additional requirements to compute, say, three- and six-month running averages as well. Discussions of rule 2 could result in requirements to include, say, a month designation with each stimulus for use in identifying inadvertent omissions in the set of sales values prior to computing their average. These changes could result in new behavior to be specified. Black box specifications are intended to encourage such discus-

Table 3.1 Black box excerpt: sales forecasting system

Black Box Rule No.	Stimulus History Condition	Current Stimulus	Response
1	History contains less than 11 monthly <sales> values for <product>	<sales>, <product>	"<sales> for <product> accepted, running average not available"
2	History contains at least 11 monthly <sales> for <product>	<sales>, <product>	average of most recent 11 monthly <sales> plus current <sales> for <product>

sions early in development, both to avoid wasting resources and to prevent developing the wrong system for the user.

3.1.2 State Box Behavior

The state box specification of a system or system component provides an intermediate view that defines its state space. State boxes encapsulate stimulus history as state data, but are procedure free. A state box maps an old state, *OS*, and a stimulus, *S*, to a new state, *NS*, and a response, *R*. The new state thus becomes the old state for the next transition. The semantics of state box behavior is a transition function written as

(old state, stimulus) → (new state, response)

or simply

$$(OS, S) \rightarrow (NS, R)$$

A state box is refined from and verified against the corresponding black box. The state represents information from the black box stimulus history that must be retained to preserve the black box specification. By retaining this information as state, the state box does not require stimulus history in its definition. Every black box has a state box description because every stimulus history can be represented as a state. Also, many different state boxes can be designed to satisfy the requirements of a given black box because different representations and access methods are possible for the state.

State boxes can be defined in a tabular format, with columns for old state, stimulus, new state, and response, plus a column to trace back to the corresponding black box rule. Consider the state box of the sales forecasting system shown in Table 3.2, which corresponds to the black box specification in Table 3.1. In this case, analysis of the black box stimulus history conditions leads to the straightforward definition of a state item named <sales file> to retain the 11 most recent sales values for each product. Each record of <sales file> can be identified by <product>, and can contain an array of 11 sales <value>. Only 11 months of sales values are required because the current stimulus will complete the total of 12 values required to compute the running average. No earlier stimuli need be retained, thus subsequent monthly stimuli will result in deletion from the state of sales values older than 11 months. Transition 1 in Table 3.2 defines the behavior required when the stimulus introduces a new product. Transition 2 defines the behavior when the product is known to the state box, but 11 months of sales values have not yet been accumulated. Transitions 1 and 2 produce literal messages as responses to the user. Lastly, transition 3 defines steady-state behavior in computing running average responses. Note that each transition requires appropriate state updates to prepare for processing subsequent stimuli. For example, transition 3 manages accumulation of state by

Table 3.2 State box excerpt: sales forecasting system

State Box Transition No.	Old State	Stimulus	New State	Response	Black Box Trace Rule No.
1	\<sales file\> does not contain record for \<product\>	\<sales\>, \<product\>	In \<sales file\>, record is added for \<product\> and \<sales\> is added as its newest \<value\>	"\<sales\> for \<product\> accepted, running average not available"	1
2	\<sales file\> contains record for \<product\> with less than 11 monthly \<value\> entries	\<sales\> \<product\>	For \<product\> record in \<sales file\>, \<sales\> is added as its newest \<value\>	"\<sales\> for \<product\> accepted, running average not available"	1
3	\<sales file\> contains record for \<product\> with 11 monthly \<value\> entries	\<sales\>, \<product\>	For \<product\> record in \<sales file\>, oldest \<value\> is deleted and \<sales\> is added as its newest \<value\>	Average of current \<sales\> stimulus plus 11 monthly \<value\> entries for \<product\>	2

deleting the oldest \<value\> and adding the current stimulus as the newest \<value\> in the \<product\> record in \<sales file\>.

A state box is verified by deriving its black box behavior and comparing the derived black box for equivalence to the original black box from which the state box was refined. The black box behavior of a state box is derived by transforming its state operations into stimulus history form.

3.1.3 Clear Box Behavior

The clear box design of a system or system component defines the processing required to achieve its corresponding state box behavior. A clear box is a computer program or set of programs that accepts a stimulus, S, and, based on the program's internal state, OS, produces a new internal state, NS, and a response, R. The processing is defined in terms of the fundamental control structures of structured programming—namely, sequence, alternation, and iteration—plus a concurrent structure if parallelism is to be introduced. A clear box defines the computation of the response and new state in terms of these control structures.

Many different clear boxes can be defined to satisfy the behavior of a given state box. The semantics of clear box behavior is a transition function written as

(old state, stimulus) → (new state, response) by procedure

or simply

$$(OS, S) \rightarrow (NS, R) \text{ by procedure}$$

Clear box procedures may reuse the services of existing black boxes, and may introduce new black boxes for subsequent refinement into state and clear box forms. Definition of a clear box is a critical step because it defines the procedure that organizes and connects the usage of the black boxes of subsystems and components at the next level in the box structure hierarchy. This explicit connection helps maintain intellectual control as development proceeds by defining the precise context of every black box use. In addition, components and their connections are derived from local processing requirements in a clear box design. In essence, the message of box structures is not "divide and conquer," but rather "divide, connect, and conquer."

A clear box is verified by abstracting its operations into a derived state box form and comparing the derived state box for equivalence with the original state box from which the clear box was refined. Clear box design and verification are discussed in detail in Chapter 4.

3.1.4 Box Structure Hierarchies

A box structure hierarchy evolves through stepwise refinement and verification as described earlier. This is a usage and not a parts hierarchy; that is, every use of a box occupies a distinct place in the hierarchy, and all processing is defined by sequential and concurrent uses of boxes. Of course, a usage hierarchy does not imply that the code is replicated wherever it is used in the implementation.

The example in Figure 3.2 depicts an initial black box that is refined into a state box and then into a clear box, with a control structure that embeds and coordinates the operations of, in this case, six black box uses at the next level. These uses could all reference the same black box, different black boxes, or some combination. Usage hierarchies of system components are helpful for maintaining intellectual control in managing system development.

3.1.5 Box Structure Principles

Four key principles that guide development and analysis of box structures (Mills, Linger, and Hevner 1986, 1987) are summarized in this section. The first two principles are enforced by the box structure refinement process; the last two principles articulate good design practices.

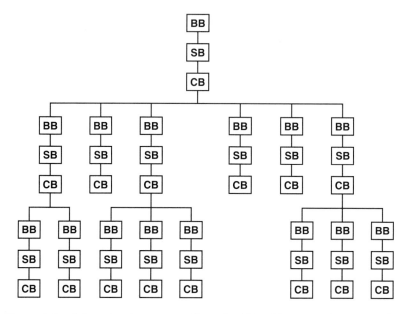

Figure 3.2   A box structure usage hierarchy. BB = black box; SB = state box; CB = clear box.

Principle of Referential Transparency: During the delegation of a system component for development, all requirements for the component should be specified completely, so that no further specification is logically required to complete the component.

A black box should define all required external behavior for a system or system component. Referential transparency is maintained when a state box implements correctly the behavior required by the black box, and similarly when a clear box implements correctly the behavior required by the state box. These three forms focus on behavior, state, and procedure respectively, yet are complete and behaviorally equivalent definitions of a system or system component, with no behavior left out. This referentially transparent hierarchy permits deferring details without losing them. Clear boxes play a key role in maintaining referential transparency by organizing and connecting the operations of embedded subsystems and components at the next level.

Effective project management requires organizing myriad details into coherent structures for delegation and development. Referential transparency in box structures permits crisp delegation and accountability by providing complete and consistent specifications of work to be done. Components can be delegated to development teams with confidence that all component commitments are specified and accounted for. In addition, referential transparency simplifies and strcamlincs communication among project members by eliminating much of the discussion and coordination required by imprecise definitions of responsibilities.

Principle of Transaction Closure: The transactions of a system or system component must be sufficient for the acquisition and retention of all its state data, and its state data must be sufficient for the completion of all its transactions.

A transaction is a description of high-level behavior that may be composed of a series of low-level transitions. For example, the transaction "reconcile bank statement" might be composed of individual transitions such as "access account," "reconcile deposits," "reconcile withdrawals," and so forth. Transaction closure defines an iterative analysis process that ensures the sufficiency of the transactions and the retained state of a system or system component during its specification. The process begins with the principal transactions carried out by primary users, and the definition of the state data needed to support those transactions. The supporting state data will require additional transactions for initialization and update, leading to more state data, and so on. The iteration continues until no additional state data requirements are identified, at which point transaction closure has been achieved.

Principle of State Migration: System data should be migrated to and encapsulated in the smallest system parts that do not require duplicating updates.

State migration enables the location and encapsulation of state data items at their proper level in a system to limit the complexity of both system specifications and the resulting system structures. For example, consider a clear box that contains state data item *T* that invokes a black box at the next level. If *T* is referenced only within the state box refinement of that black box, it can be migrated downward and encapsulated there with no duplicate updates necessary. Alternately, upward migration to a common parent box may be necessary, as a design unfolds, to eliminate duplicate updates.

Principle of Common Services: System parts with multiple uses should be considered for definition as common services. As many opportunities as possible for reuse should be created within and among system parts.

Common services are found everywhere in software systems. For example, a GUI acts as a common service for the programs that use it in managing internal state representations of user interfaces and updating displays as required. Opportunities for common service definition emerge frequently in box structure development. For example, a weather forecasting system may process measurements from a large set of distributed sensors. Operations to initialize, update, retrieve, and delete measurement data will be required at many points in the system. The measurements could be encapsulated as state in a new box structure hierarchy that provides these common services to all using programs. This design decision isolates and protects the measurement data, enhances integrity by providing controlled access, and helps prepare for future, unforeseen uses of the data. Such reuse of software components affords an opportunity to improve productivity and reliability.

3.1.6   The Box Structure Development Process

The general development process for box structure refinement and verification is summarized in the following list based on the foregoing descriptions. This process is illustrated in the security alarm example presented in this chapter and in a more extensive satellite control system example in Part III.

Box Structure Development Process

1. Define the system requirements.
2. Specify and validate the black box.
    • Define the system boundary and specify all stimuli and responses.
    • Specify the black box mapping rules.
    • Validate the black box with owners and users.
3. Specify and verify the state box.
    • Specify the state data and initial state values.
    • Specify the state box transition function.
    • Derive the black box behavior of the state box and compare the derived black box to the original black box for equivalence.
4. Design and verify the clear box.
    • Design the clear box control structures and operations.
    • Embed uses of new and reused black boxes as necessary.
    • Derive the state box behavior of the clear box and compare the derived state box to the original state box for equivalence.
5. Repeat the process for new black boxes.

It is important to note that this process can be tailored and adapted to particular project environments and objectives to make the best use of project resources. For example, behavior-rich systems may be best specified and analyzed in terms of their external behavior. In this case, black box specification should be emphasized. Subsystems that implement extensive data operations may embody simple black box behavior, but may exhibit complexities in state structure, storage, and retrieval. In this case, state box definition should be emphasized. Components that implement extensive mathematical operations may exhibit simple black box behavior and use simple state definitions, but exhibit considerable complexity in their clear box structure and operations. In this case, clear box design should be emphasized.

Large-scale systems composed of many subsystems and components will thus adopt various approaches in carrying out this process. But whatever the emphasis, system development should begin with the best possible understanding of required external behavior and agreement among stakeholders before committing further resources. It is important to note that comprehensive requirements are almost never known at the outset of system development. The box structure method is compatible with a requirements discovery and elicitation process, often carried out through incremental development of prototypes with user feedback. Even for prototypes, however, the partial set of requirements to be implemented should be known at the outset, both to achieve effective use of resources and to minimize risk.

3.2 The Sequence-Based Specification Process

A number of approaches can be used to develop specifications. The new theory of *sequence-based specification* defines one process for stepwise construction of complete, consistent, and correct black box and state box specifications, and this is the approach that is discussed in this book.

In the sequence-based specification process, all possible sequences of stimuli (stimulus histories) are enumerated systematically in a strict order, as stimulus sequences of length zero, length one, length two, and so on. As each sequence is mapped to its correct response, equivalent sequences are identified by applying a reduction rule, and the enumeration process terminates when the system has been defined completely and consistently.

Based on the work of Mills (1975), Parnas (1992), Mao (1993), Prowell (1996), and Poore (Prowell and Poore, 1998), sequence-based specification makes a tractable problem of the astronomical number of use cases arising from the combinatorial effects of software use. Through sequence enumeration, developers consider all combinations and permutations of system stimuli. Each sequence represents a scenario of use. During the stepwise process of enumeration, possible scenarios are distinguished from impossible scenarios, intended uses from erroneous uses, and reducible sequences from irreducible sequences. These irreducible sequences—*canonical sequences*—are the basis for a precise specification of software behavior that is mathematically complete and consistent, and traceably correct:

- The literal enumeration of sequences provides straightforward verification of completeness. One can follow the sequences of length one, length two, length three, and so on, to verify that all combinations and permutations of stimuli have been mapped to a response.
- The orderly enumeration of sequences ensures that a given scenario of use (i.e., sequence of stimuli) appears only once. Consistency, like completeness, is a direct consequence of enumeration.
- Every element of a sequence-based specification is traced to its origin in the requirements. If the correct response for a sequence cannot be found in the requirements, the expected behavior must be clarified and the requirements modified.

The work flow in sequence-based specification supports requirements analysis, black box specification, and state box specification in a seamless process with a substantial possibility of automated support. The steps in the work flow, described briefly in the following subsection, are exemplified in Section 3.3.

3.2.1 Black Box Definition

Tagged Requirements. Requirements are tagged (numbered) for use in verifying the correctness of each element of subsequent work products. The methodical consideration of sequences in the enumeration process forces the exposure of ambiguities and omissions in the requirements. Clarification of requirements is a natural by-product of sequence-based specification.

System Boundary Definition. The system boundary determines which components are inside and outside the system to be specified. The entities outside the system are the sources of stimuli and the destinations of responses. Identification of stimuli and responses often begins at an atomic level. After further consideration (including, perhaps, an initial enumeration), abstractions are often invented to simplify the enumeration process.

Abstractions are used to hide well-understood details, to reflect natural partitions in the problem, or to reduce a large set of elements to a smaller set. The elements of the larger set must have a well-defined mapping to the elements of the smaller set. A stimulus set (or response set) may be of mixed granularity—some atomic, some abstract. Whatever the level of granularity, the elements of the stimulus set (or response set) must be mutually exclusive.

Sequence Enumeration. Sequences are enumerated in order of length (zero stimuli, one stimulus, two stimuli, etc.), with all combinations and permutations considered systematically. As each sequence is examined, the following evaluations occur:

1. Sequences that are impossible (e.g., a stimulus prior to system start) are marked as "illegal." Any extension of an illegal sequence will itself be illegal, so sequences marked illegal are not extended further in the enumeration.

2. The correct response for each sequence is documented, as is the requirement on which it is based. If there is no requirement that addresses the sequence in question, a *derived requirement* is stated. Derived requirements represent assumptions or clarifications, and must be confirmed with the originator of the requirements.

3. Two sequences are *equivalent* if their responses to future stimuli are identical. Since extensions of the two equivalent sequences exhibit the same behavior, it is not necessary to extend both, and only the shorter is extended.

The enumeration stops when all sequences of a given length are either illegal or equivalent to a previous sequence.

The completed enumeration represents the mathematically complete and consistent, verifiably correct black box specification for the system. The specification is complete because all sequences have been mapped to a response, it is consistent because each sequence has been mapped to only one response, and it is correct on verification by domain experts that the behavior specified for each sequence and traced to the requirements is the intended behavior.

Canonical Sequence Analysis.   Legal sequences in the enumeration that are not equivalent to any previous sequence are the *canonical sequences*. The canonical sequences represent the unique conditions of system usage, and analysis of the canonical sequences yields the state space for the system, given the level of abstraction of the black box.

In canonical sequence analysis, variables are invented to encapsulate the conditions in each sequence of stimuli. These variables may be viewed as the *state data* for the system. The range of values for each variable is discovered as each canonical sequence is examined relative to each variable. The combination of variable values must be unique for each canonical sequence, such that the canonical sequences are *disjoint* when the analysis is complete.

3.2.2   State Box Definition

Each sequence in the black box specification may be thought of as a *tuple* (current stimulus, previous stimuli). The previous stimuli in each sequence in the black box are, in fact, canonical sequences. Given this fact, the creation of the state box specification for the system is a matter of assembly. Each valid (sequence → response) mapping in the black box can be replaced with a (current stimulus, state → response, state update) mapping in the state box. The

Current Stimulus: _____

Current State	Response	State Update	Black Box Trace: Sequence Prior to Current Stimulus

Figure 3.3   State box mapping table format

state box can be generated automatically from the black box, and need not be verified if generated by a certified tool.

The final form of the state box is a set of mapping tables, one per stimulus. Each mapping table is of the form shown in Figure 3.3.

The state box specification is the final specification work product. The Cleanroom box structure specification and design method continues with refinement of the state box to the clear box, in terms of full procedural design, as described in Chapter 4.

3.3 Example: Specification of a Security Alarm

A simple software-controlled security alarm depicted in Figure 3.4 is to be created for use on doors, windows, boxes, and so forth, to detect unauthorized entry. The security alarm has a detector that sends a trip signal when motion is detected. The security alarm is activated by pressing the Set button. A light in the Set button is illuminated when the security alarm is on. If a trip signal occurs

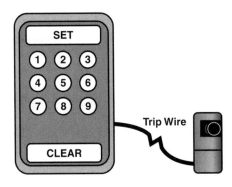

Figure 3.4   Security alarm

while the device is set, a high-pitched tone (alarm) is emitted. A three-digit code must be entered to turn off the alarm. Correct entry of the code deactivates the security alarm. If a mistake is made when entering the code, the user must press the Clear button before the code can be reentered. The security alarm will not be programmable; each unit will have a hard-coded deactivation code.

A sequence-based specification will be created for the security alarm using the stepwise process described in the preceding subsection.

3.3.1 Black Box Definition

Tagged Requirements. Tagging of requirements is the first step in creating a traceable specification, as shown in Table 3.3. Subsequent elements of the specification will be traced to their origin in the requirements through these tags.

As each step in the specification is traced to the relevant requirement, ambiguities and omissions in the requirements will be discovered. When there is no requirement to cite in a trace, a "derived" requirement will be stated and tagged as D1, D2, and so on.

System Boundary Definition. There are two possible sources of stimuli to the security alarm: the detector and the human user. The detector sends a trip stimulus and all other stimuli originate with the human user, as shown in Table 3.4.

The stimuli Trip, Set, and Clear are all atomic stimuli (i.e., discrete, low-level stimuli). The stimuli GoodDigit and BadDigit are both abstractions, representing correct and incorrect entry of digits in the three-digit code. GoodDigit represents each digit in the sequence of three digit entries that deactivate the device. BadDigit represents a digit in any other sequence of digit entries.

Table 3.3   Tagged requirements for the security alarm

Tag No.	Requirement
1	The security alarm has a detector that sends a trip signal when motion is detected.
2	The security alarm is activated by pressing the Set button.
3	The Set button is illuminated when the security alarm is set.
4	If a trip signal occurs while the security alarm is set, a high-pitched tone (alarm) is emitted.
5	A three-digit code must be entered to turn off the alarm tone.
6	Correct entry of the code deactivates the security alarm.
7	If a mistake is made when entering the code, the user must press the Clear button before the code can be reentered.

Table 3.4 Security alarm stimuli

Stimulus	Description	Requirement Trace No.
Set	Device activator	2
Trip	Signal from detector	1
BadDigit	Incorrect entry of a digit in the code	7
Clear	Clear entry	7
GoodDigit	A digit that is part of the correct entry of the three-digit code that deactivates the alarm and device	5, 6

Table 3.5 Security alarm responses

Response	Description	Requirement Trace No.
Light on	Set button illuminated	3
Light off	Set button not illuminated	6
Alarm on	High-pitched sound activated	4
Alarm off	High-pitched sound deactivated	5

Abstraction in this instance serves the purpose of hiding well-understood atomic-level details (i.e., whether a particular digit is "good" or "bad" in the context of its entry).

Two external responses are mentioned in the requirements: a light (the Set button) and an alarm. The system must start and stop each of these, as summarized in Table 3.5.

In addition to responses that are explicitly defined in the requirements, two other values are often used in sequence-based specification: the null response and illegal. The null response occurs when there is no external system response, such as when a system is ignoring or perhaps accumulating stimuli. Illegal is used when a sequence is impossible, such as when stimuli are presented before invocation.

Sequence Enumeration. Sequence enumeration involves consideration of all possible scenarios of use: sequences of length zero (the empty sequence), length one (single stimulus), length two (single-stimulus extensions of the sequences of length one), and so on. Enumeration ends when all sequences of a given length are either illegal or equivalent to a previous sequence. Again, an illegal sequence is one that is "impossible," such as *SBG* in Table 3.6 (pressing the Set button, and then a BadDigit results in there being no such thing as GoodDigit, given the definition of that abstraction). Also, one sequence is equivalent to another if the two sequences have identical future behavior. The sequence *SS* (pressing the Set button twice), for example, is marked as equivalent to the sequence *S* (pressing the Set button only once), because all future responses are the same. Note that in Table 3.6 the current responses are different. The response to *S* is to turn on the light, whereas the response to *SS* is null (because the light is already on). After the current response, however, the responses to future stimuli will be the same whether they are preceded by *S* or *SS*. Therefore, *SS* is marked as equivalent to *S* in the enumeration and need not be extended.

Questions about requirements invariably arise as sequence scenarios are considered systematically. All questions, assumptions, and so forth, are documented so that outstanding issues can be addressed and resolved.

The following symbols will be used to represent the stimuli in the enumeration given in Table 3.6.

S   Set
T   Trip
B   BadDigit
C   Clear
G   GoodDigit

In the Equivalence column, the equivalence is to a previously considered sequence. In the Requirements Trace column, a number denotes an original requirement from Table 3.3; a number prefixed with the letter D denotes a derived requirement.

Table 3.6   Security alarm sequence enumeration

Sequence	Response	Equivalence	Requirements Trace No.
Length Zero			
Empty	Null		D1
			The security alarm is initially deactivated.
Length One			
S	Light on		2, 3
T	Illegal		D1
B	Illegal		D1
C	Illegal		D1
G	Illegal		D1

continued

Table 3.6   *continued*

Sequence	Response	Equivalence	Requirements Trace No.
Length Two			
S S	Null	*S*	D2 After the device has been set, the Set button has no further effect until the device has been deactivated.
S T	Alarm on		4
S B	Null		D3 The device produces no external response to an erroneous entry.
S C	Null	*S*	D4 The device produces no external response to a Clear entry.
S G	Null		D5 The device produces no external response to correct entry of the code until all three digits of the code have been entered.
Length Three			
S T S	Null	*S T*	D2
S T T	Null	*S T*	D6 After the trip signal has set off the alarm, the trip signal has no further effect until the device has been deactivated.
S T B	Null		D3
S T C	Null	*S T*	D4
S T G	Null		D5
S B S	Null	*S B*	D2
S B T	Alarm on	*S T B*	4
S B B	Null	*S B*	D3
S B C	Null	*S*	D4, 7
S B G	Illegal		7
S G S	Null	*S G*	D2

Sequence	Response	Equivalence	Requirements Trace No.
$S\,G\,T$	Alarm on	$S\,T\,B$	4 D7 Incomplete entry of the code prior to a trip signal will be regarded as an erroneous entry that requires a Clear and a reentry of the correct code to deactivate the alarm.
$S\,G\,B$	Null	$S\,B$	D3
$S\,G\,C$	Null	S	D4
$S\,G\,G$	Null		D5
Length Four			
$S\,T\,B\,S$	Null	$S\,T\,B$	D2
$S\,T\,B\,T$	Null	$S\,T\,B$	D6
$S\,T\,B\,B$	Null	$S\,T\,B$	D3
$S\,T\,B\,C$	Null	$S\,T$	D4, 7
$S\,T\,B\,G$	Illegal		7
$S\,T\,G\,S$	Null	$S\,T\,G$	D2
$S\,T\,G\,T$	Null	$S\,T\,G$	D6
$S\,T\,G\,B$	Null	$S\,T\,B$	D3
$S\,T\,G\,C$	Null	$S\,T$	D4
$S\,T\,G\,G$	Null		D5
$S\,G\,G\,S$	Null	$S\,G\,G$	D2
$S\,G\,G\,T$	Alarm on	$S\,T\,B$	4, D7
$S\,G\,G\,B$	Null	$S\,B$	D3
$S\,G\,G\,C$	Null	S	D4
$S\,G\,G\,G$	Light off	Empty	6
Length Five			
$S\,T\,G\,G\,S$	Null	$S\,T\,G\,G$	D2
$S\,T\,G\,G\,T$	Null	$S\,T\,G\,G$	D6
$S\,T\,G\,G\,B$	Null	$S\,T\,B$	D3
$S\,T\,G\,G\,C$	Null	$S\,T$	D4
$S\,T\,G\,G\,G$	Alarm off, light off	Empty	3, 5, 6

The black box function specification for the security alarm is now mathematically complete and consistent, and subject to correctness verification.

- Every scenario has been mapped to a response, so the specification is complete.
- Every scenario has been mapped to only one response (or response set), so the specification is consistent.
- Requirements engineers can now confirm that assumptions documented as derived requirements are correct, and that the specification correctly implements both the original and the derived requirements.

In practice, the dialog between requirements engineers and specification engineers is ongoing, and issues are clarified as they arise.

Canonical Sequence Analysis.   State data encapsulates and retains the components of stimulus history that must be preserved for the system to produce correct responses. The essential components of stimulus history are identified by examining the canonical sequences in the enumeration (i.e., sequences that are not equivalent to any previous sequence). Each canonical sequence is examined to identify the unique conditions in the sequence, and state variables are invented to represent the conditions.

For example, the canonical sequence *S* in Table 3.7 is different from the Empty sequence in that the security alarm has gone from power-off to power-on. The state variable Device, with values OFF and ON, was therefore invented to encapsulate that condition. Similarly, when the sequence *ST* was examined, it was discovered to contain a condition that was not present in either the Empty or *S* sequences: The alarm has been tripped. The state variable Alarm was invented to represent the new condition, with associated values OFF and ON.

Table 3.7 contains the canonical sequences, the state variables that are required to represent the conditions in the canonical sequences, and the values of the state variables before and after the current stimulus in the sequences.

3.3.2   State Box Definition

All state variables and their possible values have now been defined. No further invention will be needed to produce the state-based specification. Table 3.8 lists the names, ranges, and initial values of the state data.

Table 3.7 Canonical sequence analysis

Canonical Sequence	State Variables	Value before Current Stimulus	Value after Current Stimulus
Empty	—	—	—
S The user has pressed the Set button to activate the device.	Device	OFF	ON
S T The device has been set and the trip signal has occurred, setting off the alarm.	Device Alarm	ON OFF	ON ON
S B The device has been set and the user has entered an invalid digit.	Device Code	ON NONE	ON ERROR
S G The device has been set and the user has entered the first digit in the code.	Device Code	ON NONE	ON 1_OK
S T B The device has been set, the trip signal has set off the alarm, and the user has entered an invalid digit. The Clear button must be pressed before the code can be entered to turn off the alarm.	Device Alarm Code	ON ON NONE	ON ON ERROR
S T G The device has been set, the trip signal has set off the alarm, and the user has entered the first digit in the code.	Device Alarm Code	ON ON NONE	ON ON 1_OK
S G G The device has been set and the user has entered the first two digits in the code.	Device Code	ON 1_OK	ON 2_OK
S T G G The device has been set, the trip signal has set off the alarm, and the user has entered the first two digits in the code.	Device Alarm Code	ON ON 1_OK	ON ON 2_OK

Table 3.8   State variables

State Variable	Range	Initial Value
Device	{OFF, ON}	OFF
Alarm	{OFF, ON}	OFF
Code	{NONE, 1_OK, 2_OK, ERROR}	NONE

The completed sequence-based specification can now be recast as a state-based specification. Whereas the black box view is expressed in terms of sequences of user inputs and system responses, the state box view is expressed in terms of (current stimulus, state) and (system response, state update). All sequences in the enumeration that end in a given stimulus will be grouped, and mapping rules of the following form will be stated:

> When the system receives the stimulus ___ and the state data values are ___, the system response is ___ and the state update is ___. This use can be traced to black box sequence ___.

These mapping rules are summarized by Tables 3.10 through 3.14, one table per stimulus. As an example, the sequences needed to construct the state-based specification for stimulus T are given in Table 3.9. This excerpt from the enumeration contains only the sequences ending in T (Trip) and their responses.

Table 3.9   Excerpt from enumeration: sequences ending in T

Sequence	Response
T	Illegal
ST	Alarm on
STT	Null
SBT	Alarm on
SGT	Alarm on
$STBT$	Null
$STGT$	Null
$SGGT$	Alarm on
$STGGT$	Null

Table 3.10   Current stimulus: Trip (T)

Tag No.	Current State	Response	State Update	Black Box Trace: Sequence Prior to T
1	Device = ON Alarm = OFF Code = NONE	Alarm on	Alarm = ON	S
2	Device = ON Alarm = ON Code = NONE	Null	—	$S\,T$
3	Device = ON Alarm = OFF Code = ERROR	Alarm on	Alarm = ON	$S\,B$
4	Device = ON Alarm = OFF Code = 1_OK	Alarm on	Alarm = ON Code = ERROR	$S\,G$
5	Device = ON Alarm= ON Code = ERROR	Null	—	$S\,T\,B$
6	Device = ON Alarm = ON Code = 1_OK	Null	—	$S\,T\,G$
7	Device = ON Alarm = OFF Code = 2_OK	Alarm on	Alarm = ON Code = ERROR	$S\,G\,G$
8	Device = ON Alarm = ON Code = 2_OK	Null	—	$S\,T\,G\,G$

The black box mapping rules of Table 3.9 are recast as a state-based specification in Table 3.10 for system behavior when the current stimulus is T.

Note that the sequences in the rightmost column of the table (the sequences prior to T) are all canonical. This is no accident. Because only the canonical sequences are extended during black box sequence enumeration, it stands to reason that any sequence prior to T is canonical. It is not necessarily the case that all canonical sequences will appear in the rightmost column, however. The canonical sequence Empty followed by T was marked as illegal in the black box enumeration, for example, so it is not included in the state box. Once a sequence has been identified as illegal (i.e., impossible), it is not carried forward in the specification.

The Current State column in Table 3.10 is populated with the state data derived during canonical sequence analysis. Because the sequences prior to T

(the rightmost column) are all canonical, the current state for each row is given by the state data associated with the canonical sequence.

An inspection of the details of the state-based specification for current stimulus T makes it apparent that there are only a few scenarios for which the system actually needs to do something. This insight will be used in the eventual implementation. The following tables are the mapping tables for the remaining stimuli. Each mapping table was derived in the manner just shown for current stimulus T.

Table 3.11   Current stimulus: Set (S)

Tag No.	Current State	Response	State Update	Black Box Trace: Sequence Prior to S
9	Device = OFF Alarm = OFF Code = NONE	Light on	Device = ON	None
10	Device = ON Alarm = OFF Code = NONE	Null	—	S
11	Device = ON Alarm = ON Code = NONE	Null	—	$S\,T$
12	Device = ON Alarm = OFF Code = ERROR	Null	—	$S\,B$
13	Device = ON Alarm = OFF Code = 1_OK	Null	—	$S\,G$
14	Device = ON Alarm = ON Code = ERROR	Null	—	$S\,T\,B$
15	Device = ON Alarm = ON Code = 1_OK	Null	—	$S\,T\,G$
16	Device = ON Alarm = OFF Code = 2_OK	Null	—	$S\,G\,G$
17	Device = ON Alarm = ON Code = 2_OK	Null	—	$S\,T\,G\,G$

Table 3.12 Current stimulus: BadDigit (B)

Tag No.	Current State	Response	State Update	Black Box Trace: Sequence Prior to B
18	Device = ON Alarm = OFF Code = NONE	Null	Code = ERROR	S
19	Device = ON Alarm = ON Code = NONE	Null	Code = ERROR	$S\,T$
20	Device = ON Alarm = OFF Code = ERROR	Null	—	$S\,B$
21	Device = ON Alarm = OFF Code = 1_OK	Null	Code = ERROR	$S\,G$
22	Device = ON Alarm = ON Code = ERROR	Null	—	$S\,T\,B$
23	Device = ON Alarm = ON Code = 1_OK	Null	Code = ERROR	$S\,T\,G$
24	Device = ON Alarm = OFF Code = 2_OK	Null	Code = ERROR	$S\,G\,G$
25	Device = ON Alarm = ON Code = 2_OK	Null	Code = ERROR	$S\,T\,G\,G$

Table 3.13 Current stimulus: Clear (C)

Tag No.	Current State	Response	State Update	Black Box Trace: Sequence Prior to C
26	Device = ON Alarm = OFF Code = NONE	Null	—	S
27	Device = ON Alarm = ON Code = NONE	Null	—	$S\,T$
28	Device = ON Alarm = OFF Code = ERROR	Null	Code = NONE	$S\,B$

continued

Table 3.13 *continued*

Tag No.	Current State	Response	State Update	Black Box Trace: Sequence Prior to C
29	Device = ON Alarm = OFF Code = 1_OK	Null	Code = NONE	$S\,G$
30	Device = ON Alarm = ON Code = ERROR	Null	Code = NONE	$S\,T\,B$
31	Device = ON Alarm = ON Code = 1_OK	Null	Code = NONE	$S\,T\,G$
32	Device = ON Alarm = OFF Code = 2_OK	Null	Code = NONE	$S\,G\,G$
33	Device = ON Alarm = ON Code = 2_OK	Null	Code = NONE	$S\,T\,G\,G$

Table 3.14 Current stimulus: GoodDigit (G)

Tag No.	Current State	Response	State Update	Black Box Trace: Sequence Prior to G
34	Device = ON Alarm = OFF Code = NONE	Null	Code = 1_OK	S
35	Device = ON Alarm = ON Code = NONE	Null	Code = 1_OK	$S\,T$
36	Device = ON Alarm = OFF Code = 1_OK	Null	Code = 2_OK	$S\,G$
37	Device = ON Alarm = ON Code = 1_OK	Null	Code = 2_OK	$S\,T\,G$
38	Device = ON Alarm = OFF Code = 2_OK	Light off	Device = OFF Code = NONE	$S\,G\,G$
39	Device = ON Alarm = ON Code = 2_OK	Alarm off Light off	Device = OFF Alarm = OFF Code = NONE	$S\,T\,G\,G$

The state box specification for the security alarm is now complete, consistent, traceable, and verifiably correct.

- The state data values, system response, and state update requirements for every scenario have been defined, so the specification is complete.
- The state data values, system response, and state update requirements for every scenario have been unambiguously defined, so the specification is consistent.
- Each element of the state-based specification can be compared to the corresponding element of the previously verified sequence-based specification to confirm that correctness has been preserved.

3.4 References

H. Mao. *The Box-Structure Development Method.* Ph.D. diss., University of Tennessee, 1993.

H.D. Mills. "The New Math of Computer Programming." *Communications of the ACM* vol. 18 (January 1975): 43–48.

H.D. Mills. "Stepwise Refinement and Verification in Box-Structured Systems." *IEEE Computer* vol. 21 (June 1988): 23–36.

H.D. Mills, R.C. Linger, and A.R. Hevner. *Principles of Information Systems Analysis and Design.* New York: Academic Press, 1986.

H.D. Mills, R.C. Linger, and A.R. Hevner. "Box-Structured Information Systems." *IBM Systems Journal* vol. 26 (1987): 395–413.

D.L. Parnas and Y. Wang. *The Trace Assertion Method of Module Interface Specification.* CRL Report No. 244. Hamilton, Ontario: Communications Research Laboratory, McMaster University, 1992.

S.J. Prowell. *Sequence-based Software Specification.* Ph.D. diss., University of Tennessee, 1996.

S.J. Prowell and J.H. Poore. "Sequence-Based Specification of Deterministic Systems." *Software—Practice and Experience* vol. 28 (March 1998): 329–344.

4

Cleanroom Software Development

4.1 Box Structure Development

The previous chapter described two functional views of a system or program, the first based on external behavior alone (black box) and the second based on a state machine (state box). This chapter describes a third view—the procedure or algorithm (clear box) to implement the state box and exhibit the specified external behavior.

The top-down iterative process by which the highest level specification of a complex system becomes a body of code that executes on a computer must address many design decisions. The box structure method does not make design decisions; however, it does encourage designers to consider the entire solution space. The solution space consists of all possible implementations—the good, the bad, and the ugly. There are solutions with fast execution times and solutions that are slow, solutions that require a lot of memory and solutions that are memory misers, solutions that will be easy to revise and maintain, as well as solutions that will be very difficult to maintain. A solution that is acceptable in one circumstance may be unacceptable in another, so the design decisions must take into account many, often conflicting, considerations.

The top-level black box description of behavior should be unique given the requirements. There is a one-to-many relationship between the black box and the possible state boxes that will mirror the required behavior. There is both control state information and data state information, and often a trade-off between the two. Minimal control state information might imply unacceptable performance, leading to a design decision with richer control information.

Likewise, there is often a trade-off between storing data in tables and recomputing values when needed. Figure 4.1 shows the general solution space with the unique black box leading to several possible state boxes, all of which will mirror the black box behavior. Box structures highlight this relationship and remind the designer to think about alternative state boxes relative to all aspects of the design. The selection of a specific state box forecloses (temporarily) many solutions and constrains, but does not fully determine, the clear box options.

There is a one-to-many relationship between a given state box and the many clear boxes or algorithms that would implement the state box. Again, the choice of clear box will constrain but not fully determine the final solution. As described in this chapter, the clear box is always defined as a structured program that may contain and connect lower level black boxes. Each of these black boxes is in turn unique, given the specifications it must meet to be referentially transparent to the clear box of which it is a part. This process of stepwise refinement results in a hierarchy of box structures, as was illustrated in Figure 3.2.

It is important always to consider a design in progress to be open to revision and reconsideration. One should never lose sight of the fact that there is an entire solution space to be considered, and a path to be chosen from the top-level black box to the final working system. It is the rule rather than the exception that better design ideas will emerge as work progresses. The first idea is

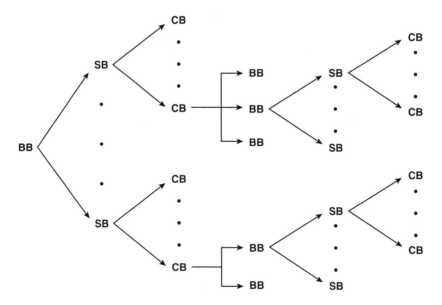

Figure 4.1 Box structure solution space. BB = black box; SB = state box; CB = clear box.

rarely the best idea. It is better to let go of a design that is working out badly, to revisit earlier design decisions and to take a better path, than to drive a bad design doggedly to conclusion. The design process should be viewed as a matter of analysis and selection—a series of choices to be made, evaluated, and possibly reconsidered.

Architecture is a powerful force in constraining the choices. If a product line architecture exists, then it is likely that certain functionality, state, and algorithms will be imposed on the solution. The designer will be required to make decisions that lead to reuse rather than new development. The box structure method does not in itself produce an architecture and does not make design decisions; these tasks are up to the designer. However, by creating an awareness of the entire solution space, box structures clarify architectural qualities and alternatives for analysis and informed decision making.

4.2 Clear Box Development

4.2.1 Clear Box Structures

A clear box defines the procedures required to implement the transition function of a state box. The stimulus and response sets, external behavior, and state of a clear box are identical to those of the corresponding state box. Clear box designs may reuse existing black boxes and introduce new black boxes, and may also define local data with no persistence. The procedures of a clear box are often organized around external services that its users (people, hardware, or other clear boxes) can invoke. For example, a data management clear box might provide services for adding, deleting, and retrieving data.

The focus of clear box design is on algorithm development. State box specifications that require little algorithmic elaboration can often be implemented directly in clear box procedures composed of `case` statements. The statements test the current stimulus and old state to determine the proper response and new state. In essence, such procedures amount to state box table look-ups that determine the appropriate transition, and verification can often be achieved by comparing individual state box transitions for equivalence with their localized implementations in the clear box statements.

However, state box specifications of algorithm-intensive systems will require extensive clear box analysis, design, and correctness verification. Such systems may exhibit simple state box specifications that nevertheless require substantial effort to implement in clear box form. These clear boxes can often result in large procedure designs, and may require definition of many new, and reuse of many existing, black boxes in their elaboration.

Clear boxes are composed of sequence, alternation, and iteration *control structures,* examples of which are depicted in Table 4.1 in graphic and design language form (Mills, Linger, and Hevner 1986). Concurrent control structures can also be introduced. The control structures are themselves composed of *function nodes,* represented in the table by g and *h,* and *predicate nodes,* represented by *p.* (Collector nodes represented by circles join the flow of control.) A function node can represent any operation, from a single assignment to an extensive computation. Any function node may itself be a new or reused black box. Every function node in a clear box may access the current state as input and may produce an updated state as output. Every predicate node may access the current state as input, but can make no changes to it. Sequence control structures can be generalized to any number of function nodes (a two-part sequence is shown in Table 4.1), or to indexed sequences that repeat execution of a function node under control of an index variable, as in a `fordo` structure. `Ifthenelse` structures can be generalized to `case` structures with multiple branches.

For ease of reference, the parts of these control structures can be given names. For example, for the `sequence`, g and *h* are referred to as `firstpart` and `secondpart` respectively. For the `ifthenelse`, *p, g,* and *h* are referred to as the `iftest`, `thenpart`, and `elsepart`. And for the `whiledo`, *p* and g are referred to as the `whiletest` and `dopart`.

Every clear box control structure exhibits a single entry line and a single exit line, with no side effects in control flow. From its entry line to its exit line, a control structure simply carries out a transformation on data. Because of this single-entry/single-exit property, these control structures correspond to mathematical functions. To illustrate, the following three-part sequence of assignments on integers t, x, and y (:= represents the assignment operation)

```
do
      t  :=  x
      x  :=  y
      y  :=  t
enddo
```

can be diagrammed as shown in Figure 4.2. At point 1 in Figure 4.2, an initial domain of t, x, and y is defined (0's represent initial values; for example, t_0 is the initial value of t). The first assignment $t := x$ changes the value of t to the initial value of x to produce the range at point 2, which in turn becomes the domain for the second assignment $x := y$, which produces the range at point 3, continuing in this manner until the final range at point 4 is reached. The overall effect of the sequence, from the domain at point 1 to the range at point 4 can thus be defined in natural language as

Table 4.1   Clear box control structures

Control Structure	Graphic Form	Design Language Form

Sequence		`do`
		    `g;`
		    `h`
		`enddo`

Ifthen		`if`
		    `p`
		`then`
		    `g`
		`endif`

Ifthenelse		`if`
		    `p`
		`then`
		    `g`
		`else`
		    `h`
		`endif`

Whiledo		`while`
		    `p`
		`do`
		    `g`
		`enddo`

Dountil		`do`
		    `g`
		`until`
		    `p`
		`enddo`

Dowhiledo		`do`
		    `g`
		`while`
		    `p`
		`do`
		    `h`
		`enddo`

Set t to the initial value of x and exchange the initial values of x and y

or equivalently in terms of a concurrent assignment as

```
t, x, y := x, y, x
```

In a concurrent assignment, all variables or expressions on the right are assigned simultaneously to the position-respective variables on the left. That is, simultaneous assignments are made of x to t, y to x, and x to y. In set notation, {(<t,x,y>, <x,y,x>)} is the sequence-free function definition for the three-part sequence. The definition is independent of context. Even if the sequence was embedded in a large clear box, the function definition would be identical. All clear box control structures implement domain-to-range mappings as illustrated in the sequence example in Figure 4.2.

4.2.2 Clear Box Abstraction and Documentation

Control structures can be read and understood in terms of their net effect on data from entry to exit and documented as function definitions. These definitions, called *program functions,* express the final values of variables as functions of initial values, and are determined by *function abstraction.* They can be expressed in a variety of forms, from natural language to mathematics. Program functions are *function equivalent* to their corresponding control structures.

The systematic process of reading and abstracting programs can be used to recover missing or incomplete documentation. In particular, legacy systems and reused components that are expressed in structured form can be read and abstracted to document their designs and to help recover embedded business rules for improved maintenance and evolution.

To illustrate, the control structures in Table 4.2 (w, x, y, and z are positive integers) can be read and analyzed to abstract their program functions as shown. The program function of sequence can be determined by mental composition of its individual operations. In this case, the value of w computed by the first operation can be substituted into the occurrence of w in the second operation. An ifthenelse program function can be determined by summarizing its true and false operations into a single expression. In this case, the true and false operations are seen to carry out a common mathematical operation. Determina-

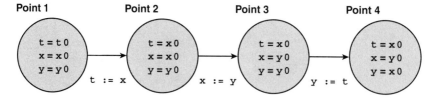

Figure 4.2 Domain-to-range mappings for the three-part sequence

tion of program functions for `whiledo` and other iteration control structures may require more analysis, but can often be derived by summarizing the results of mental execution of several iterations in a single expression. In this case, if x is initially odd, its value is reduced by two each iteration until it reaches one and the loop terminates. If x is initially even, its value is reduced by two each iteration until it reaches zero, and the loop likewise terminates. This program function is conveniently expressed in the table as a two-part *conditional rule* of the form

(condition 1 → rule 1 |

condition 2 → rule 2)

where each condition is a predicate that defines the circumstances under which the corresponding rule (assignment) is to be executed, and the vertical bar (|) represents "or." In this case, if x is initially odd, its final value is set to one; otherwise, if x is initially even, its final value is set to zero. (In general, conditional rules can have any number of parts.)

When all conditions of a conditional rule are pairwise disjoint for all pairs, the rule is called a *disjoint rule*, and the order of evaluation of the conditions does not affect the outcome. Disjoint rules are very useful in expressing program functions. Note also that a state box defines a possibly large disjoint rule with conditions that evaluate the stimulus and old state to determine the response and new state.

The program functions of the `sequence`, `ifthenelse`, and `whiledo` structures in Table 4.2 are sequence free, alternation free, and iteration free respectively. That is, the program functions of these structures abstract control flow to define their net effect on data in a single step from entry to exit.

Table 4.2 Program function examples

Control Structure	Program Function

do
  w := abs(x)
  z := max(w, y)
enddo
	w, z := abs(x), max(abs(x), y)

if
  x < y
then
  z := x
else
  z := y
endif
	z := min(x, y)

while
  x > 1
do
  x := x - 2
enddo
	(*initial* x *odd* → x := 1 |
	initial x *even* → x := 0)

The single-entry/single-exit property of control structures and their function nodes is critical to scalability in clear box abstraction, design, and verification. For this reason, clear box designs should avoid language features that can interfere with this property (e.g., goto statements that permit arbitrary branching logic). Single-entry/single-exit control structures enable a natural scalability for creating large designs while retaining intellectual control over their structure and function. Specifically, control structures can be nested and sequenced again and again in clear box designs as necessary to implement a state box transition function.

To illustrate, consider the clear box procedure design in Figure 4.3. At the lowest level of design, the net effect from entry to exit of while q do i enddo can be abstracted to a loop-free program function named A, and the net effect of do g; h enddo can be abstracted to a sequence-free program function named B. Now the ifthenelse can be treated at a higher but function-equivalent level of abstraction as if p then A else B endif, with no details of its constituent sequence and whiledo required, and in turn can be abstracted to a program function named C. Now do C; k enddo can be treated at a higher but again function-equivalent level of abstraction with no details of the constituent ifthenelse required. The net effect of this sequence can be abstracted to program function D to define the overall program function of the entire clear box. Thus, clear box designs define a natural hierarchy of abstractions that record the

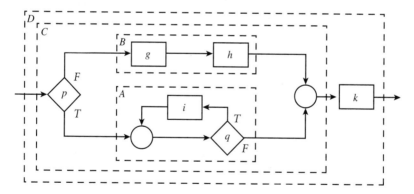

Program Function	Defines Effect of
A	whiledo: while q do i enddo
B	sequence: do g; h enddo
C	ifthenelse: if p then A else B endif
D	sequence: do C; k enddo

Figure 4.3   Abstraction hierarchy of a clear box

full functional effect of abstracted operations at each level, with no reference to their procedural details required, but no behavior unaccounted for in the abstractions. This hierarchy of abstractions exists within an algebra of functions, where replacement of a control structure by its program function is the sole operation, and keywords do, if, and so forth, act as function operators. Function abstraction is a complete and systematic method for recovering program documentation for understanding and maintenance.

4.2.3   Clear Box Design with Intended Functions

The process of reading and abstracting control structures to recover the previously described program functions is reversed for procedure design. In this case, the functions are called *intended functions.* Clear box designs are elaborated through stepwise refinement of intended functions, which define the required net effect on data of their subsequent control structure refinements. The initial intended function for a clear box refinement is a state box specification. Intended functions internal to clear box refinements may be embedded in their design text according to the design language syntax depicted in Table 4.3. Square brackets ([ ]) are used in Table 4.3 to delimit the intended functions. Comment delimiters can be employed for this purpose in implementation languages. The overall intended function of each control structure, denoted by [f], is attached to its entry point. Intended functions internal to control structures are attached to their keywords. For example, in the ifthenelse structure, intended functions [g] and [h] are attached to keywords then and else respectively to document the net effect of operations g and h respectively.

Table 4.3   Intended functions in control structures

Control Structure	Intended Function Placement

Sequence	[f]
	do
	    g;
	    h
	enddo

Ifthen	[f]
	if
	    p
	then [g]
	    g
	endif

continued

Table 4.3 *continued*

Control Structure	Intended Function Placement

Ifthenelse	[f]
	if
	   p
	then [g]
	   g
	else [h]
	   h
	endif

Whiledo	[f]
	while
	   p
	do [g]
	   g
	enddo

Dountil	[f]
	do [g]
	   g
	until
	   p
	enddo

Dowhiledo	[f]
	do [g]
	   g
	while
	   p
	do [h]
	   h
	enddo

Figure 4.4 depicts the refinement process for an intended function on the left operating on integer variables, itself embedded in a larger design not shown. This function is refined in the first step into a sequence of two operations in the center of the figure, themselves expressed as intended functions for further refinement. (Variable b is local to the design and not referenced outside it, and thus is not mentioned in the original intended function.) Note that the original intended function propagates to this sequence refinement to document its net effect on data. The two new intended functions are next refined in the second step into, in this case, ifthenelse control structures on the right of the figure, and are likewise propagated to these refinements to document their designs.

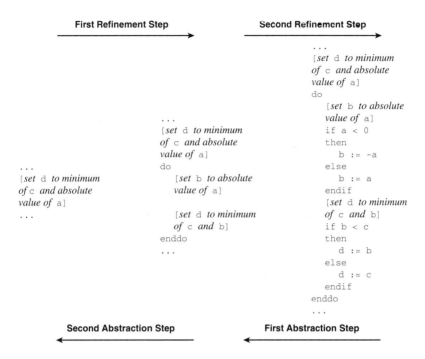

First Refinement Step

Second Refinement Step

```
                                                    . . .
                                                    [set d to minimum
                                                    of c and absolute
                                                    value of a]
                                                    do
                                                        [set b to absolute
                            . . .                           value of a]
                            [set d to minimum           if a < 0
                            of c and absolute           then
                            value of a]                     b := -a
                            do                          else
        . . .                   [set b to absolute          b := a
        [set d to minimum           value of a]         endif
        of c and absolute                               [set d to minimum
        value of a]                 [set d to minimum   of c and b]
        . . .                       of c and b]         if b < c
                            enddo                       then
                                . . .                       d := b
                                                        else
                                                            d := c
                                                        endif
                                                    enddo
                                                    . . .
```

Second Abstraction Step

First Abstraction Step

Figure 4.4   Stepwise refinement with intended functions

Figure 4.4 also depicts two abstraction steps that correspond to reading the control structures to derive their program functions. The abstracted program functions and the intended functions should be equal. Although this simple example can be readily understood by direct reading of its control structures, in larger designs intended functions play a critical role in preserving design intention for verification and maintenance. It is easy for the eye and mind to summarize five or 10 lines of design mentally, but not so easy to summarize 50 or 100 lines. It is clear that a correctness relationship exists between intended functions and their control structure refinements, as discussed next.

It is also important to note that clear box refinement is not a lockstep process. The top-level structure of a design cannot be created without a good understanding of how it will be refined into lower level structures. Design is an iterative, creative process; as understanding improves, better ideas emerge. Insights at lower levels may lead to revisions at higher levels. The critical point is that the *last intellectual pass* through a design should be top down to validate and verify its intended function definitions and refinement steps.

4.3 Clear Box Verification

4.3.1 The Correctness Questions

Clear box correctness verification is a mathematics-based method for demonstrating that a procedure meets its specification. Just as the correctness of a long-division computation is not demonstrated by rechecking the division, but rather by multiplication, so too the correctness of a procedure is not demonstrated by rechecking its refinement, but rather by other means. The clear box verification method widely used in Cleanroom development is called *function–theoretic correctness verification*. Using the function–theoretic approach, every control structure in a procedure is verified to do what its intended function specifies. An entire procedure has been verified when all its constituent control structures have been verified. Verifications are typically carried out in team reviews.

The Correctness Theorem (Linger, Mills, and Witt 1979) defines correctness questions for every clear box control structure, as depicted in Table 4.4. The number of questions to be asked and answered for each control structure is one for sequence structures, two for alternation structures, and three for iteration structures. Because procedures of any size contain a virtually infinite number of execution paths, verification by tracing paths is impossible. However, despite the number of paths they define, procedures are composed of a finite number of control structures. By verifying every control structure in a few steps (three or fewer for the structures in Table 4.4), procedure verification is reduced to a systematic process with a practical total number of steps. The correctness questions can be applied at varying levels of rigor, ranging from verbal proofs in team reviews to detailed written proofs. The level of rigor employed is a business decision based on risks and rewards. Experience has shown that verbal proofs in team reviews are very effective in developing high-quality software.

The correctness questions in the table follow directly from analysis of execution paths in the corresponding control structures. For the `sequence`, the only path that exists is g followed by h; so for correctness, the composition of these function nodes must do f, the intended function of the `sequence`.

For the `ifthen`, when p is true, the only path is through g; so for correctness, g must do f in this case. When p is false, the only path is through nothing (the identity function), so for correctness doing nothing must do f in this case; that is, f must already have been done when p is false. Analysis of the `ifthenelse` is similar, except when p is false, the only path is through h, so for correctness h must do f in this case.

The correctness of iteration structures can often be difficult to prove directly. Fortunately, the correctness of an iteration that terminates can be deter-

Table 4.4 Correctness questions for clear box control structures

Control Structure	Design Language	Correctness Question (for all possible inputs to f)

Sequence	[f]
	do
	  g;
	  h
	enddo
		(1) Composition question:
		    Does g followed by h do f?

Ifthen	[f]
	if
	  p
	then
	  g
	endif
		(1) Iftest true question:
		    When p is true, does g do f?
		(2) Iftest false question:
		    When p is false, does doing nothing do f?

Ifthenelse	[f]
	if
	  p
	then
	  g
	else
	  h
	endif
		(1) Iftest true question:
		    When p is true, does g do f?
		(2) Iftest false question:
		    When p is false, does h do f?

Whiledo	[f]
	while
	  p
	do
	  g
	enddo
		(1) Termination question:
		    Is termination guaranteed?
		(2) Whiletest true question:
		    When p is true, does g followed by f do f?
		(3) Whiletest false question:
		    When p is false, does doing nothing do f?

Dountil	[f]
	do
	  g
	until
	  p
	enddo
		(1) Termination question:
		    Is termination guaranteed?
		(2) Whiletest true question:
		    When p after g is false, does g followed by f do f?
		(3) Whiletest false question:
		    When p after g is true, does g do f?

Dowhiledo	[f]
	do
	  g
	while
	  p
	do
	  h
	enddo
		(1) Termination question:
		    Is termination guaranteed?
		(2) Whiletest true question:
		    When p after g is true, does g followed by h followed by f do f?
		(3) Whiletest false question:
		    When p after g is false, does g do f?

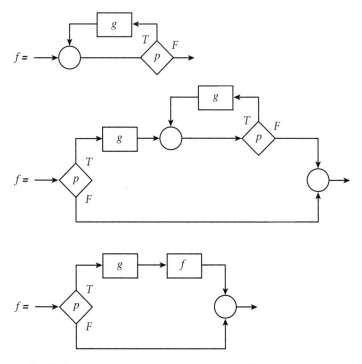

Figure 4.5 Deriving the `whiledo` correctness question

mined by verifying a simpler but equivalent `ifthenelse` structure derived through transformations on execution paths of the iteration. For example, consider the `whiledo` control structure shown in graphic form in the top display of Figure 4.5. In the middle display, an equivalent `ifthenelse` has been constructed with the `whiletest` *(p)* as its predicate. For the true branch of the `ifthenelse`, one step *(g)* of the iteration is executed, followed by reentry to the `whiledo` itself, just as in execution of the original `whiledo`. For the false branch, nothing is done, likewise just as in execution of the original `whiledo`. This new `ifthenelse` is thus execution equivalent to the `whiledo` in the top display. But the `whiledo` on the true branch of the new `ifthenelse` is postulated to be equivalent to *f*; so in the lower display, it is replaced by *f*. Thus, the correctness of a `whiledo` is reduced to the correctness of an `ifthenelse` and a `sequence`. The correctness questions for the `whiledo` can now be derived by analysis of the execution paths of the `ifthenelse`. The true path requires that *g* followed by *f* must do *f*, and the false path requires that doing nothing must do *f*.

In illustration of the true-case correctness question, consider the following `whiledo`:

[*read remaining records from file, if any*]
```
while
```
    [*records remain*]
```
do
```
    [*read next record*]
```
enddo
```

The correctness question is: When the `whiletest` is true, does *g* followed by *f* do *f*? It is expressed as

When [*records remain*] is true,

does [*read next record*] followed by [*read remaining records from file, if any*]

do [*read remaining records from file, if any*]

The answer is yes, because given an initial nonempty state of the file (guaranteed by the predicate evaluation of true), [*read next record*] (representing *g)* will result in one fewer record left to be read, resulting in either an empty or nonempty file, and [*read remaining records from file, if any*] (representing *f)* will either complete the reading of a nonempty file or do nothing if the file is already empty. Thus the `sequence` *(g* followed by *f)* has the same effect as the intended function [*read remaining records from file, if any*] *(f)*, given the same initial state of the file.

Note that in addition to the true and false questions for the `whiledo`, a third question is required to show that the iteration terminates. Termination arguments are often based on some monotonic property of the iteration that eventually results in failure of the test. For example, the iteration here that reads consecutive records from a file is guaranteed to terminate when the file is exhausted. Analysis for the `dountil` and `dowhiledo` structures is similar.

4.3.2   A Correctness Verification Example

Consider the following clear box procedure and how to verify it. Such a procedure could be a low-level subroutine in a large clear box design. As such, its overall intended function (lines 1–2) would be involved in verification of the higher level procedures that invoke it. The procedure accepts as arguments an integer array named `emp` (for employee number) of `n` elements, an integer named `id` (for identification), and an integer named `i`. (Array `emp` is guaranteed to be in ascending sorted order.) The intended function of the procedure requires that `i` be set to the location in `emp` that matches `id`, if any; otherwise, `i` is to be set to `0`. The procedure implements a binary search for the value of `id` in `emp`. The intended functions of the procedure, delimited by square brackets, are expressed in an informal yet concise style. Because some operations are self-evident, not every control structure carries an intended function.

```
1    [if possible, set i such that emp(i) = id and 1 <= i <= n,
     otherwise set i to 0]
2    procedure search(id, i: integer; emp(1..n): array of integer)
3        bot, top, mid: integer

4        i := 0
5        bot := 1
6        top := n

7        [if possible, set i so that emp(i) = id and bot <= i <= top,
8        otherwise leave i unchanged]
9        while
10           bot <= top & i = 0

11       [if id = emp((bot + top)/2), set i to (bot + top)/2,
         otherwise
12       if id > emp((bot + top)/2), set bot to (bot + top)/2 + 1,
         otherwise
13       if id < emp((bot + top)/2), set top to (bot + top)/2 - 1]
14       do
15           mid := (bot + top)/2
16           if
17               emp(mid) = id
18           then
19               i := mid
20           else [if id > emp(mid), set bot to mid + 1, otherwise
21                 if id < emp(mid), set top to mid - 1]
22               if
23                   emp(mid) < id
24               then
25                   bot := mid + 1
26               else
27                   top := mid - 1
28               endif
29           endif
30       enddo
31   endprocedure
```

The verification will be carried out by asking and answering the correctness questions, just as is done in a team review. The control structures can be verified in any order (e.g., top down, bottom up, or in some combination). After all the control structures have been verified, no matter the order, the entire procedure is verified. The following verification is carried out in top-down order.

The sequence at lines 4 through 8.   Consider the sequence of three assignments at lines 4 through 6, followed by the intended function at lines 7 and 8:

```
4   i := 0
5   bot := 1
6   top := n
7   [if possible, set i so that emp(i) = id and bot <= i <= top,
8   otherwise leave i unchanged]
```

The sequence correctness question requires that the composition of operations in this four-part sequence satisfy the intended function given at line 1:

```
1   [if possible, set i such that emp(i) = id and 1 <= i <= n,
    otherwise set i to 0]
```

Proof reasoning: At line 7, bot and top can be replaced by their prior values from lines 5 and 6; namely, 1 and n respectively. Then the intended function at lines 7 and 8 becomes

```
7   [if possible, set i such that emp(i) = id and 1 <= i <= n,
8   otherwise leave i unchanged]
```

as is required by the intended function at line 1. Also, i is set to 0 at line 4 and is left unchanged by the intended function at lines 7 and 8 unless id is found in emp, also as required. Thus, the sequence appears to be correct.

The whiledo at lines 9 through 13, 30.   The intended function for the whiledo is given at lines 7 and 8, and for its dopart at lines 11 through 13. Note that the dopart intended function defines the net effect of all the operations in its refinement at lines 14 through 29, and thus participates in the verification in place of these operations. The structure to be verified is thus

```
9   while
10      bot <= top & i = 0
    (do)
11      [if id = emp((bot + top)/2), set i to (bot + top)/2,
        otherwise
12      if id > emp((bot + top)/2), set bot to (bot + top)/2 + 1,
        otherwise
13      if id < emp((bot + top)/2), set top to (bot + top)/2 - 1]
30  enddo
```

The `whiledo` correctness question is composed of three parts that must be proved to show that the `whiledo` satisfies its intended function at lines 7–8:

```
7   [if possible, set i so that emp(i) = id and bot <= i <= top,
8   otherwise leave i unchanged]
```

Proof reasoning: First, termination (`whiletest` evaluates false) is guaranteed because on each iteration, either `id` is found in `emp` and `i` is set to a nonzero value, or either `bot` is increased or `top` is decreased, so that eventually the `whiletest` will fail and the loop will terminate. Second, for the `whiletest` true case, the two-part `sequence` of operations defined by the `dopart` intended function *(g)* followed by the `whiledo` intended function *f* (recall the definitions of *f* and *g* from Table 4.4)

```
11   [if id = emp((bot + top)/2), set i to (bot + top)/2,
     otherwise
12   if id > emp((bot + top)/2), set bot to (bot + top)/2 + 1,
     otherwise
13   if id < emp((bot + top)/2), set top to (bot + top)/2 - 1]
7    [if possible, set i so that emp(i) = id and bot <= i <= top,
8    otherwise leave i unchanged]
```

must satisfy the `whiledo` intended function *(f):*

```
7   [if possible, set i so that emp(i) = id and bot <= i <= top,
8   otherwise leave i unchanged]
```

To see this, note that performing the first part of the sequence (the `dopart` intended function at lines 11–13) will either find `i` in `emp` (line 11) or will exclude a portion of `emp` from further search (where `i` is guaranteed not to be found) by adjusting the value of `top` or `bot` as required (lines 12 and 13). Thus, the `dopart` function may find `i`, but if not it will not prevent finding `i` if possible in performing the second part of the sequence (the `whiledo` intended function at lines 7–8), which now searches that part of `emp` where `i` may still be found. Also, the `dopart` intended function (lines 11–13) and the `whiledo` intended function (lines 7 and 8) do not change the value of `i` unless it is found in `emp`. Thus, the two-part `sequence` appears to be equivalent to the `whiledo` intended function, as is required.

Third, for the `whiletest` false case, doing nothing must do the intended function. When the `whiletest` is false, either `i` has already been set to the appropriate value (line 11) or the entire array has been searched (each iteration, lines 11 and 12 exclude successive portions of the sorted array where `id` is guaranteed not to be found, until finally no portions remain to be excluded—the entire array has been searched) and id has not been found. In either case, doing nothing is the appropriate action to satisfy the intended function.

The dopart at lines 11 through 21, 30.   The intended function for the dopart is given at lines 11 through 13, and the intended function for the nested ifthenelse is given at lines 20 and 21. Note that a sequence with firstpart an assignment to mid and secondpart an ifthenelse is verified here. Such combined analysis of control structures in verification is useful when proof arguments are simplified as a result:

```
11  [if id = emp((bot + top)/2), set i to (bot + top)/2,
    otherwise
12  if id > emp((bot + top)/2), set bot to (bot + top)/2 + 1,
    otherwise
13  if id < emp((bot + top)/2), set top to (bot + top)/2 - 1]
14  do
15      mid := (bot + top)/2
16      if
17          emp(mid) = id
18      then
19          i := mid
20      else [if id > emp(mid), set bot to mid + 1, otherwise
21              if id < emp(mid), set top to mid - 1]
29      endif
30  enddo
```

Proof reasoning: Given the assignment at line 15, the ifthenelse can be rewritten as

```
16  if
17      emp(bot + top)/2 = id
18  then
19      i := ((bot + top)/2)
20  else [if id > emp((bot + top)/2), set bot to ((bot + top)/2) + 1,
        otherwise
21          if id < emp((bot + top)/2), set top to ((bot + top)/2) - 1]
29  endif
```

Thus, the iftest at line 17 and assignment at line 19 perform the first part of the intended function at line 11, and the embedded intended function at lines 20 and 21 performs the remaining two parts of the intended function at lines 12 and 13, as required.

The `ifthenelse` at lines 20 through 28. This control structure is correct by direct inspection of the true and false correctness questions.

```
20  else [if id > emp(mid), set bot to mid + 1, otherwise
21  if id < emp(mid), set top to mid - 1]
22  if
23      emp(mid) < id
24  then
25      bot := mid + 1
26  else
27      top := mid - 1
28  endif
```

Having completed the proof arguments for all the control structures in the search procedure, the correctness of the entire procedure can now be asserted. The level of proof reasoning illustrated here is typically carried out verbally in team reviews, stepping through each correctness question in turn, with group agreement required for correctness. This process of acquiring team consensus is extremely effective in producing high-quality software because team fallibility is far less than individual fallibility. Additional rigor is always available for verifying life-, mission-, and enterprise-critical software through mathematics-based intended functions and written proofs of the correctness questions.

4.3.3 Verification in Practice

To make verification as practical as possible (fast and effective), several aspects of formal verification described earlier must be adapted to each situation. For example, one would need a correctness condition for every language construct used to have a formal basis for doing function abstraction correctly in terms of transformations on the data space visible to the structure. It is often beneficial for a team to agree to use a limited subset of the programming language and to write constructs uniformly. As a practical matter, it would be wise to have a style guide for team coding practices that is as simple and as limited as the situation allows.

The methods described earlier for verification are the very same methods used to reverse-engineer code. However, there is a vast difference in level of effort between verification of code that has been designed in full knowledge that its authors must verify the code, and verification of code written by others with no verification anticipated (reverse engineering). The sequence enumeration leads to black box and state box specifications that can serve as the intended functions to be coded. Further design decisions made at the clear box level may change these intended functions somewhat; however, in general, intended functions can be represented in the code by reference to the state box specifications.

Finally, the verification process will be conducted by a team reading the code, mentally posing and answering correctness questions, abstracting the program function of various constructs, and comparing that program function with the intended function. Function abstraction and comparison with the intended function is the essence of verification. Given straightforward and uniform coding practices, teams become very effective at the cognitive pattern matching of mental and verbal verification, which is also known as *proof by direct assertion.* In practice, a team would only "go to the board" when there is controversy regarding the actual transformation on data or the comparison with the specification.

Successful verification does not mean that the code will not change. Verification sessions often lead to insights for better designs, and sometimes the better idea justifies redesign of the code, which should be reverified. Errors found, of course, lead to code changes and repeated verification. The verification process can consume substantial resources; however, this resource allocation is very cost-effective because of the nearly total elimination of rework after the code goes into testing.

Stavely (1999) gives an intuitive and thorough treatment of design and verification using intended functions.

4.4 Example: The Security Alarm Clear Box

The state-based specification for the security alarm will now be used for clear box design. The security alarm illustrates a clear box that can be developed from the state box with little algorithmic elaboration required. However, as the example illustrates, substantial thought should be applied to the architecture of clear boxes to provide flexibility for future business needs.

4.4.1 Design Strategies

An obvious design strategy, though not necessarily the best one, is simply to use a high-level switch structure to send each stimulus to a lower level component. Four lower level components would be needed: one each for Trip, Set, Digit, and Clear. The lower level components would perform the actions specified in the tables presented earlier. Another obvious design strategy, again not necessarily the best one, is to use a high-level switch structure based on the current values of state data. There is no compelling reason for this choice, but it would be easy to produce.

These two options are so straightforward that the code could be generated directly from the tables, with no design decisions required. As modifications and enhancements are made in the future, only the specification needs to be maintained. Code could always be generated at the level of abstraction of the specification. If, on the other hand, the product is to be part of a product line, with related products containing similar components, then separation of concerns may be a design priority to facilitate reuse across the product line. A modular, extensible architecture based on device objects may be desired.

4.4.2   Flexible Architecture for Product Evolution

The simple security alarm might be the base product in a prospective line of consumer security devices. The following features might be included in the plan for derivative products:

- User-programmable codes
- A device status window
- Event data storage
- Devices with multiple trip mechanisms
- Alarms with various characteristics (e.g., time-out, signal type, volume level)
- Connectivity to other devices

This list could be elaborated to all conceivable features of derivative products. A software architecture that isolates each aspect of the device will accommodate product evolution by allowing changes to parts while preserving the integrity of the whole. The important aspects of the security alarm might be described as the device display, the code, and the alarm. Three principal components will be defined for the security alarm clear box architecture: a `DisplayManager`, a `CodeManager`, and an `AlarmManager`.

4.4.3   Security Alarm Clear Box Design

The clear box for the security alarm is a set of components that collectively implements the state box specification developed in Chapter 3 and summarized in Tables 3.10 to 3.14. The clear box is expressed in an object-oriented pseudo code. The pound symbol (#) precedes each comment in the clear box. Some comments include numbers that are preceded by *SB* (for state box), followed by tag numbers as defined in Tables 3.10 through 3.14. These comments are traces to the intended functions.

The security alarm state box can be considered as a disjoint conditional rule that defines 39 transitions. Examination shows that transition 9 defines initialization whereas transitions 38 and 39 define finalization. After initialization, a loop will monitor events and produce responses as indicated in all other transitions of the state box.

A clear box implementation of state variables invented during state box development often involves some variation on their state box form. In this example, the state variables are implemented as follows.

1. The Set stimulus activates the device. All device behavior occurs when the device is active, as seen in the state box tables by the fact that the Device state variable is always ON and corresponds to `LightStatus`.

2. The state variable Alarm is implemented as the variable `AlarmStatus` in the `AlarmManager` component.

3. The state variable Code is implemented as the variable `EntryStatus` in the `CodeManager` component.

```
Security Alarm;
#----------------------------------------------------------------
#                          Declarations
#----------------------------------------------------------------
# Constants
CLEAR constant 0;            # no error or alarm
STOP constant -1;            # stops main loop on correct code
TRIPSIGNAL constant -99;     # hardware trip wire signal
SET constant -100;           # Set button on keypad pressed
# Variables
Event integer init (CLEAR); # any keypad entry or hardware signal
SecurityStatus boolean init (CLEAR); # alarm on or off
#----------------------------------------------------------------
#                          Main Program
#----------------------------------------------------------------
# start the device; SB 9
DisplayManager (Start);

while (Event != STOP)
do
    # get next user input or hardware signal
    get (Event);

    switch (Event);

        # SB 10-17
        case (SET);
            # do nothing

        # SB 1-8
        case (TRIPSIGNAL)
            AlarmManager (Query, SecurityStatus);
            if (SecurityStatus = CLEAR)
            then
```

```
                    # SB 1,3,4,7
                    AlarmManager (Start);
                    # SB 4,7
                    CodeManager (Alert, Event);
                # else do nothing; SB 2,5,6,8
                endif

          # SB 18-37
          default
              CodeManager (Evaluate, Event);
              # CodeManager will return STOP if code entry is
                complete

      endswitch
enddo

# SB 38,39
AlarmManager (Stop);
DisplayManager (Stop);

# end of Security Alarm main program
#                          OBJECT TEMPLATES
# DisplayManager (Service)
# AlarmManager (Service, Data)
# CodeManager (Service, Data)

DisplayManager (DisplayService);
#-----------------------------------------------------------------
#                              Data
#-----------------------------------------------------------------
# Constants
ON constant 1;                # light is on
OFF constant 0;               # light is off

# State data
LightStatus boolean static init (OFF); # device activation light
#-----------------------------------------------------------------
#                            Services
#-----------------------------------------------------------------
# SB 9
Start;
    LightStatus := ON;
```

```
# SB 38-39
Stop;
    LightStatus := OFF;


# end DisplayManager


AlarmManager (AlarmService, Status);
#------------------------------------------------------------------
#                                Data
#------------------------------------------------------------------
# Constants
ON constant 1;              # alarm is on
OFF constant 0;             # alarm is off


# State data
AlarmStatus boolean static init (OFF); # alarm activation status
#------------------------------------------------------------------
#                             Services
#------------------------------------------------------------------
# SB 1,3,4,7
Start;
    AlarmStatus := ON;


Query;
    Status = AlarmStatus;


# SB 39
Stop;
    AlarmStatus := OFF;


# end AlarmManager


CodeManager (CodeService, Event);
#------------------------------------------------------------------
#                                Data
#------------------------------------------------------------------
# Constants
NONE constant 0;            # no keypad entry
1_OK constant 1;            # first correct digit in code entered
2_OK constant 2;            # second correct digit in code entered

CLEAR constant 0;           # Clear button on keypad pressed
COMPLETE constant -1;       # correct code entered
ERROR constant -2;          # error in code entry
```

```
# State data
CodeCombination array static init([1]:=7;[2]:=5;[3]:=7]) # code is 757
EntryStatus   integer static init (NONE); # code entry status
#-------------------------------------------------------------------
#                               Services
#-------------------------------------------------------------------
# SB 4,7
Alert;
    if ((EntryStatus = 1_OK) | (EntryStatus = 2_OK))
    then EntryStatus := ERROR;
    endif

# SB 18-37
Evaluate;
    if (Event = CLEAR)
    then
        # clear button has been pressed; SB 26-33
        EntryStatus := NONE;

    else
        # digit has been pressed
        switch (EntryStatus);

        case (NONE)
            # SB 34,35
            if (Event = CodeCombination[1])
            then EntryStatus := 1_OK;
            # SB 18,19
            else EntryStatus := ERROR;
            endif

        case (1_OK)
            # SB 36,37
            if (Event = CodeCombination[2])
            then EntryStatus := 2_OK;
            # SB 21,23
            else EntryStatus := ERROR;
            endif

        case (2_OK)
            # SB 38,39
            if (Event = CodeCombination[3])
            then
```

```
                    EntryStatus :- NONE;
                    Event := COMPLETE;
              # SB 24,25
              else EntryStatus = ERROR;
              endif
          default;
              # if EntryStatus = ERROR, do nothing; SB 20,22


       endswitch

    endif
# end CodeManager
```

4.4.4   Correctness Verification of Clear Box

Verification of the security alarm clear box is done by abstracting the program function and then comparing the results with the state box specification, followed by analyzing the correctness conditions. At the risk of belaboring the issue, many details are written out here that in practice would be dispatched quickly in team review. Increasingly, however, full documentation of correctness verification is being required in safety-critical and high-business-risk applications.

The verification fundamentals described earlier are used, with effects on data presented in <before, after> and tabular forms. The column titles in Tables 4.5 through 4.7 give the names of all the variables mentioned in the code of the object. Each row of the table represents the status of all variables on exit. The rightmost column contains a trace to the state box row being implemented, and an asterisk is used to flag partial or distributed implementation. Thus the effects on data are fully summarized and the effect of any use of the object is easily seen. The program function of each of the three objects is abstracted before that of the main program. Logic symbols are & for logical and, | for or, and ~ for not. Dashes indicate no change and x represents don't know or don't care. All tables are written out here; in practice, perhaps only that of the `CodeManager` would be written.

The program function of `CodeManager` is a bit more complex than the others. Each numbered row has two rows within it; the upper represents the data space before execution and the lower represents the data space after execution.

`CodeManager` makes essentially 10 transformations in monitoring user attempts to enter a correct three-digit code to turn off the device. Row 8 changes `Event` to -1 to indicate success. Row 1 shows that an alarm signal will disrupt a disarm code in progress, whereas row 2 shows that no code in progress results in no change to the data space. Row 3 shows that `SET` initializes and `CLEAR` resets progress status, and a newly entered, correct three-digit code is required. Row 4

Table 4.5 Program function of `DisplayManager`

Display Service	LightStatus	State Box Trace Row No.
Start	1	9
Stop	0	38*, 39*

Table 4.6 Program function of `AlarmManager`

Alarm Service	Status	AlarmStatus	State Box Trace Row No.
Start	-	1	1, 3, 4*, 7*
Query	0|1	-	
Stop	-	0	39*

shows that a good first digit (meaning the correct digit at the right time) records progress, otherwise it results in an error (row 5). Row 6 shows that a good second digit records progress, otherwise it results in an error (row 7). As noted earlier, a good third digit results in `Event` being set to –1; otherwise, it results in an error (row 9). All other inputs result in no change to the data space, as indicated in row 10.

The visible data space of the device is a pair `<LightStatus, AlarmStatus>`. The overall structure of the top-level procedure is a four-part `sequence` with correct behavior:

```
<OFF, OFF>
DisplayManager
<ON, OFF>
While-do-loop
<ON, x>
AlarmManager
<ON, OFF>
DisplayManager
<OFF, OFF>
```

When the device is turned on, `DisplayManager` turns on the light `<OFF, OFF>` to `<ON, OFF>`. `Event` is defaulted to `CLEAR`, and so the loop is always entered.

Within the loop, (1) further instances of `SET` have no effect; (2) `TRIPSIGNAL` will turn on the alarm and tell the `CodeManager` (so that if disarming is in

Table 4.7 Program function of `CodeManager`

Row No.	Service	Event	EntryStatus	CodeCombination[1]	CodeCombination[2]	CodeCombination[3]	State Box Trace
1	Alert	x -	1|2 -2	7 -	5 -	7 -	4*, 7*
2	Alert	x -	~(1|2) -	7 -	5 -	7 -	1*, 3*
3	Evaluate &	0 -	x 0	7 -	5 -	7 -	26-33
4	Evaluate &	7 -	& 0 1	7 -	5 -	7 -	34, 35
5	Evaluate &	~7 -	& 0 -2	7 -	5 -	7 -	18, 19
6	Evaluate &	5 -	& 1 2	7 -	5 -	7 -	36, 37
7	Evaluate &	~5 -	& 1 -2	7 -	5 -	7 -	21, 23
8	Evaluate &	7 -1	& 2 0	7 -	5 -	7 -	38, 39
9	Evaluate &	~7 -	& 2 -2	7 -	5 -	7 -	24, 25
10	Evaluate &	other -	& other -	7 -	5 -	7 -	20, 22

progress it will be interrupted, if the alarm is off; if the alarm is on, then it will have no effect); (3) all other values of `Event`s will be given directly to the `CodeManager` to evaluate. It is possible for the loop to terminate. This happens when and only when `CodeManager` sets `Event` to `-1`, whereupon the loop terminates immediately and the device behavior is <ON, x>.

On exiting the loop, `AlarmManager` is called and the device goes from <ON, x> to <ON, OFF>. `DisplayManager` is called and the device goes from <ON, OFF> to <OFF, OFF>. This analysis is easily restated directly in terms of correctness questions in a further illustration of verification methods.

The overall structure of the top-level procedure is a four-part `sequence`, with `firstpart`, `thirdpart`, and `fourthpart` object service invocations and with `secondpart` a `whiledo`. The `sequence` correctness question requires that the composition of these four parts must carry out the intended function; in this case, successive transitions of the state box itself. Inspection shows that `firstpart` correctly implements transition 9, start-up. Likewise `thirdpart` and `fourthpart` correctly implement transitions 38 and 39, with the assumption that `whiledo` terminates. For correctness, `secondpart` `whiledo` must carry out all state box transitions other than 9, 38, and 39, and must also terminate on completion of a correct code only. These assumptions define the required, intended function of the `whiledo`.

The `dopart` of `whiledo` is a two-part `sequence`, with `firstpart` a `get` statement that obtains the current stimulus, and `secondpart` a `switch` statement that processes it. This `sequence` is correct by inspection with the provision that `secondpart` processing is correct.

`Secondpart` is comprised of three cases that are based on the current stimuli. The first case deals with the Set stimulus, and inspection shows that this case correctly implements transitions 10 through 17.

The second case, TRIPSIGNAL, is composed of a `sequence` of `AlarmManager` and an `ifthenelse`. The `iftest` composes the `AlarmManager` with either the `thenpart` or the `elsepart`. If the alarm is off, it is turned on no matter what the current state, as required by transitions 1, 3, 4, and 7, and `CodeManager` is invoked to set `EntryStatus` to `-2` if a code entry was in progress, as required by transitions 4 and 7. If the alarm is on, there is no response or state change as required by transitions 2, 5, 6 and 8. Thus, the second case correctly handles transitions 1 through 8.

The third case deals with all other stimuli and is composed of `CodeManager`, which directly implements transitions 18 through 37. Thus, `dopart` correctly implements transitions 1 through 8 and 10 through 37, and sets the loop exit conditions. Given this analysis, the three `whiledo` correctness conditions—termination, `whiletest` true, and `whiletest` false—can be addressed. The clear box appears to be a correct implementation of the state box.

4.5 References

R.C. Linger, H.D. Mills, and B.I. Witt. *Structured Programming: Theory and Practice.* Reading, MA: Addison-Wesley, 1979.

H.D. Mills, R.C. Linger, and A.R. Hevner. *Principles of Information Systems Analysis and Design.* Orlando, FL: Academic Press, 1986.

A.M. Stavely. *Toward Zero-Defect Programming.* Reading, MA: Addison-Wesley, 1999.

5

Cleanroom Software Certification

A statistical approach to software testing was developed both by Harlan Mills (Mills, Dyer, and Linger 1987) and colleagues at IBM, and by John Musa (1993) and colleagues at AT&T. The terminology used by Mills and Musa differed slightly, but their ideas were similarly drawn from scientific approaches to product testing and certification in mature engineering disciplines. In other industries, products are typically certified under protocols in which random samples of the product are drawn, tests characteristic of operational use are applied, analytical or statistical inferences are made, and products meeting a standard are "certified" as fit for use.

The Cleanroom approach to software testing and certification—statistical testing based on a usage model—is the application of such a protocol to software (Poore and Trammell 1998). In statistical testing, an operational usage model of the software is developed, test cases are generated randomly from the usage model, and test results are interpreted according to mathematical and statistical models to yield measures of software quality and test sufficiency. Traditional forms of structural testing are complementary with Cleanroom statistical usage testing, and need not be abandoned. However, many organizations have found that usage testing is a more economical and efficient approach to developmental testing, and it results in higher reliability of fielded software.

5.1 Benefits of Statistical Testing Based on a Usage Model

Statistical usage testing of a software system produces measures of product and process quality for management decision making throughout the life cycle.

Because a usage model is based on specifications rather than code, the insights that result from model building can be used to make informed management decisions in the early stages of a project when the opportunity to prevent problems is greatest. The following are key benefits of usage modeling and statistical testing.

Validation of Requirements. A usage model is an external view of the system specification that is readily understandable by system engineers, developers, customers, and end users. Interfaces and requirements are often simplified or clarified when the usage model (including possible inputs, possible sequencing of inputs, and expected outputs) is reviewed systematically in the context of operational use.

Resource and Schedule Estimation. Standard calculations on a usage model provide data for effort, schedule, and cost projections, such as the minimum number of tests required to cover all states and transitions in the model. "What-if" analyses can be conducted to bound the best and worst case outcomes of testing based on failure data.

Crafted, Nonrandom Test Cases. Special test cases, perhaps required by contract or regulation, can be determined by examining the model to be sure that certain sequences are tested. Existing test cases can be mapped to the model to assess omissions or redundancy. The usage model becomes a reference model for all testing required or desired.

Automated Test Case Generation. A minimal coverage test script (the minimal number of test events for complete coverage of the usage model) and random test cases (based on the usage probability distribution) can be generated automatically from a usage model. Model coverage testing ensures a minimal level of function before random testing begins, and random testing provides a basis for estimating operational reliability.

Effective, Efficient Testing. Faults are not equally likely to cause failures. Faults that are on frequently traversed paths have a higher probability of causing failures than faults that are on infrequently traversed paths. This simple fact is the primary motivation for random testing: Faults are discovered in roughly the order in which they would cause failures in the field. The test budget is spent in a way that maximizes the increase in operational reliability resulting from testing.

Focused Testing (Biased Sampling). Usage models support biased sampling of sequences of special interest, such as infrequently used but critical functions. Separate models can be developed for these functions, or the original model may be transformed, sampled, and the results corrected to remove the bias.

Quantitative Test Management.   Statistical testing based on a usage model provides quantitative criteria for management decisions about completion of testing and system release. The sufficiency of testing can be measured as the statistical difference between expected usage (as represented in the usage model) and tested usage (as recorded in testing).

Estimate of Reliability.   Using a statistical testing protocol, a valid estimate of expected operational performance can be derived from the performance of the software during testing. The actual test results (i.e., correct and incorrect performance on each input) are recorded as weights on the usage model, and calculations on the model provide estimates of reliability in operational use.

5.2 Theoretical Foundations of Statistical Testing

5.2.1   Populations and Samples

In statistical testing, software testing is viewed as a problem to be solved by statistical methods. A subset of all possible uses of the software is generated, and performance on the subset is used as a basis for conclusions about general operational performance. In other words, a "sample" is used to draw conclusions about a "population."

The premise that must be accepted as a starting point in this analogy is that it is not possible to test *all* ways in which software may be used. This is apparently not a premise that can be assumed as obvious. In discussing software testing strategies with testing practitioners, it is not uncommon to hear someone say, "We *have* to test every possible use of the software; the kind of software we develop could have catastrophic consequences if it is not tested completely." The following simple examples are intended to demonstrate the impossibility of testing all possible scenarios of use.

Software with a bounded but large input sequence length has a finite but astronomical number of possible usage scenarios. The combinatorial growth in possible input sequences yields a testing problem of surprising magnitude for even a small application, as shown in the example in Table 5.1 from Wiener (1994). The example assumes a system in which (1) a usage scenario has at least one input and at most 10 inputs, (2) 20 different inputs are possible, and (3) inputs may be repeated. Such a system would be small indeed by today's standards.

If each scenario in this example could be tested in one second, the system would require more than 300,000 years to test. If 100 scenarios could be tested per second, the testing time is reduced to 3,000+ years. If 100 scenarios could

Table 5.1 Scenarios

Length of Input Sequence	No. of Possible Usage Scenarios	
1	20	= 20
2	20 x 20	= 400
3	20 x 20 x 20	= 8,000
4	20 x 20 x 20 x 20	= 160,000
5	20 x 20 x 20 x 20 x 20	= 3,200,000
6	20 x 20 x 20 x 20 x 20 x 20	= 64,000,000
7	20 x 20 x 20 x 20 x 20 x 20 x 20	= 1,280,000,000
8	20 x 20 x 20 x 20 x 20 x 20 x 20 x 20	= 25,600,000,000
9	20 x 20 x 20 x 20 x 20 x 20 x 20 x 20 x 20	= 512,000,000,000
10	20 x 20 x 20 x 20 x 20 x 20 x 20 x 20 x 20 x 20	= 10,240,000,000,000
Total usage scenarios		10,778,947,368,420

be tested per second on each of 100 copies of the software, testing time is reduced to 30+ years. Exhaustive testing is simply an impossible task, even when the number of usage scenarios is finite.

Software with an unbounded input sequence length has a theoretically infinite number of possible usage scenarios. For software with only two user inputs, A and B, the possible scenarios of use (i.e., scenarios that begin with invocation and end with termination) are A, B, AA, AB, BB, BA, AAA, AAB, ABA, BAA, BBB, and so on.

There is really no question about whether all possible scenarios of use will be tested. They will not. The only questions are how the population of uses will be characterized and how a subset of test cases will be drawn. A random sample of test cases from a properly characterized population, if applied to the software with proper experimental control, will allow valid generalization of conclusions from testing to operational use. Any other set of test cases, no matter how thoughtfully constructed, will not.

5.2.2 Stochastic Nature of Software Use

Software use can be viewed as a stochastic process (i.e., a series of events that unfold over time in a probabilistic way). A Markov process is a stochastic process that obeys the Markov property, in which the next event in a series can be determined based on the present, without reference to the past. Markov theory has been applied to developing and analyzing software usage models (Whittaker and Poore 1993, Whittaker and Thomason 1994), and mathematical programming has been applied to model optimization (Walton, Poore, and Trammell 1993). Software use can be modeled as a finite state, discrete-parameter Markov chain, and the standard analytical results for Markov chains can be interpreted to yield insights about long-term operational use. Given a usage model as a system of constraints (Walton 1995), mathematical programming can then be used to generate the optimal model for an objective function (for example, the model that "covers" all usage states and state transitions with the fewest test cases). The formalisms used in Cleanroom software certification provide a sound theoretical foundation for current practice and ongoing advances in technology.

5.3 Statistical Usage Testing in Practice

A software usage model characterizes operational use of a software system (i.e., the population from which a statistically correct sample of test cases can be drawn). Statistical testing is ordinarily discussed within the context of normal usage conditions, but other usage contexts (e.g., stress conditions, hazardous conditions, maintenance conditions) may be specified as well.

5.3.1 Usage Specification

The first step in usage model development is to characterize general operational conditions and perhaps stratify classes of usage. Software is "used" by a "user" in some "environment." The definitions of *user, use,* and *environment* define the operational environment to which inferences about the software apply. If multiple usage contexts are important, separate models that are tailored for each context may be used. Stratification of usage is a technique for characterizing usage in as granular a fashion as necessary to describe the variation in operational conditions.

A user of the software may be a person, a hardware device, or other software, and each user type may be further stratified if necessary. Human users, for example, might be classified by job type, access privileges, or experience in the domain.

A use of the software may be a work session, a transaction, a telephone call, or any other unit of service. A use may be bounded by power-on/power-off, invocation/termination, switchhook-up/switchhook-down, or any other appropriate start/finish events defining an instance of usage.

A usage environment can be characterized by platform, single user versus multiuser, concurrent applications, system load, integrity of externally provided data, and other factors.

5.3.2   Usage Model Development

The initial structure of a usage model follows directly from the software specification. The Cleanroom approach to specification provides a common point of departure for both the development work described in the previous chapter and the certification work described in this chapter. In particular, the canonical sequences identified during specification define the initial state space for the usage model.

A usage model may be represented as a graph in which the nodes represent usage states and the arcs represent stimuli that cause transitions between usage states. Note that it is states of use (e.g., "signed on," "transaction initiated," etc.) that are referred to here, and not internal states of the software. Graphical usage models are easily understood by developers and potential users, who often participate in usage model review. Graphical representation aids in system understanding but is generally only used for small systems or for high-level representation of large systems. Usage models for large systems are often defined abstractly at first, with automated support for model expansion through submodels and transformation of abstract stimuli to associated atomic stimuli. Usage models may also be represented as tables or matrices, with rows and columns representing states, and each cell representing the probability of the row state being followed by the column state.

The structure of a usage model represents *possible* use of the software. A probability distribution is next imposed on the structure to represent *expected* use of the software under specified conditions. Transition probabilities between states in the usage model may be based on field data if available, on estimates from customer interviews, or on instrumentation of prior system versions. The probabilities associated with states and state transitions in a usage model may be set to reflect either routine or nonroutine conditions.

5.3.3   Usage Model Analysis and Test Planning

As mentioned, state transition graphs or matrices are common forms for representing usage models. Such structures are also common forms for representing Markov chains. Although usage models may be represented in other forms, Markov chain usage models are prominent in Cleanroom practice due to the insights that may be gained from calculations on a Markov chain. Standard calculations on a Markov chain provide expected values for measures that are highly useful in test planning, such as

- Average number of events in a use (test case)
- Long-run state occupancy (i.e., percentage of total usage time)
- Average number of uses (test cases) before a given usage state occurs

These results—available from the model alone (i.e., prior to software design and implementation)—have application throughout the software life cycle. They may be used to prune the specification, gauge complexity, focus verification efforts, identify frequencies of events, plan the test schedule, and determine the upper bound on inferences about reliability.

5.3.4 Test Case Generation and Testing

After the usage model has been developed, test cases can be generated automatically by traversing the usage states of the model, guided by the transition probabilities associated with the exit arcs from each state. Because each arc is associated with a particular stimulus to the system, the traversal results in an accumulation of successive stimuli that represents a particular test case. The test cases constitute a *script* for use in testing. They may be annotated during test planning to include instructions for conducting and evaluating tests, and they may be annotated during testing to record results and observations. Test cases may be applied by human testers or used as input to an automated test tool.

Several assumptions underlie the validity of inferences from a statistical experiment. In general, proper control of the testing process may be safeguarded by the following four practices.

1. Each version of the software is tested in a unique statistical experiment. Data from a given version may be used to estimate the reliability of that version only. Data across versions are used to characterize the testing process. Data used in reliability models are used to estimate the reliability of the product; data used in reliability growth models are used to estimate the effectiveness of the process.

2. The specification, environmental conditions, and the basis for evaluation of performance are held constant for each version of the software that is tested.

3. Test cases are run as generated. One does not "pick and choose" among test cases.

4. Test staff members are trained to ensure a common understanding of all test materials and policies. Performance of human testers is monitored throughout testing to prevent "drift." Regular communication among test team members is scheduled to review results and discuss matters that may affect test judgment.

The actual behavior of the software under test is compared with the specified behavior by either human or automated means. The behavior of the software is checked on each transition, and failures are recorded by software version, test case number, and transition number. All test data and test scripts are archived.

5.3.5   Metrics for Test Sufficiency and Product Quality

The usage model that generates test cases is called the *usage chain*. The expected long-run occupancy of each state is calculated from the usage chain during model analysis. During the testing phase, a second chain (called the *testing chain)* is used to track actual state traversals during testing. The testing chain begins as a copy of the usage chain structure, with a counter on each arc that is initially zero (indicating that no use of the software has yet occurred). As test cases are applied, the counters associated with the arcs are incremented to record state transitions (if the software performs the transition to the usage state successfully) during testing.

A comparison of the usage and testing chains is made on an ongoing basis during testing to gauge the difference between expected and actual usage. The difference is given as the value of a measure called the *discriminant,* which reflects the degree to which the testing experience has become representative of expected usage. The value for the discriminant generally tends toward zero (but not monotonically) as testing progresses without failures. The value will plateau at stages of testing, with the specific values dependent on the specific models and the amount of testing done. When, in the judgment of the test engineers, the value is low enough to indicate that the testing experience is sufficiently similar to expected field performance such that further testing is not worth its cost, testing should stop.

As testing progresses and failures occur, the structure of the testing chain is augmented with *failure states.* The reliability of the software, which may be calculated at any point in testing, is the probability of taking a random walk through the testing chain from invocation to termination without encountering a failure state. In other words, reliability is the probability that every event in a complete usage scenario will be processed successfully. Reliability is calculated from the testing chain.

If no failures occur during testing, the reliability calculation yields 1.0, which must be interpreted as "no information" and not as a reliability estimate. When testing shows no failures, other reliability measures should be used, such as presented by Poore, Mills, and Mutchler (1993) or Miller (1992).

Statistical testing based on a usage model is an appropriate protocol for software testing. It is grounded in sound scientific principles, has been reduced to reasonable engineering practice, and produces conclusions that are independently confirmable.

5.4 Example: Security Alarm

5.4.1 Usage Model

The canonical sequences identified during security alarm specification define the state space for the usage model. The canonical sequences for the security alarm that were discovered in Chapter 3 are presented again in Table 5.2. Each canonical sequence is named to represent the usage state.

The usage model may be drawn using the canonical sequences as states. The ordering of states can be determined by referring to the canonical sequences, and the full set of possible stimuli given in the sequence enumeration in Chapter 3 can be used to define all possible transitions (arcs) among states. Figure 5.1 is a graphical depiction of the usage model for the security

Table 5.2   Canonical sequences for the security alarm

Canonical Sequence	Description	Usage State Name
Empty	—	Software Not Invoked
S	The user has pressed the Set button to activate the device.	Ready
$S\,T$	The device has been set and the trip signal has occurred, setting off the alarm.	Alarm
$S\,B$	The device has been set and the user has entered an invalid digit.	Entry Error
$S\,G$	The device has been set and the user has entered the first digit in the code.	1_OK
$S\,T\,B$	The device has been set, the trip signal has set off the alarm, and the user has entered an invalid digit. The Clear button must be pressed before the code can be entered to turn off the alarm.	Alarm and Entry Error
$S\,T\,G$	The device has been set, the trip signal has set off the alarm, and the user has entered the first digit in the code.	Alarm and 1_OK
$S\,G\,G$	The device has been set and the user has entered the first two digits in the code.	2_OK
$S\,T\,G\,G$	The device has been set, the trip signal has set off the alarm, and the user has entered the first two digits in the code.	Alarm and 2_OK

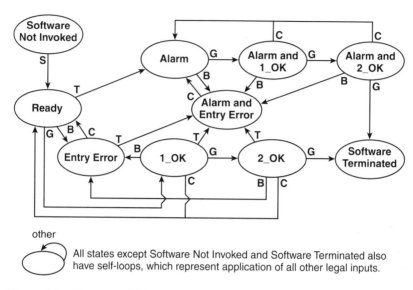

other

All states except Software Not Invoked and Software Terminated also have self-loops, which represent application of all other legal inputs.

Figure 5.1   Usage model for security alarm

alarm. Stimuli that have no effect on the usage state are represented in a self-loop in each state. From the Alarm state, for example, the Set button may be pressed, but it has no effect (does not change state of use); the usage state is still Alarm.

The next step in usage modeling is assignment of usage probability values for each arc in the model. In this case, all stimuli that can produce a state change will be regarded as equally likely except for the Trip stimulus, which will be assumed to be less likely than other stimuli. The Trip stimulus will be assigned a 0.05 probability from the Ready, Entry Error, 1_OK, and 2_OK states. The Trip stimulus has no effect in other states because the alarm is already on. (Stimuli that do not produce state changes are the "other" stimuli associated with self-loops in Figure 5.1.)

In the Ready state, for example, the Trip stimulus has a 0.05 probability of occurring, a GoodDigit and BadDigit in the security code each has a 0.45 probability of occurring, and all other stimuli (in this case, Set and Clear) have a (collective) 0.05 probability of occurring. Probabilities are assigned to all the outgoing arcs of each state.

Given the usage model structure and the usage probabilities, an analysis of the usage model can be performed to produce data that can be used throughout the life cycle. Table 5.3 presents the analytical values for the model. Formulas for all analytical results presented in this chapter are found in Whittaker and Thomason (1994).

Test planning is one primary use of analytical data from the usage model. The average length of a test case, for example, may be used to establish upper and lower bounds on the testing schedule. The expected average test case length for the security alarm is 48. Each test case might be estimated to require 15 minutes to test. The target level of system reliability to be demonstrated in testing might be 0.95 reliability at the 99% confidence level. Using simple hypothesis testing, a total of 90 test cases must be performed to meet that requirement (Poore, Mills, and Mutchler 1993). Assuming there are no failures during testing, a total of 22.5 hours will be needed to perform the 90 test cases. If an equivalent amount of time is needed for pre- and post-test activity, then the minimum total test schedule may be estimated to be 45 hours. An upper limit may be estimated as well by assuming longer elapsed time for test cases and/or a distribution of failures across test cases.

The minimum amount of random testing required to visit all usage states is being driven by the 2_OK state. Fifty-eight usage events (transitions) are expected before its first occurrence—a greater number than for any other state. A reduction in time to achieve state coverage is possible if the probability of stimuli leading to the 2_OK state is increased. Further consideration of this probability assignment is warranted (and may or may not lead to a decision to alter the probability to achieve a shorter schedule for state coverage).

Data from model analysis may also be used to focus development activity. For example, the expected long-run occupancy of the Alarm, and Alarm and Entry Error states represent half the usage probability mass (0.293 + 0.215 =

Table 5.3   Analysis of the security alarm usage model

State	Long-run Occupancy	Expected Transitions until State First Occurs	Probability of Occurrence in a Single Use
Software Not Invoked	0.020	48.860	1.000
Ready	0.111	1.000	1.000
Entry Error	0.074	9.763	0.835
1_OK	0.053	13.820	0.832
2_OK	0.017	58.330	0.527
Alarm	0.293	18.363	0.756
Alarm and 1_OK	0.147	21.521	0.756
Alarm and 2_OK	0.049	32.047	0.756
Alarm and Entry Error	0.215	21.102	0.714
Software Terminated	0.020	47.860	1.000

0.508). The development activity related to these usage states should receive particularly rigorous verification. Conversely, states with extremely low occupancy rates may represent functions that might even be pruned from the specification in some applications.

5.4.2 Testing

After the usage model and the analysis have been reviewed and determined to be a viable basis for testing, test cases are generated. The first test suite generated is usually the *minimal arc coverage* suite, which traverses the model in the fewest possible steps required to achieve model coverage. Model coverage testing accomplishes several goals. The model is further confirmed to be accurate, the ability to evaluate all responses is confirmed, and the readiness of the software for random testing is established. Random testing enables measurement of the reliability of the software. If the quality of the software is so poor that it cannot survive arc coverage testing in a reasonable period of time, then the software is not ready for random testing.

After the software has successfully passed the arc coverage test, random test cases are generated. Each test case is a random walk through the usage model. Each state in the model has a set of exit arcs, with each arc representing a stimulus. During a random walk through the model, a random number is generated at each state, and a stimulus is chosen based on the probabilities associated with the exit arcs from that state.

Table 5.4 depicts a sample test case for the security alarm that was generated randomly from the usage model. The initial state is Software Not Invoked. The only stimulus that is possible in that state is Set, so regardless of the random number generated, Set will be the next stimulus. The Set stimulus leads to the Ready state, which has four exit arcs (i.e., four possible stimuli). As mentioned earlier, the probabilities associated with the exit arcs are T (Trip), 0.05; G (GoodDigit), 0.45; B (BadDigit), 0.45; and any other stimulus, 0.05. In the following test case, the random number generated at the Ready state resulted in the G stimulus being selected. Random selection of stimuli continues at each state until the Software Terminated state is reached, signaling the end of the test case.

As testing proceeds, the performance of the software on each test case is recorded. If the software processes each test event correctly, the test case is recorded as a "pass." If there is a failure, the test case number and the transition number of the failure are recorded. Failure data and usage model analyses are used together to produce metrics for test sufficiency and product quality.

5.4.3 Measures of Test Sufficiency

The sufficiency of testing for the security alarm is quantified in two ways. The simplest measure of sufficiency is model coverage. Only two random test cases

Table 5.4   A randomly generated test case

Stimulus No.	Stimulus	Next State
1	S	Ready
2	G	1_OK
3	G	2_OK
4	C	Ready
5	B	Entry Error
6	C	Ready
7	B	Entry Error
8	C	Ready
9	G	1_OK
10	G	2_OK
11	G	Software Terminated

will be required to cover all states in the model on average. Fifteen test cases will be required to cover all arcs in the model. Again, a test case is a random walk through the usage model beginning with Software Not Invoked and ending with Software Terminated.

The column headed D(U,T) in Table 5.5 is the discriminant described earlier. The value is not defined until all arcs have been traversed; consequently, this column has no value for the first 14 scripts. When test cases are generated randomly from the model, they are of course generated in a manner that reflects the probabilities in the usage model. As the randomly generated test cases continue to accumulate usage events in proportion to usage probabilities, the use of the software in testing becomes more and more like the profile of usage that is expected to occur in the field. The discriminant—a measure of the similarity between expected and tested use—decreases during testing and eventually stops changing at some significant digit of interest. In the example in Table 5.5, the value of the discriminant is generally decreasing, but has not yet converged. The specific stopping criterion is a matter of experience in a particular domain, engineering judgment, and the testing budget and schedule.

In Table 5.5 no failures were assumed to have occurred during testing. An alternative scenario will now be assumed, in which a failure in the software's processing of the trip signal occurs. In this scenario, the software fails to set off the alarm when a trip signal occurs immediately after a bad digit has been entered.

The same 30 randomly generated test cases will again be considered, with failures as recorded in Table 5.6. The failures are *stop failures* rather than *continue*

Table 5.5 Test sufficiency: no-failures case

Script No.	Result	D(U,T)	% States Visited	% Arcs Traversed
1	Pass	—	60.000	22.581
2	Pass	—	100.000	58.065
3	Pass	—	100.000	67.742
4	Pass	—	100.000	67.742
5	Pass	—	100.000	70.968
6	Pass	—	100.000	77.419
7	Pass	—	100.000	87.097
8	Pass	—	100.000	90.323
9	Pass	—	100.000	93.548
10	Pass	—	100.000	96.774
11	Pass	—	100.000	96.774
12	Pass	—	100.000	96.774
13	Pass	—	100.000	96.774
14	Pass	—	100.000	96.774
15	Pass	0.0059	100.000	100.000
16	Pass	0.0055	100.000	100.000
17	Pass	0.0036	100.000	100.000
18	Pass	0.0035	100.000	100.000
19	Pass	0.0037	100.000	100.000
20	Pass	0.0037	100.000	100.000
21	Pass	0.0037	100.000	100.000
22	Pass	0.0036	100.000	100.000
23	Pass	0.0039	100.000	100.000
24	Pass	0.0036	100.000	100.000
25	Pass	0.0037	100.000	100.000
26	Pass	0.0038	100.000	100.000
27	Pass	0.0034	100.000	100.000
28	Pass	0.0028	100.000	100.000
29	Pass	0.0020	100.000	100.000
30	Pass	0.0019	100.000	100.000

failures, meaning that a test case is discontinued on failure, and the remaining transitions in the test case are not executed.

The failure data indicate that the software failed six times. In test cases 3, 7, 12, 27, 28, and 29, a trip signal immediately followed a bad digit, and the software did not set off the alarm. Given this scenario, the measures of test sufficiency are different. As shown in Table 5.7, all arcs in the model have not been covered after 30 test cases, and the value of the discriminant cannot be computed. Clearly, the measures of test sufficiency do not support product release.

As is apparent by the presentation of the no-failure and the one-failure scenarios, it is possible to pose what-if scenarios and determine bounds on the testing schedule given assumptions about the performance of the software during

Table 5.6   Failure data

Test Case No.	Transition No.	Stop or Continue?
3	5	Stop
7	21	Stop
12	27	Stop
27	16	Stop
28	9	Stop
29	16	Stop

Table 5.7   Test sufficiency: one-failure case

Script No.	Result	D(U,T)	% States Visited	% Arcs Traversed
1	Pass	—	60.000	22.581
2	Pass	—	100.000	58.065
3	Fail	—	100.000	58.065
4	Pass	—	100.000	58.065
5	Pass	—	100.000	61.290
6	Pass	—	100.000	70.968
7	Fail	—	100.000	77.419
8	Pass	—	100.000	83.871
9	Pass	—	100.000	90.323

continued

Table 5.7 *continued*

Script No.	Result	D(U,T)	% States Visited	% Arcs Traversed
10	Pass	—	100.000	93.548
11	Pass	—	100.000	93.548
12	Fail	—	100.000	93.548
13	Pass	—	100.000	93.548
14	Pass	—	100.000	93.548
15	Pass	—	100.000	96.774
16	Pass	—	100.000	96.774
17	Pass	—	100.000	96.774
18	Pass	—	100.000	96.774
19	Pass	—	100.000	96.774
20	Pass	—	100.000	96.774
21	Pass	—	100.000	96.774
22	Pass	—	100.000	96.774
23	Pass	—	100.000	96.774
24	Pass	—	100.000	96.774
25	Pass	—	100.000	96.774
26	Pass	—	100.000	96.774
27	Fail	—	100.000	96.774
28	Fail	—	100.000	96.774
29	Fail	—	100.000	96.774
30	Pass	—	100.000	96.774

testing. Measures of test sufficiency may be used prior to testing, in test planning, and during testing for test management.

5.4.4 Measures of Product Quality

Continuing the scenario in which one failure occurs during testing, measures of product quality are generated and summarized in Table 5.8 for the same 30 random test cases. As noted earlier, the reliability calculation will be 1.0 (no information) until a failure is recorded.

Because no failures occurred in the first two test cases, there is no failure data to use in calculating the MTTF for those two test cases. Similarly, the reliability of the software is reported as 1.0 as long as the software has exhibited no failures.

The first failure occurs in test case 3, so the MTTF (the average number of test cases until a failure occurs) at that point is approximately three. By the fifth

Table 5.8 Security alarm: one-failure case

Script No.	Result	Mean Time to Failure	Reliability
1	Pass	—	1.000
2	Pass	—	1.000
3	Fail	3.000	0.667
4	Pass	4.000	0.750
5	Pass	5.000	0.800
6	Pass	6.000	0.833
7	Fail	3.500	0.714
8	Pass	4.000	0.750
9	Pass	4.500	0.778
10	Pass	5.000	0.800
11	Pass	5.500	0.818
12	Fail	4.000	0.750
13	Pass	4.333	0.769
14	Pass	4.667	0.786
15	Pass	5.000	0.800
16	Pass	5.333	0.813
17	Pass	5.667	0.824
18	Pass	6.000	0.833
19	Pass	6.333	0.842
20	Pass	6.667	0.850
21	Pass	7.000	0.857
22	Pass	7.333	0.864
23	Pass	7.667	0.870

continued

Table 5.8   *continued*

Script No.	Result	Mean Time to Failure	Reliability
24	Pass	8.000	0.875
25	Pass	8.333	0.880
26	Pass	8.667	0.885
27	Fail	6.750	0.852
28	Fail	5.600	0.821
29	Fail	4.833	0.793
30	Pass	5.000	0.800

test case, the MTTF has risen to five, because only one failure has been seen in five test cases. When the second failure occurs in test case 7, the MTTF decreases sharply because two failures have now been seen in seven test cases, for a MTTF of 3.5.

Because statistical testing is based on a model of the specification, these measures of product quality, like measures of test sufficiency, may be generated for various scenarios of software performance long before the software actually exists. Product quality projections (based on what-if scenarios) provide data for reliability planning early in the software life cycle, and product quality estimates (based on performance during testing) provide additional stopping criteria for testing.

5.5 References

K.W. Miller, et al. "Estimating the Probability of Failure When Testing Reveals No Failures." *IEEE Transactions on Software Engineering* vol. 18 (January 1992): 33–43.

H.D. Mills, M. Dyer, and R.C. Linger. "Cleanroom Software Engineering." *IEEE Software* vol. 4 (September 1987): 19–24.

J. Musa. "Operational Profiles in Software Reliability Engineering." *IEEE Software* vol. 10 (March 1993): 14–32.

J.H. Poore, H.D. Mills, and D. Mutchler. "Planning and Certifying Software System Reliability." *IEEE Software* vol. 10 (January 1993): 88–99.

J.H. Poore and C.J. Trammell. "Application of Statistical Science to Testing and Evaluating Software Systems," in *Statistics, Testing, and Defense Acquisition,* ed. M. Cohen, et. al. (Washington: National Academy Press, 1998).

G.H. Walton. *Generating Transition Probabilities for Markov Chain Usage Models.* Ph.D. diss., University of Tennessee, 1995.

G.H. Walton, J.H. Poore, and C.J. Trammell. "Statistical Testing of Software Based on a Usage Model." *Software Practice and Experience* vol. 25 (January 1993): 97–108.

J.A. Whittaker and J.H. Poore. "Markov Analysis of Software Specifications." *ACM Transactions on Software Engineering and Methodology* vol. 2 (January 1993): 93–106.

J. Whittaker and M. Thomason. "A Markov Chain Model for Statistical Software Testing." *IEEE Transactions on Software Engineering* vol. 20 (October 1994): 812–824.

L.R. Wiener. *Digital Woes: Why We Should Not Depend on Software.* Reading, MA: Addison-Wesley, 1994.

PART II

The Cleanroom
Software Engineering
Reference Model

6

The Cleanroom
Reference Model

6.1 An Introduction to the CRM

The Cleanroom Software Engineering Reference Model (Linger and Trammell 1996), or CRM, was developed at the Software Engineering Institute, Carnegie Mellon University, as part of a study to map Cleanroom into the Capability Maturity Model for Software, or CMM (Linger, Paulk, and Trammell 1996). The CRM is expressed in terms of a set of 14 Cleanroom processes and 20 associated work products. It embodies the principal technologies and processes of Cleanroom, and is intended as a guide for Cleanroom project management and performance, process assessment and improvement, and technology transfer and adoption, as well as a baseline for continued evolution of Cleanroom practice. It is a comprehensive road map to Cleanroom project performance for software teams trained in Cleanroom methods. The CRM is organized into processes for software project management, specification, development, and testing. Other processes essential to product success, such as marketing, distribution, installation, and customer support are beyond the scope of the project management and technology focus of the CRM. The 14 processes are as follows:

Cleanroom Management Processes
- Project Planning Process
- Project Management Process
- Performance Improvement Process
- Engineering Change Process

Cleanroom Specification Processes
- Requirements Analysis Process
- Function Specification Process
- Usage Specification Process
- Architecture Specification Process
- Increment Planning Process

Cleanroom Development Processes
- Software Reengineering Process
- Increment Design Process
- Correctness Verification Process

Cleanroom Certification Processes
- Usage Modeling and Test Planning Process
- Statistical Testing and Certification Process

The CRM is a high-level process template that is intended to be tailored and adapted for specific organizational environments and project requirements. Existing organizational and project policies and standards should be taken into account in defining the tailored processes. For example, if a requirement exists to program in a specific language, the relationship of that language to box structure specification and design semantics and formats should be defined, and any specializations of the correctness conditions for verifying language constructs should be specified and documented. Such process adaptations and implementation procedures should be documented in the *Cleanroom Engineering Guide.* Tables 6.1 through 6.4 provide summaries of key tasks in each process, and enumerate the principal work products produced.

Table 6.1 Cleanroom management processes

Cleanroom Process	Process Description	Principal Work Products
Project Planning	Define and document plans for a Cleanroom project, and revise as necessary to accommodate changes. Review plans with the project team, peer groups, and the customer for agreement.	*Cleanroom Engineering Guide, Software Development Plan*
Project Management	Manage the Cleanroom incremental development and certification process to deliver software and associated work products on schedule and within budget. Establish and train Cleanroom teams, and define quality objectives and team performance expectations. Initiate and track Cleanroom processes.	*Project Record*

Cleanroom Process	Process Description	Principal Work Products
	Meet process performance standards and product quality objectives, and improve team performance. Use the quantitative measurements of product and process performance produced by statistical testing and certification of successive increments for objective management decision making.	
Performance Improvement	Evaluate and improve Cleanroom team performance continually, based on conformance with the *Software Development Plan,* process control standards, and causal analysis of software failures. Analyze and pilot promising improvements in software processes and tools, and introduce them to the project as appropriate.	*Performance Improvement Plan*
Engineering Change	Correct and change the evolving software system and associated work products using a protocol that preserves correctness and integrity. Implement engineering change control for all changes.	*Engineering Change Log*

Table 6.2 Cleanroom specification processes

Cleanroom Process	Process Description	Principal Work Products
Requirements Analysis	Analyze and define initial customer requirements for the software system, as well as requirements changes arising from customer assessment of evolving increments. Express requirements in user terms and review with the customer for agreement.	*Software Requirements*
Function Specification	Define the required external behavior of a software system in all possible circumstances of use based on the *Software Requirements.* Express the specification in box structure form. Create complete, consistent, and correct specifications, and review with the customer for agreement.	*Function Specification*
Usage Specification	Define all classes of users, major patterns of usage, and usage environments for a software product based on the *Software Requirements.* Create complete, consistent, and correct usage specifications, and review with the customer for agreement.	*Usage Specification*

continued

Table 6.2 *continued*

Cleanroom Process	Process Description	Principal Work Products
Architecture Specification	Analyze architectural assets and define the architectural strategy for the software product, including major components, high-level structure, and software design strategies and conventions. Review with the customer for agreement.	*Software Architecture*
Increment Planning	Create an incremental development and certification plan for the software product such that the increments implement user function, accumulate into the final system, execute in the system environment, and permit system-atic feedback on process control and product function and quality. Maintain referential transparency between increment specifications and their design decompositions. Use incre-mental development to reduce or eliminate risks and to maintain intellectual control.	*Increment Construction Plan*

Table 6.3   Cleanroom development processes

Cleanroom Process	Process Description	Principal Work Products
Software Reengineering	Prepare reused software for incorporation into a software product. Restructure and document the functional semantics of the reused soft-ware as necessary to maintain intellectual control and to avoid unforeseen failures in execution. Determine the fitness for use of reused software as necessary through sta-tistical testing to achieve project certifica-tion goals.	*Reengineering Plan, Reengineered Software*
Increment Design	Design and code the increments for a soft-ware product through stepwise decomposition of box structures, typically from stimulus history-based black box specifications into state-based state box specifications, and then into procedure-based clear box designs containing lower level black boxes for further refinement. Prepare designs for correctness verification by embedding intended function definitions that specify the effect on data of corresponding control structure decompositions.	*Increment Design*

Cleanroom Process	Process Description	Principal Work Products
Correctness Verification	Carry out function–theoretic correctness verification of designs, typically through verbal proofs of correctness in team reviews, to identify and to correct software faults prior to first execution. Document all faults found and rereview their corrections.	*Increment Verification Report*

Table 6.4 Cleanroom certification processes

Cleanroom Process	Process Description	Principal Work Products
Usage Modeling and Test Planning	Create the usage models to be used for software testing and certification. Express the models in terms of software usage states and probabilities of transition between them. Develop the models to satisfy objectives such as certification for expected operational use or certification of infrequently used functions with high consequences of failure. Employ usage model statistics to provide insight into system complexity and the testing effort required to meet quality objectives. Develop a statistical test plan, prepare the test environment, and generate the statistical test cases.	*Usage Models, Increment Test Plan, Statistical Test Cases*
Statistical Testing and Certification	Demonstrate the fitness for use of the software in a formal statistical experiment. Execute statistical test cases under experimental control, evaluate results, and initiate engineering change activity if failures are encountered. Compare the values of certification measures obtained in statistical testing with certification goals to assess the software's fitness for use. Compare measures of testing progress to process control standards to assess the likelihood of reaching certification goals with planned schedules and resources.	*Executable System, Statistical Testing Report, Increment Certification Report*

The purpose and content of the work products produced by the Cleanroom processes are defined in the following sections.

Cleanroom Engineering Guide.   The *Cleanroom Engineering Guide* is created in the Project Planning Process. It defines the adaptation and refinement of the Cleanroom processes to meet project-specific requirements. It includes process definitions; work product definitions; and local policies, procedures, templates, and forms that define how a project will be conducted. It identifies the facilities, hardware and software environments, and tools to support Cleanroom operations, and defines guidelines for their use. It also defines relationships among Cleanroom processes.

An organization-level *Cleanroom Engineering Guide* constitutes the "standard software process" required by the CMM Level 3 Organization Process Definition Key Process Area (KPA). The *Cleanroom Engineering Guide* may be successively refined and elaborated for use by organizational divisions, product lines, and specific projects. At each level, the guide is tailored for standards, technologies, languages, and other aspects of the development environment at that level.

The *Cleanroom Engineering Guide* for a project constitutes the "tailored version of the organization's standard software process" required by the CMM Level 3 Integrated Software Management KPA. The tailored guide also documents the "plans for the project's software engineering facilities and support tools" required by the CMM Level 2 Software Project Planning KPA.

Configuration Management Plan.   See *Software Development Plan.*

Engineering Change Log.   The *Engineering Change Log* is created and maintained in the Engineering Change Process. It is the record of all engineering change requests, along with their evaluations, impacts, and status.

Executable System.   The *Executable System* is created in the Statistical Testing and Certification Process. It is the executable form of the accumulating increments to be used for testing and customer evaluation.

Function Specification.   The *Function Specification* is created in the Function Specification Process. It documents (1) software boundaries and interfaces with hardware, other software, and human users, and (2) the external view of a system in terms of mapping all possible stimuli to their corresponding responses in all possible circumstances of use, including correct and incorrect, frequent and infrequent, and nominal and stress usage conditions.

The *Function Specification* is a precise statement of the *Software Requirements* often expressed as a mathematical function. The domain of the function is all possible stimulus histories and the range is all correct responses. The mathematical form of the *Function Specification* as a set of mapping rules provides a flexible yet verifiable basis for function decomposition.

From the customer's perspective, the *Function Specification* is the definitive statement of functional requirements for the software. From a development perspective, the *Function Specification* is the top-level black box in the box structure usage hierarchy that will be fully realized in the *Increment Design*.

Increment Certification Report. The *Increment Certification Report* is created in the Statistical Testing and Certification Process. It contains values for measures of certification goals (the desired "ends") and measures of process control (the efficiency of "means" based on historical performance). Certification measures may include reliability and confidence, MTTF, representativeness of the test case sample, and other measures of product quality. Process control measures may include reliability growth rate, error rate per unit volume of code, and other measures of process performance.

The *Increment Certification Report* documents the quantitative basis for management decisions made regarding the testing process. Continuation of testing, cessation of testing for engineering change or reengineering, and certification of the software are justified on the basis of product and process measures. The *Increment Certification Report* documents the "analysis of data on defects identified in testing" required by the CMM Level 3 Software Product Engineering KPA. It also documents the "results of the project's quantitative process management activities" required by the CMM Level 4 Quantitative Process Management KPA.

Increment Construction Plan. The *Increment Construction Plan* is created in the Increment Planning Process. It specifies the number of increments into which a Cleanroom Project will be divided, the functions that will be implemented in each increment, and the schedule and resources allocated for each increment. The *Increment Construction Plan* is used by management to assign tasks, track progress, and monitor product quality and process control.

The earliest version of the *Increment Construction Plan* may be based on the customer's *Statement of Work* and/or the *Software Requirements.* This version will contain assumptions that will be explored further in the course of preparing the *Risk Analysis Plan* and the *Reuse Analysis Plan.* A sound basis for increment planning will exist when the *Function Specification* and the *Usage Specification* have been prepared. The *Increment Construction Plan* should be considered preliminary until these two work products are available. The *Increment Construction Plan* is also influenced by the *Software Architecture.* The *Increment Construction Plan* documents the "software life cycle with predefined stages of manageable size" required by the CMM Level 2 Project Planning KPA.

Increment Design. The *Increment Design* is created in the Increment Design Process. It is the box structure implementation of a set of functions named in the *Increment Construction Plan* and defined in the *Function Specification*. The *Increment Design* is a hierarchy of components in which each component is represented in black box (history-based), state box (state-based), and clear box (procedure-based) forms.

Clear boxes in the *Increment Design* may contain new black boxes that are either implemented or stubbed. In each *Increment Design,* some previously stubbed functions are implemented.

Increments are cumulative. An *Increment Design* is the sum of all specification, design, and code to date. The final *Increment Design* is the completed product.

Increment Evaluation Report. The *Increment Evaluation Report* is originated by the customer. It is the customer's documentation of feedback from increment execution and evaluation.

Increment Test Plan. The *Increment Test Plan* is created in the Usage Modeling and Test Planning Process. It contains all information needed by the certification team for the Statistical Testing and Certification Process, including schedules, staffing, training, hardware and software environments, data collection forms, test case evaluation procedures, certification goals, and statistical models. The *Increment Test Plan* is the "plan for system testing to demonstrate that the software satisfies its requirements" required by the CMM Level 3 Software Product Engineering KPA.

Increment Verification Report. The *Increment Verification Report* is created in the Correctness Verification Process. It is the record of experience during the Correctness Verification Process, including participants, number of verification sessions, time spent in each session, faults found during each session, and any other information relevant to the assessment of the correctness of the design. Data for sessions in which engineering changes are verified are also included in the *Increment Verification Report.*

In addition to raw data, the *Increment Verification Report* may contain other measures that provide indications of process control. Such measures may include percentage of engineering changes that are found to be incorrect, the distribution of faults with regard to severity and type, and the number of faults found per unit volume of code. The *Increment Verification Report* constitutes the "data on the conduct and results of peer reviews" required by the CMM Level 3 Peer Reviews KPA. It also documents the "data on defects identified in peer reviews" required by the CMM Level 3 Software Product Engineering KPA.

Measurement Plan. See *Software Development Plan.*

Performance Improvement Plan. The *Performance Improvement Plan* is created in the Performance Improvement Process. It defines plans to improve team performance by refining the current *Cleanroom Engineering Guide* and/or exploring the use of new software technologies.

The *Performance Improvement Plan* contains an analysis of the cause of each failure that occurred during statistical testing and includes plans to prevent the recurrence of the underlying problem. It also documents the comparison of current performance with planned or historical performance for the measures defined in the *Measurement Plan.*

The *Performance Improvement Plan* documents the "causal analysis meetings" and "revisions to the project's defined software process resulting from defect prevention actions" required by the CMM Level 5 Defect Prevention KPA, the "incorporation of appropriate new technologies into a project's defined software process" required by the CMM Level 5 Technology Change Management KPA, and the "plan for software process improvement" required by the CMM Level 5 Process Change Management KPA.

Project Mission Plan. See *Software Development Plan.*

Project Organization Plan. See *Software Development Plan.*

Project Record. The *Project Record* is created in the Project Management Process and is updated in all processes. It includes actions, reviews, decisions, measures, and other events throughout a project. The *Project Record* contains formal documents, such as contracts and reports, and informal correspondence, such as meeting notes or records of phone conversations. It is the archive of documentation about all project events that are not captured in other Cleanroom work products. It is a flexible, tailorable work product that is the Cleanroom vehicle for fulfilling project documentation requirements not met by other work products.

Reengineering Plan. The *Reengineering Plan* is created in the Software Reengineering Process. It includes the tasks, schedules, and resources required to prepare existing artifacts for reuse in the current project. The *Reengineering Plan* elaborates the technical aspects of the *Reuse Analysis Plan.* It defines specific investigations required to make decisions about the reusability of a component and/or adaptations required to reuse a component in the current system.

Reuse Analysis Plan. See *Software Development Plan.*

Reengineered Software. The *Reengineered Software* is created in the Software Reengineering Process. It consists of specifications, designs, code, usage models, and/or testing artifacts produced during the reengineering of reused components.

Risk Analysis Plan.   See *Software Development Plan.*

Schedule and Resource Plan.   See *Software Development Plan.*

Software Architecture.   The *Software Architecture* is created in the Architecture Specification Process. *The Software Architecture* identifies the conceptual architecture, expressed in terms of principal software components and their relationships; the module architecture, expressed in terms of layers of functional decomposition; and the execution architecture, expressed in terms of dynamic software operation (Soni, Nord, and Hofmeister, 1995).

The *Software Architecture* serves as a vehicle for analyzing application and service domains, reference architectures, reusable assets, communication protocols, standards, and software design strategies. It is a principal input to the Increment Planning and Increment Design Processes.

Software Development Plan.   The *Software Development Plan* is created in the Project Planning Process, and is used in the Project Management Process for task initiation, performance tracking, and quantitative process management. The *Software Development Plan* is the "software project plan" required by the CMM Level 2 Software Project Planning KPA, and is the "software development plan" to be used in the CMM Level 2 Software Project Tracking and Oversight KPA. The *Software Development Plan* consists of the following project management plans.

The *Project Mission Plan* defines the overall mission, goals, and objectives of the system and the Cleanroom development project.

The *Project Organization Plan* defines the structure, responsibilities, and relationships of the Cleanroom project organization and peer organizations. It is the "documented plan to communicate intergroup commitments and coordinate and track the work performed" required by the CMM Level 3 Intergroup Coordination KPA.

The *Work Product Plan* defines the Cleanroom work products to be produced by the project. It constitutes the "identification of software work products" required by the CMM Level 2 Software Project Planning KPA.

The *Schedule and Resource Plan* defines estimates for overall tasks, schedules, milestones, budgets, and resources for Cleanroom work product development. It documents the "estimates of size, effort, schedule, cost, and critical computer resources" required by the CMM Level 2 Software Project Planning KPA.

The *Measurement Plan* defines product and process measurements, standards, and goals for managing the project, including those for Cleanroom software certification and statistical process control. It defines the "plan for quantitative process management" and the "strategy for data collection and analysis" required by the CMM Level 4 Quantitative Process Management KPA.

The *Reuse Analysis Plan* identifies sources of reusable assets, and asset acquisition and evaluation tasks. It also identifies opportunities to reuse domain models, reference architectures, software specifications, designs, code, and usage models. The *Reuse Analysis Plan* is a management plan for identification of assets. A related work product, the *Reengineering Plan,* is a technical plan for evaluation and adaptation of assets.

The *Risk Analysis Plan* defines methods for risk analysis, identifies project risks, and describes strategies for risk management and avoidance. It constitutes the "identification, assessment, and documentation of risks associated with the cost, resource, schedule, and technical aspects of the project" required by the CMM Level 2 Software Project Planning KPA.

The *Standards Plan* identifies and defines the application of external standards that will be used in the project.

The *Training Plan* identifies project training requirements, including training in the application domain, development environments, and Cleanroom technology and processes. This plan is the "training plan" required by the CMM Level 3 Training Program KPA.

The *Configuration Management Plan* defines requirements for change control of designated work products. This plan is the "software configuration management plan" required by the CMM Level 2 Software Configuration Management KPA.

Software Requirements. The *Software Requirements* are created in the Requirements Analysis Process. They define the functional, usage, performance, and environmental requirements for a software system to be developed using the Cleanroom process. Included among these requirements are operational constraints such as dependencies on other systems, capacity requirements, and reliability requirements. The *Software Requirements* are typically documented in user terms, and are the principal input to the Function Specification and Usage Specification Processes, in which requirements are defined in the more precise terms essential to software development and certification.

The *Software Requirements* are the "documentation of allocated requirements" required by the CMM Level 2 Requirements Management KPA.

Standards Plan. See *Software Development Plan.*

Statement of Work. The *Statement of Work* is originated by the customer. It is the "documented and approved statement of work for the software project" required by the CMM Level 2 Software Project Planning KPA.

Statistical Test Cases. The *Statistical Test Cases* are created in the Usage Modeling and Test Planning Process. *Statistical Test Cases* are generated randomly from a usage model for use in statistical testing of an increment. Once generated, test cases may undergo postprocessing to add information for human testers or for an automated test tool. Such information may include additional instructions (e.g., events to initiate in the background), invocation of independent data feeds, or pointers to the relevant "oracle" for evaluation of responses.

Each statistical test case is a complete usage scenario given as a sequence of user inputs, beginning with a predefined initial event and ending with a predefined terminal event. The *Statistical Test Cases* become a script for testing, and may be annotated during testing to record responses and their evaluations.

Statistical Testing Report.   The *Statistical Testing Report* is created in the Statistical Testing and Certification Process. It is the record of experience in testing, and includes participants, number of compilation sessions, faults found during compilation, number of testing sessions, number of test cases executed during each session, failures observed during test case executions, faults found during investigation of failures, time required to correct each fault, and any other information relevant to assessment of the correctness of the executing software.

The *Statistical Testing Report* documents the "data on defects identified in testing" and the "performance of system testing to demonstrate that the software satisfies its requirements" required by the CMM Level 3 Software Product Engineering KPA.

Training Plan.   See *Software Development Plan.*

Usage Models.   The *Usage Models* are created in the Usage Modeling and Test Planning Process. A usage model is a formal representation of software use, often expressed as a Markov chain. It defines the usage states of the software and the probabilities of transitions between usage states. When software is to be certified for normal operational use, usage probabilities are based on expected use. When the customer requires certification for other usage conditions, the probabilities reflect those conditions. Usage model analysis provides numerous insights into software usage characteristics that are useful in making management and technical decisions. Usage models are also used as test case generators.

Usage Specification.   The *Usage Specification* is created in the Usage Specification Process. It is a description of the expected users, usage scenarios, and usage environments of the software. It contains definitions of high-level usage models that record this information, as well as the results of model analysis for management decision making.

Work Product Plan.   See *Software Development Plan.*

6.2 Cleanroom Process Definition Format

The 14 Cleanroom processes are defined in Chapters 7 through 10 in terms of the following augmented entry, task, verification, exit (ETVX) format:

Objectives—The objectives section defines the outcomes of effective process performance.

Entry—The entry section defines the entry criteria that must be satisfied for the process to be initiated, and lists the work products that must be available as inputs to the process.

Tasks—The tasks section defines work to be carried out in performing the process. The order of the tasks is generally, but not strictly, sequential. Some tasks may be concurrent with other tasks.

Verification—The verification section defines steps for verifying that the process has been properly executed and the associated work products meet project objectives.

Measurement—The measurement section defines Cleanroom measures for assessing the performance of the process and the characteristics of the work products. The measures provided in the measurement section are either characteristic of or integral to Cleanroom software engineering. Many other measures not provided in the measurement section may also be useful or even required in a given project.

Exit—The exit section defines the exit criteria that must be satisfied for the process to be terminated. The exit criteria generally involve completion and verification of work products, but may also be stated in terms of quantitative or qualitative conditions of work products.

In addition to these formatting conventions, boxed text appears in the process definitions to (1) explain Cleanroom terms and concepts, (2) recommend specific implementation techniques, (3) provide examples, and (4) point to further information. Accordingly, the boxes are labeled Explanation, Recommendation, Example, or Reference. In some instances the boxed text summarizes key Cleanroom principles and technologies discussed in Part I. This summarization is intended to make the Cleanroom process definitions more self-contained, and helps to relate specific technologies to their application points in the process.

6.3 Common Cleanroom Process Elements

The common objectives, participants, entry criteria, tasks, verification, measures, and exit criteria in Cleanroom processes are defined here as common Cleanroom process elements. These elements are part of every Cleanroom process. Rather than being restated in each process, the common elements have been "factored out" and stated once to avoid repetition and to achieve more compact definitions of the Cleanroom processes described in the remaining chapters in Part II. The people responsible for each of the Cleanroom management, specification, development, and certification processes (i.e., the "process owners") should include these common elements in their process responsibilities.

Common Objectives

Objective 1   **Work products created or updated in the process are traceable to the entry work products from which they were derived.**

Objective 2   **Defects in work products created or updated in the process are identified through peer review and are eliminated.**

Common Entry

Entry 1   **The *Cleanroom Engineering Guide* and the *Software Development Plan* (developed in the Project Planning Process), and the *Project Record* are available.**

Entry 2   **When the process is reentered for changes to work products, the reentry is consistent with the Engineering Change Process and the *Configuration Management Plan.***

Common Tasks

Task 1   **Ensure that all participants understand process requirements as documented in the *Cleanroom Engineering Guide.***

Task 2   **Create work products according to the formats defined in the *Cleanroom Engineering Guide.***

Task 3   **Make changes to work products in compliance with the Engineering Change Process and the *Configuration Management Plan.***

Task 4   **Document project activity in the *Project Record.***
Document information that will not be recorded in other work products in the *Project Record.* Specifically, document process beginning and ending dates, staff assignments, process review dates and data, measurements, and other key events and decisions.

Common Verification

Verification 1   **Review the status of the process with management, the project team, peer groups, and the customer.**
These verification activities include confirming that the process was performed as defined in the *Cleanroom Engineering Guide.*

Verification 2   **Review work products created or updated during the process with the project team.**
Work products are verified against properties defined for them in the *Cleanroom Engineering Guide.* Work products under review are verified to be fully traceable to the work products from which they were derived.

EXPLANATION: Peer review

Peer review is a key to intellectual control of work by Cleanroom teams. The work of an individual team member is regarded as a draft until there is team consensus that the work is correct and of acceptable quality.

Every Cleanroom work product is peer reviewed, yielding substantial benefits. Differing interpretations of requirements are uncovered, conventions are established, errors are detected, opportunities for economy are identified, understandability is tested, and expertise is shared. The results benefit the project, the product, and the team members alike.

REFERENCE: CMM Peer Reviews and Defect Prevention
KPAs

If compliance with these KPAs is an organizational objective,
their specific requirements should be reviewed when this verification step is tailored for organizational or project use.

Common Measurement

Measurement 1   **Measure the process.**

Measure process performance in terms such as deviations
in resource and schedule actuals from plans.

Measure the effectiveness of a review in terms of the percentage of all defects originating prior to the review that are
found in the review. These percentages are determined, of
course, after execution testing.

Measurement 2   **Measure the product.**

Measure the size and stability of work products that define
the software (i.e., the *Software Requirements,* the *Function
Specification,* the *Usage Specification,* the *Software Architecture,* the *Usage Models,* the *Increment Design,* and the
Executable System*).

Measure the quality of work products that define the software in terms of the percentage of execution failures that are
traced to defects in the work products. These percentages are
determined, of course, after execution testing.

Common Exit

Exit 1   **Tasks and verification activities have been completed and
the *Project Record* has been updated.**

6.4 References

R.C. Linger and C.J. Trammell. *Cleanroom Software Engineering Reference Model, Version 1.0.* CMU/SEI-96-TR-022. Pittsburgh: Software Engineering Institute, Carnegie Mellon University, 1996.

R.C. Linger, M.C. Paulk, and C.J. Trammell. *Cleanroom Software Engineering Implementation of the CMM for Software.* CMU/SEI-96-TR-023. Pittsburgh: Software Engineering Institute, Carnegie Mellon University, 1996.

D. Soni, R. Nord, and C. Hofmeister. "Software Architecture in Industrial Applications," in *Proceedings of the 17th International Conference on Software Engineering,* ed. R. Jeffrey and D. Notkin (New York: Association for Computing Machinery, 1995), 196–207.

7

Cleanroom Management Processes

7.1 Project Planning Process

The purpose of the Project Planning Process is to tailor the CRM (or the organizational reference model) for the project, to define and document plans for the Cleanroom project, and to review the plans with the customer, the project team, and peer groups for agreement. The work products of the Project Planning Process are the *Cleanroom Engineering Guide* and the *Software Development Plan.* Both are revised as necessary during the project to accommodate customer needs and project performance. The *Cleanroom Engineering Guide* defines a tailoring of the Cleanroom processes to meet project-specific process requirements. The *Software Development Plan* is the repository for project management plans, including mission, organization, work products, schedules, resources, measurements, reuse analysis, risk analysis, standards, training, and configuration management. The *Software Development Plan* is used in the Project Management Process for task initiation, performance tracking, and quantitative process management. The *Cleanroom Engineering Guide* and the *Software Development Plan* form the basis for defined, repeatable, managed, and optimized performance of Cleanroom activities.

Objectives

Objective 1   **Cleanroom software engineering processes are tailored for the project and documented.**

Objective 2   **The software project plans are defined and documented.**

Objective 3   **The customer, the project team, and peer groups agree to the Cleanroom processes and project plans.**

Entry

The process begins when one of the entry criteria is satisfied.

Entry 1   A new or revised *Statement of Work* and/or *Software Requirements* exist for the software project.

Entry 2   The *Software Development Plan* and/or *Cleanroom Engineering Guide* require revision or elaboration at the beginning of a new increment or as necessary.

Entry work products are available.

Tasks

Task 1   **Create the *Cleanroom Engineering Guide.***
Use the CRM or the organizational Cleanroom Software Engineering Reference Model, if any, as the basis for defining or revising the project's *Cleanroom Engineering Guide,* including

1. Project-specific tailoring and refinement of the Cleanroom processes. Define and document clear process implementation guidance for the Cleanroom project.
2. Identification and documentation of facilities, hardware and software environments, and tools to support Cleanroom processes, with guidelines for their use.

> REFERENCE: CMM Organization Process Definition,
> Integrated Software Management, Software
> Product Engineering, and Software Quality
> Management KPAs
>
> If compliance with these KPAs is an organizational objective,
> their specific requirements should be reviewed when the
> Cleanroom processes are tailored for organizational or project use.

Task 2

Create the *Software Development Plan.*

> REFERENCE: CMM Software Project Planning KPA
>
> If compliance with this KPA is an organizational objective,
> its specific requirements should be reviewed when the *Software Development Plan* is developed.

Use the *Statement of Work* and/or *Software Requirements* to define or revise the *Software Development Plan,* including the following plans:

1. *Project Mission Plan:* Define the overall mission, goals, and objectives of the software product and the Cleanroom development project.

2. *Project Organization Plan:* Define the structure, responsibilities, and relationships of the Cleanroom project organization. Identify points of contact in customer and peer organizations.

> REFERENCE: CMM Intergroup Coordination KPA
>
> If compliance with this KPA is an organizational objective,
> its specific requirements should be reviewed when the *Project Organization Plan* is developed.

3. *Work Product Plan:* Define the Cleanroom work products and customer deliverables to be produced during the project.

4. *Schedule and Resource Plan:* Define estimates for overall schedules, milestones, and budgets. Define staffing, system, and other resource requirements. These estimates will be refined in the Increment Planning Process.

5. *Measurement Plan:* Define product and process measures for managing the project, including goals for Cleanroom software certification and standards for statistical process control. Define the use of measures in project reviews and decision making.

EXPLANATION: Quantitative management decisions

A quantitative basis for management decisions regarding product quality and process control is a hallmark of Cleanroom. The organizational database of project measures that accumulates over time becomes increasingly useful in planning and managing activities. A historical baseline of product measures (e.g., size, stability, and quality) and process measures (e.g., conformance to plans and effectiveness of reviews) provides a basis for estimating schedules, budgets, and resources; defining process control standards for work in progress; and defining certification goals for increment and product certification.

REFERENCE: CMM Quantitative Process Management KPA

If compliance with this KPA is an organizational objective, its specific requirements should be reviewed when the *Measurement Plan* is developed.

---

6. *Reuse Analysis Plan:* Define methods for identifying and evaluating opportunities to reuse existing assets and create new, reusable assets. Reusable assets include domain models, reference architectures, software specifications, designs, implementations, and usage models. Define specific opportunities for reuse.

7. *Risk Analysis Plan:* Define methods for identifying and managing risks throughout the project. Define specific management and technical risks associated with the project.

8. *Standards Plan:* Identify and define the application of external standards that will be used in the project.

9. *Training Plan:* Identify project training requirements, including training in the application domain, development environments, and Cleanroom technology and processes.

REFERENCE: CMM Training Program KPA

If compliance with this KPA is an organizational objective, its specific requirements should be reviewed when the *Training Plan* is developed.

---

10. *Configuration Management Plan:* Identify the work products to be maintained under configuration control. Define procedures for change management and configuration control of the work products.

REFERENCE: CMM Software Configuration Management KPA

If compliance with this KPA is an organizational objective, its specific requirements should be reviewed when the *Configuration Management Plan* is developed.

Verification

Verification 1   **Review the *Cleanroom Engineering Guide* for agreement.**
Review the *Cleanroom Engineering Guide* with the project team and peer groups to obtain commitments to Cleanroom processes and team performance objectives.

Review the *Cleanroom Engineering Guide* with the customer. Modify and rereview as necessary to obtain concurrence.

Verification 2   **Review the *Software Development Plan* for agreement.**
Review the *Software Development Plan* with the project team and peer groups to obtain commitments to project plans and schedules.

Review the *Software Development Plan* with the customer. Modify and rereview as necessary to obtain concurrence.

Measurement

(See Section 6.3, Common Cleanroom Process Elements.)

Exit

The process is complete when the exit criteria are satisfied.

Exit 1   The *Software Development Plan* and the *Cleanroom Engineering Guide* have been completed and reviewed with the project team, peer organizations, and the customer, and commitments have been obtained.

7.2 Project Management Process

The purpose of the Project Management Process is to manage the Cleanroom project to deliver the software on schedule and within budget. Management responsibilities include managing interactions with the customer and peer organizations; establishing and training Cleanroom teams; initiating, tracking, and controlling planned Cleanroom processes; eliminating or reducing risks; revising plans as necessary to accommodate changes and actual project results; and continually improving Cleanroom team performance. Cleanroom management is guided by quantitative measurements of process and product performance as defined in the *Measurement Plan*—in particular, the measurements produced by statistical testing and certification of successive increments throughout the project life cycle.

Overall project processes, schedules, and resource allocations are managed according to the *Schedule and Resource Plan.* The *Increment Construction Plan,* created in the Increment Planning Process, provides detailed schedules for managing increment development and certification within the overall schedules. The *Risk Analysis Plan* defines risks to be managed.

An important aspect of Cleanroom project management is establishing and enforcing standards of performance for Cleanroom operations. The Cleanroom development process is designed for defect prevention through mathematically based specification, design, and correctness verification. Development teams are expected to produce fault-free software that implements specified behavior. The Cleanroom testing process is designed for scientific certification of software fitness for use through statistical testing. Certification teams are expected to produce valid statistical estimates of software quality, not to attempt to test in quality.

Objectives

Objective 1   **The project plan is implemented using a tailored Cleanroom process, and schedules, budgets, and quality objectives are met.**

Objective 2   **The project is performed under statistical quality control.**

Objective 3   **The delivered software meets the customer's requirements and is statistically certified to be fit for its intended use.**

Entry

The process begins when the entry criteria are satisfied.

Entry 1   The *Software Development Plan* and the *Cleanroom Engineering Guide* have been completed, reviewed, and agreed to by the project team, peer groups, and the customer.

All project work products are available for use in this process as they are developed.

Tasks

Task 1   **Manage customer interaction.**

Establish and maintain communication with points of contact in customer organizations. Maintain all information received from the customer.

Conduct reviews with the customer on project status and plans.

Establish procedures for customer evaluation of completed software increments.

Task 2   **Manage peer organization interaction.**

Establish and maintain communication with points of contact in peer organizations.

Conduct reviews with peer organizations on project status and plans.

Task 3   **Form, staff, and train the Cleanroom teams.**

Create a Cleanroom organizational structure composed of four functions:

1. Management team led by the project software manager
2. Specification team led by the chief specification engineer
3. Development team led by the chief development engineer
4. Certification team led by the chief certification engineer

Provide team training in the application domain, development environment, and Cleanroom software engineering as defined in the *Training Plan.*

Task 4   **Initiate Cleanroom processes.**

Initiate Cleanroom processes defined in the *Cleanroom Engineering Guide,* as required by the *Software Development Plan*—in particular, the processes, schedules, and resource allocations defined in the *Schedule and Resource Plan* and the *Increment Construction Plan.* Document process initiation in the *Project Record.*

Task 5   **Monitor Cleanroom process performance and work products through measurement, and take corrective action when necessary.**

Record measurements of process and product performance over the life of the project as defined in the *Measurement Plan.*

Use measurements to monitor performance with respect to plans. Inspect work products to assess adherence to the process. Measurements from the Correctness Verification and the Statistical Testing and Certification Processes are especially important in assessing product quality and team performance.

Address performance shortfalls or windfalls. Identify schedule and quality deviations, and implement corrective actions. Revise project plans when necessary through the Project Planning, Increment Planning, Project Management, and Performance Improvement Processes.

Maintain consistency among related work products produced by the Cleanroom processes in accordance with the *Configuration Management Plan.*

REFERENCE: CMM Software Project Tracking and Oversight
and Quantitative Process Management KPAs

If compliance with these KPAs is an organizational objective, their specific requirements should be reviewed when this task is tailored for organizational or project use.

Task 6   **Manage project risks.**

Identify and manage risks according to the *Risk Analysis Plan.* Use the Cleanroom incremental development and certification process as a risk management strategy.

Task 7   **Manage Cleanroom team performance.**

Manage team performance and implement improvements in Cleanroom processes defined in the *Performance Improvement Plan.*

Verification

(See Section 6.3, Common Cleanroom Process Elements.)

Measurement

(See Section 6.3, Common Cleanroom Process Elements.)

Exit

The process is complete when the exit criteria are satisfied.

Exit 1   The Cleanroom software development project has been completed and the *Project Record* has been completed.

7.3 Performance Improvement Process

The purpose of the Performance Improvement Process is to evaluate and improve team performance continually in the application of Cleanroom and other software technologies and processes, and to evaluate and introduce appropriate new technologies and processes.

Frequent and objective evaluation of team performance is essential to achieve continuous improvement. Causal analysis of deviations from plans can provide early identification of risks. Causal analysis of faults found through the Correctness Verification and the Statistical Testing and Certification Processes can identify areas that require improvement through better process definition, increased emphasis, and/or additional training.

Process and product evaluations during review, verification, testing, and certification activities provide an objective basis for justifying and targeting process improvements. Improvements can be introduced within a project at specific milestones, such as initiation of successive increments, and across projects through coordinated organizational process improvement. New technologies and processes can be evaluated in pilot applications for their impact on productivity and quality, and introduced in a systematic manner if proved effective.

Objectives

Objective 1   **The performance of the Cleanroom team is continuously improved.**

Objective 2   **New Cleanroom and other software technologies and processes are evaluated and introduced as appropriate, and produce improvement in process performance and product quality.**

Entry

The process begins when one of the entry criteria is satisfied.

Entry 1   A process step, a software increment, or a work product has been completed and a team review is scheduled.

Entry 2   New Cleanroom technologies and/or processes are to be evaluated.

Entry 3   Shortfalls in Cleanroom process performance or work product quality have been identified.

Supporting work products are available.

The *Increment Verification Report, Statistical Testing Report, Increment Certification Report,* and *Engineering Change Log,* if any, define measures of Cleanroom process performance and software product quality.

New Cleanroom or other software technology and process documentation, if any, may be evaluated.

Tasks

Task 1

Evaluate Cleanroom team performance and develop improvement plans.

Evaluate project performance with respect to the *Software Development Plan,* and apply trend and causal analysis to deviations.

Apply causal analysis to faults found in the Correctness Verification and the Statistical Testing and Certification Processes to identify the steps in which they were introduced and to determine why they occurred.

Compare process and product measurements with historical team performance to assess process control.

Develop plans to improve team performance, including additional training, improved tools and procedures, and revised Cleanroom processes, and document the plans in the *Performance Improvement Plan.*

REFERENCE: CMM Process Change Management KPA

If compliance with this KPA is an organizational objective, its specific requirements should be reviewed when this task is tailored for organizational or project use.

Task 2

Evaluate new technologies and processes, and develop implementation plans.

Identify new Cleanroom and other software technologies and processes, and evaluate their impact on current Cleanroom processes. Conduct experiments in the project environment to measure their effectiveness.

Develop plans for the introduction of proved new technologies and processes, and document them in the *Performance Improvement Plan* work product.

Schedule new technology and process introductions for the start of subsequent increments or subsequent projects as appropriate.

REFERENCE: CMM Technology Change Management KPA

If compliance with this KPA is an organizational objective, its specific requirements should be reviewed when this task is tailored for organizational or project use.

Verification

(See Section 6.3, Common Cleanroom Process Elements.)

Measurement

Measurement 1   **Measure performance improvement.**
Assess the effect of process and technology changes by examining trends in measures defined in the *Measurement Plan* across successive increments.

Exit

The process is complete when the exit criteria are satisfied.

Exit 1   The *Performance Improvement Plan* has been applied and the recommendations have been implemented. Any changes, such as revisions to the *Software Development Plan* or *Cleanroom Engineering Guide,* have been completed.

7.4 Engineering Change Process

The purpose of the Engineering Change Process is to plan and perform additions, changes, and corrections to work products in a manner that preserves correctness and is consistent with the *Configuration Management Plan.*

Proposed changes to work products are documented in the *Engineering Change Log.* The status of the changes (e.g., proposed, approved, rejected, scheduled, in progress, completed) is updated throughout the process. Changes are made with full engineering rigor and discipline using the Cleanroom processes. The highest level of specification or design affected by a change is identified as the starting point for any respecification, redesign, reverification, recertification, and any other revision activity.

Objectives

Objective 1   **Additions and changes to work products occur in a manner that preserves correctness and is consistent with the *Configuration Management Plan.***

Entry

The process begins when one of the entry criteria is satisfied.

Entry 1

An *Increment Verification Report, Statistical Testing Report,* or report from field use identifies software faults or failures that require correction.

Entry 2

New requirements or insights require engineering changes to be made to work products.

Entry work products and the following work products are available.
The *Software Development Plan, Increment Construction Plan,* and *Reengineering Plan* may be affected by engineering change activity.

Tasks

Task 1

Document proposed engineering changes in the *Engineering Change Log.*

Task 2

Evaluate the impact of proposed engineering changes.
Analyze the scope and impact of proposed changes on project work products, and approve or reject them based on the analysis.

Task 3

Identify the Cleanroom processes required to perform the engineering changes.
Define the Cleanroom process sequencing and scheduling required to perform approved engineering changes, and if necessary revise the *Software Development Plan,* the *Increment Construction Plan,* and/or the *Reengineering Plan.*

Task 4

Apply the Cleanroom processes to perform the engineering changes.
Apply Cleanroom processes to incorporate the engineering changes at the highest level of specification affected, reengineer subsequent levels of decomposition, and reverify all affected work products for correctness. Maintain the correctness and integrity of all affected work products as the engineering changes are made, and satisfy the requirements of the *Configuration Management Plan.*

Verification

Verification 1   **Confirm the consistency of engineering change decisions with the *Configuration Management Plan*.**

Measurement

Measurement 1   **Use measurements from other Cleanroom processes.**
Use measurements defined for each Cleanroom process initiated through the Engineering Change Process.

Exit

The process is complete when the exit criteria are satisfied.

Exit 1   The required engineering changes have been completed, the necessary work products have been revised, and the *Engineering Change Log* has been updated.

8

Cleanroom Specification Processes

8.1 Requirements Analysis Process

The purpose of the Requirements Analysis Process is to define requirements for the software product, including function, usage, environment, and performance; and to obtain agreement with the customer on the requirements as the basis for function and usage specification. The specification team creates the *Software Requirements* document as the repository of all requirements information. Elicitation and analysis of requirements is carried out in close cooperation with the customer and peer engineering organizations, and the requirements are typically documented in user terms.

Requirements analysis may identify opportunities to simplify the customer's initial product concept and to reveal requirements that the customer has not addressed. Early simplification and clarification of requirements can result in schedule and resource savings throughout the development process.

The *Software Requirements* are the customer's requirements. They are the basis for customer acceptance of the product. The *Software Requirements* are the principal input to the Function Specification and Usage Specification Processes, in which they are elaborated into the mathematically complete and consistent form essential to intellectual control over development and certification. These processes in turn produce the *Function Specification* and *Usage Specification,* which serve as the developer's technical specifications for the software product.

Requirements are reconfirmed or clarified throughout the incremental development and certification process. The customer executes completed increments and provides feedback on the evolving system.

Objectives

Objective 1 **Software requirements—including function, usage, environment, and performance—are clearly stated, internally consistent, technically feasible, and testable.**

Objective 2 **The customer agrees with the software requirements as the basis for software specification.**

Objective 3 **The software requirements are reconfirmed or clarified at the completion of software increments through customer evaluation.**

> REFERENCE: CMM Requirements Management KPA
>
> If compliance with this KPA is an organizational objective, its specific requirements should be reviewed when the Requirements Analysis Process is tailored for organizational or project use.

Entry

The process begins when one of the entry criteria is satisfied.

Entry 1 The *Statement of Work* or other initial artifact, such as a statement of allocated system requirements, is available.

Entry 2 Changes, including additions and corrections to the *Software Requirements,* are proposed.

Entry 3 A completed increment is ready for customer execution and evaluation.

Entry work products and the following supporting work products are available.

The *Engineering Change Log* and the *Increment Evaluation Report,* if any, contain customer feedback from increment execution and may identify proposed changes to requirements.

Tasks

Task 1   **Define the software requirements.**

Understand and analyze the *Statement of Work,* the customer's environment, and the context and mission of the product to be developed.

Define requirements, including software function and usage, hardware and software configurations and environments, interfaces, operational constraints, dependencies, and goals for reliability, capacity, and performance.

EXPLANATION: Sources of requirements

Requirements come from many different sources depending on the nature of the product.

- Software that is part of an embedded system or larger software system will be defined on the basis of allocated requirements from the system of which it is a part.

- A product that is part of a product line may inherit requirements related to architecture, interfaces, standard components, and so forth.

- Marketing, manufacturing, distribution, and other peer organizations may be a source of requirements.

- Industry standards, regulatory standards, export standards, and other commercial or contractual standards can influence requirements.

All relevant sources of requirements should be identified for the system under development.

EXPLANATION: Prototyping

If the requirements definition is insufficient for software specification, initial software increments can be specified and developed as prototypes to obtain user feedback for establishing the requirements.

Simplify requirements and investigate alternatives to improve usability and to reduce development and certification effort.

Document requirements and associated assumptions in the *Software Requirements* work product.

Task 2

On completion of each increment, reconfirm or clarify requirements through customer evaluation of the executable system.

Monitor customer execution and evaluation of completed software increments to confirm existing *Software Requirements* or to identify proposed changes.

Verification

Verification 1

Review the evolving *Software Requirements* work product.

Conduct frequent specification team reviews of the evolving *Software Requirements* for clarity, consistency, feasibility, and testability. Make simplification of requirements an explicit objective.

Verification 2

Validate the *Software Requirements* work product with the customer and peer organizations.

Review the *Software Requirements* with the customer and affected peer organizations for agreement on the basis for software specification.

Measurement

(See Section 6.3, Common Cleanroom Process Elements.)

Exit

The process is complete when the exit criteria are satisfied.

Exit 1

The new or changed *Software Requirements* are complete and verified, and approved by the customer as the basis for further development.

EXPLANATION: Formal baselining of requirements

It is often the case that requirements cannot be "baselined" and established as the basis for acceptance of the product by the customer until well into the Function Specification, Usage Specification, and Architecture Specification Processes. The Requirements Analysis Process and the aforementioned processes are often concurrent—not sequential—processes.

8.2 Function Specification Process

The purpose of the Function Specification Process is to specify the complete functional behavior of the software in all possible circumstances of use and to obtain agreement with the customer on the specified function as the basis for software development and certification.

The specification team creates the *Function Specification* document to satisfy the software requirements. It expresses the requirements in a mathematically precise, complete, and consistent form. The required behavior of the software for every user scenario, however likely or unlikely to occur, is defined in the specification. The specification is an unambiguous definition of the external behavior of the software. No invention of external behavior should be required in subsequent software development.

The *Function Specification* is based on the *Software Requirements*. After the specification has been completed and validated, it becomes the definitive statement of functional behavior for the software. The specification defines the capabilities to be created through incremental software development. It also serves as the basis for usage specification and usage model development in incremental software certification.

For large systems, a strategy of incremental specification is usually necessary. In this approach, software increments are iteratively specified, developed, and certified. This permits user feedback on observed increment behavior in execution, and can help to elicit requirements that may have proved difficult to define. The Function Specification Process is ongoing. Whenever the evolving *Function Specification* is sufficient to support increment planning and development of an increment, that development can be initiated.

Objectives

Objective 1   **The required behavior of the software in all possible circumstances of use is defined and documented.**

Objective 2   **The function specification is complete, consistent, correct, and traceable to the software requirements.**

Objective 3   **The customer agrees with the function specification as the basis for software development and certification.**

Entry

The process begins when one of the entry criteria is satisfied.

Entry 1   The *Software Requirements* have been partially or fully completed.

> EXPLANATION: Incremental function specification
>
> All software requirements must eventually be defined to permit complete function specification. Often, all requirements are not fully understood at the outset, and a strategy of incremental function specification based on partial requirements definition may be necessary.
>
> In large-scale developments, incremental function specification is often a desirable strategy for pacing development, maintaining intellectual control, and eliciting customer feedback.

Entry 2   The *Function Specification* requires revision for changes to the *Software Requirements* or for changes from increment specification, development, or certification.

Entry work products and the following supporting work products are available.

The *Engineering Change Log* describes proposed changes, if any. The *Usage Specification,* if any, is used as a check on the completeness and consistency of the *Function Specification.*

Tasks

Task 1

Define the format and notation of the *Function Specification.*

EXAMPLE: *Function Specification* format

The mathematical definition of a black box specification prescribes certain elements with a format that must be specified. For example, a black box specification can be formatted as tables (with columns for current stimulus, conditions on stimulus history, and responses), enumerations of input sequences and responses, disjoint conditional rules, or other formalisms appropriate to the application. The notation definition should include project conventions for naming and typing.

Task 2

Define all software boundaries and stimulus–response interfaces with hardware, other software, and human users.

Specify stimuli from hardware devices and associated responses and protocols.

Specify stimuli from external software and associated responses, including formats of files and messages.

Specify stimuli from user interfaces and associated responses, including details of presentation and interaction.

RECOMMENDATION: Specification of human user interfaces

The details of human user interfaces should be established during function specification, not deferred for completion during development. The *Function Specification* defines the complete external behavior of the software, which is closely coupled to user interfaces.

Document the software boundaries and external stimuli and responses in the *Function Specification* work product.

Task 3

Specify the required external behavior of the software in the black box function form of stimulus history mappings to corresponding responses.

Specify the required external behavior of the software in all possible circumstances of use.

EXPLANATION: "All possible circumstances of use"

The *Function Specification* defines the required behavior of the software for all uses, including correct and incorrect, frequent and infrequent, and nominal and stress conditions. Responses for all possible stimulus histories should be specified.

EXPLANATION: Mathematical function

"Function" refers to a mathematical function. A mathematical function defines a mapping from a domain to a range. In a black box specification, the domain is the set of all possible sequences of inputs (all stimulus histories), and the range is the set of all correct responses. A mathematically "complete" specification is one in which all possible stimulus histories have been mapped to their corresponding responses. A mathematically "consistent" specification is one in which no history has been mapped to more than one response. A "correct" specification is one in which the domain, range, and mapping have been properly specified in the judgment of domain experts.

REFERENCE: Software specification based on mathematical function theory

See Mills (1986, 1988) and Mills, Dyer, and Linger (1987).

RECOMMENDATION: Prudent exceptions to black box specification

The black box specification has a state- and procedure-free form that is extremely useful for validating requirements and driving incremental development and certification. In some cases, however, state box and even clear box specifications can be considered when they are more natural alternatives. Black box specifications are generally best, and are well worth the effort to develop.

Use abstractions such as specification functions in the black box specification to maximize understandability, limit complexity, and maintain intellectual control.

EXPLANATION: Specification functions

"Specification functions" are a common form of abstraction used in scaling up black box specifications for large systems. Specification functions define conditions or operations that are used to simplify function mappings. They appear in the mappings as named placeholders. For example, in a specification for a database, a specification function named "delete-ok" operating on stimulus history might define conditions for which a "delete" stimulus should produce a deletion; namely, that the record to be deleted had been added somewhere in the history of use and not subsequently deleted.

Simplify external software behavior whenever possible to improve usability and to reduce the development and certification effort.

Document the black box mapping of stimulus histories to responses and associated assumptions in the *Function Specification* work product.

Verification

Verification 1

Verify the completeness, consistency, correctness, and clarity of the evolving *Function Specification* work product in frequent team reviews.

Verification 2

Verify the completed *Function Specification* work product with the customer and the project team.

Review the *Function Specification* with the customer, the development and certification teams, and affected peer groups for agreement as the basis for incremental development and certification.

Measurement

(See Section 6.3, Common Cleanroom Process Elements.)

Exit

The process is complete when the exit criteria are satisfied.

Exit 1   The *Function Specification* has been completed, verified against the *Software Requirements,* and agreed to by the customer as the basis for software development.

8.3 Usage Specification Process

The purpose of the Usage Specification Process is to identify and to classify software users, usage scenarios, and environments of use; to establish and to analyze the highest level structure and probability distributions for software usage models; and to obtain agreement with the customer on the specified usage as the basis for software certification.

The specification team creates the *Usage Specification* based on the *Software Requirements* and the evolving *Function Specification.* The information in the *Usage Specification* defines the scope of the testing effort and serves as the basis for incremental usage model development. It also assists in completing and validating the *Function Specification.*

Analysis of high-level usage models provides early guidance for allocation of development and testing resources. The analysis can provide estimates of relative long-run usage of specified software functions, which can help prioritize development activities. It can also help estimate testing resource and schedule requirements. Usage model analysis can be carried out prior to software development, before resources are committed to increment development and certification. This analysis is an effective management tool for reducing the risk of inaccurate resource and schedule estimates.

Objectives

Objective 1   **The users, usage scenarios, and usage environments of the software are defined and documented to clarify the specification, establish development priorities, and provide a basis for initial test planning.**

Objective 2   **The customer agrees with the usage specification as the basis for usage model development and software certification.**

Entry

The process begins when one of the entry criteria is satisfied.

Entry 1   The *Software Requirements* and the *Function Specification* have been partially or fully completed.

> EXPLANATION: Incremental usage specification
>
> All software requirements and function specifications must eventually be defined to permit a complete usage specification. Often, all requirements are not fully understood at the outset, and the strategy of incremental usage specification based on a partial requirements definition may be necessary. In large-scale developments, incremental usage specification is often a desirable strategy for pacing development, maintaining intellectual control, and eliciting customer feedback.

Entry 2   The *Usage Specification* requires revision for changes to the *Software Requirements* or *Function Specification,* or for changes from increment specification, development, or certification.

Entry work products and the following supporting work product are available.
The *Engineering Change Log* describes proposed changes, if any.

Tasks

Task 1   **Define the format and notation of the *Usage Specification.***
The *Usage Specification* is often represented as a high-level Markov chain. Naming and documentation conventions are established for encoding usage information as elements of the chain.

EXPLANATION: Markov chain

Software use is treated as a stochastic process that can be described as a Markov chain. A Markov chain can be represented as a directed graph, in which the nodes are states of use and the arcs are stimuli that cause transitions between states.

In the Usage Modeling and Test Planning Process, the high-level *Usage Specification* is refined to produce detailed Markov chain *Usage Models*. Additional explanation of Markov chains is given in that process.

Task 2

Specify the expected usage of the software through progressive stratification of usage characteristics.

EXPLANATION: Stratification of usage characteristics

Variation in usage can be described as a hierarchy of progressively narrower categories of usage. A heterogeneous user population, for example, may be subdivided into a set of more homogeneous user classes. This stratification of usage results in a better understanding of software usage requirements and provides a high-level basis for test planning.

Identify and classify all hardware, software, and human users of the software.

Identify the expected proportion of each class of user within the set of expected users.

EXAMPLE: User classifications

Hardware user classifications include sensors, actuators, and other peripheral devices. Software user classifications include operating systems, databases, and other controlling or supporting software. Human user classifications include job type, access privileges, and experience level.

EXPLANATION: Contribution of usage specification to
function specification

Identification of users, usage scenarios, and environments of use in the Usage Specification Process contributes to the completeness and correctness of function definition in the Function Specification Process.

The users of the software are the sources of stimuli and the targets of responses. The completeness of the set of identified users is a necessary condition for the correctness of the domain defined in the *Function Specification.* The principle of *transaction closure* in Cleanroom black box specification refers to the requirement that all possible uses by all possible users be identified.

For each class of user, identify and classify all scenarios of use, including starting and ending events.

Identify the expected proportion of each class of scenarios within the set of expected scenarios.

EXAMPLE: Use classifications

Usage scenarios are defined by considering main and supporting user functions, routine and nonroutine use, safe and hazardous use, and other dimensions that stratify and organize usage patterns.

Because statistical testing is based on random sampling of the population of possible uses, the definition of a "use" is critical to the validity of the testing process. A use begins and ends with predefined events that are appropriate to the application; for example, invocation to termination, switchhook-up to switchhook-down, power-up to power-down, main menu to main menu, transaction start to transaction end, and so on.

For each class of user and class of use, identify and classify expected hardware and software environments for the software system.

Identify the expected proportion of each class of environment within the set of expected environments.

EXAMPLE: Environment classifications

Usage environments can be classified in terms of characteristics such as computer and network configuration, capacity, and performance; system and support software capabilities and resource requirements; data rates and volumes; and support for concurrency.

EXPLANATION: Operational use as the context for certification

Cleanroom testing is performed as a statistical experiment in which tested use of the software should reflect operational use to the greatest extent possible. Careful characterization of operational environments permits their accurate simulation in testing, which in turn permits valid estimates of fitness for use of the software in the operational environments.

REFERENCE: Usage specification

See Walton, Poore, and Trammell (1995).

Document the results in the *Usage Specification* work product.

Task 3   **Represent usage information as high-level Markov chains. Analyze the models, and make recommendations based on analysis of usage model statistics.**

EXPLANATION: Relationship of usage specification to usage modeling

Usage specification is a system-level activity. Detailed usage modeling parallels lower-level development activity. The high-level usage model developed during the Usage Specification Process is the top level of the usage model(s) developed during the Usage Modeling and Test Planning Process.

Identify any areas in which the functions defined in the *Function Specification* result in excessive complexity and cost in usage model development. Make recommendations for possible simplification.

Evaluate software functions in terms of probability of use. Make recommendations on development priorities.

Analyze usage statistics to estimate resources and schedules required to achieve certification goals.

Verification

Verification 1

Verify the evolving *Usage Specification* work product in specification team reviews.

Conduct frequent specification team reviews of the evolving *Usage Specification* for completeness, consistency, correctness, and clarity.

Verification 2

Verify the completed *Usage Specification* work product with the customer and the project team.

Review the *Usage Specification* with the customer, the certification team, and affected peer groups for agreement as the basis for usage model development and software certification.

Measurement

Measurement 1

Apply standard calculations to Markov chain usage models to derive high-level operational profiles of the software.

EXPLANATION: Usage model calculations

Standard calculations on Markov chain usage models provide estimates of long-term software usage behavior. The calculations may be interpreted to identify patterns of use, usage features, probabilities of particular usage events, and insights relevant to both development and test planning. Further discussion of usage model analysis is provided in the discussion of the Usage Modeling and Test Planning Process.

Exit

> **The process is complete when the exit criteria are satisfied.**

Exit 1   The *Usage Specification* has been completed, verified, and agreed to by the customer as the basis for detailed usage modeling and test planning.

8.4 Architecture Specification Process

The purpose of the Architecture Specification Process is to define the conceptual model, the structural organization, and the execution characteristics of the software. Architecture definition is a multilevel activity that spans the life cycle of the project. Architecture may be inherited from a domain or product line, evolve within the constraints of the system of which it is a part, or wholly originate in the software project.

The Cleanroom aspect of architecture specification is in decomposition of the history-based black box *Function Specification* into state-based state box and procedure-based clear box descriptions. This high-level box structure of the software identifies and connects principal components, including their state encapsulations and operations. It is the beginning of a referentially transparent decomposition of the *Function Specification* into box structure hierarchies, and will be used during increment development. The architecture may take a variety of forms, including functional, object based, and so on.

Key dimensions of an architecture are a conceptual architecture, expressed in terms of major software components and their relationships; a module architecture, expressed in terms of layers of functional decomposition; and an execution architecture, expressed in terms of dynamic software operation (Soni, Nord, and Hofmeister 1995). The architecture is a vehicle for incorporating existing reference models, components, protocols, standards, and software design strategies. Architecture specification spans the development life cycle.

The *Software Architecture* is a principal input to the Increment Planning and the Increment Design Processes.

Objectives

Objective 1   **The architectural strategy leverages existing assets and supports reuse plans.**

Objective 2   **The architectural structure of the software is defined as the complete behavior and interaction of its principal components.**

Objective 3   **The customer agrees with the software architecture as the basis for software development.**

Entry

The process begins when one of the entry criteria is satisfied.

Entry 1   The *Software Requirements* and the *Function Specification* are partially or fully completed.

Entry 2   The *Software Architecture* requires revision for changes to the *Software Requirements* or *Function Specification,* or for changes from increment specification, development, or certification.

Entry work products and the following supporting work products are available.

The *Engineering Change Log* describes proposed changes, if any. The *Usage Specification* is used to clarify requirements and constraints on the software architecture.

The *Reengineered Software,* if any, is used to define the use of reengineered components in the architecture.

Tasks

Task 1   **Identify architectural assets.**

Identify and analyze architectural assets applicable to the software, including existing domain models, reference architectures, components, communication protocols, standards, and design strategies and conventions.

Record the asset analysis in the *Software Architecture* work product.

Task 2   **Define a strategy for the software architecture.**

Define a strategy for the architecture based on the *Software Requirements,* the *Function Specification,* the analysis of the architectural assets, and the requirements derived from higher level system or subsystem design.

Document the strategy in the *Software Architecture.*

Task 3

Specify the top-level box structure of the software architecture.

Decompose the history-based black box specification of required external behavior defined in the *Function Specification* into top-level, state-based state box and procedure-based clear box forms based on the architecture strategy.

For the state box, invent principal state elements and operations required to achieve specified black box behavior.

For the clear box, invent procedures for operations on state elements required to achieve specified state box behavior. Within the clear box, invent and connect principal software components, usually defined as black boxes, whose subsequent state box decompositions will encapsulate state at the next level.

Continue the decomposition until the architecture is fully elaborated.

The completed software architecture represents hierarchies of box uses, wherein every use of a box is represented explicitly in a hierarchy.

Document the architecture in the *Software Architecture* work product.

Task 4

Analyze and validate the software architecture.

Perform simulations and analysis as necessary to ensure that performance, reliability, usability, and other software requirements can be met by the architecture.

Document the analysis in the *Software Architecture* work product.

Verification

Verification 1

Verify the evolving *Software Architecture* work product in team reviews.

Conduct frequent team reviews of the evolving *Software Architecture* to ensure that it meets requirements.

Use the Correctness Verification Process to verify that the representation of the *Software Architecture* in top-level box structure form is complete, consistent, and correct.

Verification 2

Verify the completed *Software Architecture* work product with the customer and the project team.

Review the *Software Architecture* with the customer, the development and certification teams, and the affected peer

groups for agreement as the basis for incremental development and certification.

Measurement

(See Section 6.3, Common Cleanroom Process Elements.)

Exit

The process is complete when the exit criteria are satisfied.

Exit 1   The *Software Architecture* has been completed, verified, and
                  agreed to by the customer.

8.5 Increment Planning Process

The purpose of the Increment Planning Process is to allocate customer requirements defined in the *Function Specification* to a series of software increments
that satisfy the *Software Architecture,* to define schedule and resource allocations for increment development and certification, and to obtain agreement with
the customer on the increment plan.

The *Increment Construction Plan* is created by the specification team for
use by management to assign tasks, track progress, and monitor product quality
and process control in the Project Management Process. It is revised as necessary to incorporate changes or to accommodate actual project performance. In
the incremental process, a software system grows from initial to final form
through a series of increments that implement user function, execute in the system environment, and accumulate into the final system. The first increment is
an *end-to-end executable subset* (i.e., initial user state to final user state) of the
functional behavior on which later increments can be built. When the final
increment is in place, the system is complete. By providing a series of accumulating subsets of the software that grow in capability, the incremental process
reduces risk and permits early and continual user evaluation and feedback. If
the customer prefers delivery of the final system only, incremental development
can still be used by the development organization for management control, risk
mitigation, and to support development needs such as hardware and software
co-design.

Incremental development and certification avoids the risks associated with
a separate integration step late in a project life cycle. Increments are typically

developed in top-down fashion, often with concurrent engineering of increments. Each increment is a composition of functions and interfaces specified in prior increments. This approach permits continual testing and quality assessment as the software evolves into final form.

Objectives

Objective 1 **The incremental development and certification plan supports intellectual control of the work, statistical quality control of the process, and risk management of the overall project.**

Objective 2 **The increment plan ensures ongoing clarification of requirements through user execution and evaluation of increments.**

Objective 3 **The customer agrees with the increment plan as the basis for software development and certification.**

Entry

The process begins when one of the entry criteria is satisfied.

Entry 1 The *Software Requirements, Function Specification, Usage Specification, Software Architecture, Reuse Analysis Plan, Risk Analysis Plan,* and *Schedule and Resource Plan* are partially or fully complete. These work products are the basis for developing the *Increment Construction Plan,* as well as a source of revisions to it.

Entry 2 The *Increment Construction Plan* requires revision for changes from development or certification activity, or as a result of new or changed requirements.

Entry work products are available.

Tasks

Task 1 **Partition software functions into a series of increments for development and certification.**

Define the functional content of a series of software increments that implement user function, execute in the system environment, and accumulate into the final system.

EXPLANATION: "Accumulate into the final system"

Cleanroom increments accumulate in a top-down fashion. The *Function Specification* and *Software Architecture* provide the high-level structure for a series of increments that grow from the structure. From the beginning, embedded specifications with executable stubs are used as placeholders for functions planned for later increments. In this way, all testing occurs in a system environment. Traditional integration testing is unnecessary.

Use the *Software Requirements* to identify software requirements or system engineering factors that may influence the definition of increment content.

Use the *Function Specification* and the *Software Architecture* to identify required software functions and their dependent relationships as a basis for defining increment content.

Use the *Reuse Analysis Plan* to identify reused components and allocate them to appropriate increments.

Use the *Risk Analysis Plan* to identify risks that influence increment content. Plan increment content to avoid or manage risks, with emphasis on addressing risks early in the project.

Use the *Usage Specification* to define increment content in consideration of usage probabilities; specifically, to incorporate functions with high usage probabilities into early increments.

Identify special components, such as complex algorithms requiring extensive analysis, for independent development and certification prior to incorporation into the accumulating increments. These components can be incorporated as reusable assets in the overall increment plan.

Document the required functional content of the increments in the *Increment Construction Plan.*

Task 2   **Refine the *Schedule and Resource Plan* by allocating schedules and resources to incremental development and certification.**

Within the overall constraints of the *Schedule and Resource Plan,* allocate development and certification schedules and resources for each increment.

Provide for overlapping or parallel development of increments as necessary to meet schedules based on the availability of development resources.

Define schedule points for measurement of software quality and process control, and for customer evaluation of increments.

Document schedule and resource allocations in the *Increment Construction Plan* work product.

REFERENCE: Increment planning

See Trammell, Pleszkoch, Linger, and Hevner (1996).

Verification

Verification 1   **Review the *Increment Construction Plan* with the customer, the development and certification teams, and affected peer groups for agreement as the basis for incremental development and certification.**

Measurement

(See Section 6.3, Common Cleanroom Process Elements.)

Exit

The process is complete when the exit criteria are satisfied.

Exit 1   The *Increment Construction Plan* has been completed, verified, and agreed to by the customer as the plan for software development and certification.

8.6 References

H.D. Mills. "Mathematical Foundations for Structured Programming," in *Software Productivity* (New York: Dorset House, 1988), 115–178.

H.D. Mills. "Structured Programming: Retrospect and Prospect." *IEEE Software* vol. 3 (November 1986): 58–66.

H.D. Mills, M. Dyer, and R.C. Linger. "Cleanroom Software Engineering." *IEEE Software* vol. 4 (November 1987): 19–25.

D. Soni, R. Nord, and C. Hofmeister. "Software Architecture in Industrial Applications" in *Proceedings of the 17th International Conference on Software Engineering,* eds. R. Jeffrey and D. Notkin (New York: Association for Computing Machinery, 1995): 196–207.

C.J. Trammell, M.G. Pleszkoch, R.C. Linger, and A.R. Hevner. "The Incremental Development Process in Cleanroom Software Engineering." *Decision Support Systems* vol. 17 (April 1996): 55–71.

G.H. Walton, J.H. Poore, and C.J. Trammell. "Statistical Testing Based on a Usage Model." *Software—Practice and Experience* vol. 25, no. 1 (January 1995): 97–108.

9

Cleanroom Development Processes

9.1 Software Reengineering Process

The purpose of the Software Reengineering Process is to prepare reused software for incorporation into the software product. Reused software can originate in Cleanroom or non-Cleanroom environments, and can include commercial products, customer-furnished software, and components from previous software developments. Software may be reused as is, reused through interface controllers such as wrappers, or reused after reengineering.

Reused software must satisfy two principal Cleanroom requirements. First, the functional semantics and interface syntax of reused software must be understood and documented, to maintain intellectual control and to avoid unforeseen failures in execution. If specification and design documentation for reused software is incomplete, its functional semantics can be recovered through function abstraction and correctness verification. The completeness and correctness of specifications for reused software must satisfy project specification standards.

Second, the fitness for use of reused software must be either known or determined to achieve the project's certification goals. Usage models can be developed for reused software, and its fitness for use can be determined through statistical testing. The reliability of reused software must satisfy project certification goals.

The results of the Software Reengineering Process are recorded in the *Reengineering Plan* and *Reengineered Software* work products.

Objectives

Objective 1 **Reengineered software satisfies requirements for the software product in which it is used.**

Objective 2 **Reengineering activity enables intellectual control over the reengineered software.**

Objective 3 **Reengineered software is certified to be fit for its intended use as necessary to meet certification goals for the software product in which it is used.**

Entry

The process begins when one of the entry criteria is satisfied.

Entry 1 Candidate reusable assets identified in the *Reuse Analysis Plan* are to be evaluated and possibly reengineered for use in the software product.

Entry 2 The *Reengineering Plan* and/or the *Reengineered Software* require revision for changes from specification, development, or certification activities.

Entry work products and the following supporting work products are available.
Reused software and its supporting documentation are used as the basis for creating the *Reengineered Software.*
The *Engineering Change Log* describes proposed changes. The *Software Requirements, Function Specification, Usage Specification, Software Architecture,* and *Increment Construction Plan* are used to define requirements for reengineering reused software.

Tasks

Task 1 **Analyze candidate reused software and its documentation to develop a reengineering plan.**
Analyze specifications, designs, and implementations of reused software to evaluate the completeness and correctness

of documentation of its functional semantics, and the extent of reengineering necessary to satisfy software product requirements.

Analyze the usage models, test plans, test procedures, test results, and actual usage of reused software to evaluate the basis for its reliability estimates.

Conduct a cost/benefit analysis with respect to project certification goals and future software maintenance responsibilities to determine appropriate resource allocations to reengineering activities.

If necessary, develop a plan for reengineering reused software to satisfy functional requirements, recover functional semantics, and/or assess fitness for use.

Define and document reengineering tasks, schedules, and resources in the *Reengineering Plan* work product.

Task 2 | **Recover the functional semantics of reused software using function abstraction techniques.**

If reused software implementations are not structured, transform them into structured form using program structuring techniques to permit function abstraction.

Carry out stepwise abstraction of structured implementations as necessary and document embedded intended functions. Continue abstraction until specifications of external behavior in all possible circumstances of use have been defined.

Document the functional semantics of reused software in the *Reengineered Software* work product.

Task 3 | **Reengineer reused software to meet software product requirements.**

Respecify, redesign, and reimplement reused software as necessary to meet requirements using the Function Specification, Increment Design, and Correctness Verification Processes.

Document the reengineering of reused software in the *Reengineered Software* work product.

Task 4 | **Recover the functional semantics of reused software using experimental execution.**

If the source code of reused software is not available, conduct experimental executions as necessary to derive an understanding of its functional semantics.

> RECOMMENDATION: Use of Commercial Off-the-Shelf
> Software (COTS) or Application
> Program Interfaces (APIs)
>
> If neither specifications nor source code are available, execution experiments can be used to understand the semantics of the software. The use of COTS, API, or otherwise "sealed" software in the product under development should be restricted to functions that are well understood.

Document the functional semantics of reused software in the *Reengineered Software* work product.

Task 5 | **Certify the fitness for use of reused software.**
Create usage models and conduct statistical testing as necessary to certify the fitness for use of reused software with respect to project certification goals. Use the Usage Modeling and Test Planning Process and the Statistical Testing and Certification Process.

Document certification results in the *Reengineered Software* work product.

Verification

Verification 1 | **Verify the *Reengineered Software* work product.**
Carry out correctness verification in team reviews as necessary to ensure correctness of abstracted specifications and/or redeveloped software. Use the Correctness Verification Process.

Measurement

Measurement 1 | Measure the fitness for use of the reengineered software using the Cleanroom certification processes and associated measures.

Exit

The process is complete when one of the exit criteria is satisfied.

Exit 1

The *Reengineered Software* has been completed, including any necessary redevelopment to meet requirements, abstraction of functional semantics, and certification of fitness for use.

Exit 2

Reengineering activity has revealed that the candidate software is not fit for use in the product, and project plans must be changed.

9.2 Increment Design Process

The purpose of the Increment Design Process is to design and code a software increment that satisfies the *Increment Construction Plan, Function Specification,* and *Software Architecture*; and conforms to Cleanroom design principles and quality criteria. The development team documents each increment in the *Increment Design* work product.

Increments are designed and implemented as usage hierarchies through box structure decomposition. This process preserves referential transparency between successive decompositions to maintain intellectual control. Increment designs can be expressed in object, functional, or other forms. Each increment is based on a prior specification. Increment specifications are expressed in stimulus history-based black box and state-based state box forms. Increment designs and implementations are expressed in procedure-based clear box forms that can introduce new black boxes for further decomposition. Reused or reengineered components are incorporated as planned.

Team reviews during the Increment Design Process focus on issues such as design strategies, simplification, verifiability, maintainability, reuse, and conformance to style. In the complementary Correctness Verification Process, the team focuses exclusively on correctness. Specifications, designs, and implementations evolve in the Increment Design Process, and intended functions are embedded in clear box procedure decompositions to permit effective correctness verification. The team performs correctness verification as the last intellectual pass through the work.

The development team does not execute the increment implementation. First execution is performed by the certification team in the Statistical Testing and Certification Process after the development team has completed verification in the Correctness Verification Process.

Objectives

Objective 1   **The increment design and implementation satisfy the** *Function Specification,* **the** *Software Architecture,* **and the** *Increment Construction Plan.*

Objective 2   **The increment design and implementation are a verifiably correct decomposition of required functions.**

Objective 3   **Intellectual control over increment design and implementation is maintained through team reviews.**

Entry

The process begins when one of the entry criteria is satisfied.

Entry 1   The *Software Requirements, Function Specification, Usage Specification, Software Architecture, Reengineered Software,* and *Increment Construction Plan* are sufficient for increment design, and a software increment is scheduled for development or change. These work products are the basis for developing the *Increment Design,* as well as a source of revisions to it.

Entry 2   An *Increment Verification Report* or *Increment Certification Report* identifies faults or failures requiring correction of the *Increment Design.*

Entry work products and the supporting work product are available.
The *Engineering Change Log* describes proposed changes.

Tasks

Task 1   **Review the work products that are the basis for the increment design.**
Review the *Increment Construction Plan* to identify the user functions to be implemented in the increment.
Review the *Function Specification* for definitions of the user functions to be implemented in the increment.
Review the *Software Architecture* for the architectural strategy to be maintained in the increment.

Task 2

Design and implement the software increment as a usage hierarchy through box structure decomposition.

EXPLANATION: Box structure usage hierarchy

Box structure decomposition results in a usage hierarchy of objects, modules, and other units of code. The box structure hierarchy for an increment is the completed increment. The box structure hierarchy for the final increment is the completed software product.

Decompose history-based black box specifications into state-based state box specifications with equivalent behavior in all circumstances of use.

Decompose state box specifications into procedure-based clear box designs with equivalent behavior in all circumstances of use. Introduce new black box uses in clear box designs as necessary.

Create clear box designs as structured procedures that fully define control and data relationships among new black box uses and other design elements.

Repeatedly decompose new black boxes into state box and clear box forms. Continue decomposition until designs can be implemented with no further invention required.

Maintain referential transparency between decompositions for intellectual control.

EXPLANATION: Referential transparency

Cleanroom minimizes the risk of integration faults through development based on the mathematical principle of referential transparency. Referential transparency in box structure hierarchies requires that the black box specifications embedded in clear boxes at each level of decomposition define precisely the required functional behavior of their subsequent decompositions into state and clear boxes. With referential transparency, intellectual control is maintained and independent work at lower levels can proceed without concern for functional interactions at higher levels.

Incorporate components from the *Reengineered Software* work product into the increment as planned.

Attach intended functions to the control structures in clear box procedure designs for use in correctness verification.

EXPLANATION: Intended functions

Intended functions are a key Cleanroom concept and are essential to achieving Cleanroom objectives. An intended function is a definition of the full functional effect on data of the control structure (`sequence`, `ifthenelse`, `whiledo`, etc.) to which it is attached. Intended functions typically appear as comments in the clear box. They are often expressed in black box or state box form, particularly as conditional rules, and are used in verifying their control structure expansions.

If necessary, translate designs into the implementation language and review for correct translation.

Refer to the *Usage Specification* document for information about the operational environment. Refer to the *Increment Verification Report* or *Increment Certification Report* for faults or failures requiring correction.

Document the design and code in the *Increment Design* work product.

REFERENCE: Box structure specification and design

See Mills (1986, 1988) and Mills, Dyer, and Linger (1987).

Task 3   **Improve the *Increment Design* through team reviews.**

Conduct frequent development team reviews of the evolving *Increment Design* to discuss design strategies and improvements, and to assess characteristics including understandability, verifiability, and maintainability. Make design simplification and style compliance explicit review objectives for efficient correctness verification. Redesign for simplicity when cost effective.

EXPLANATION: Writing for verification

Correctness verification is only possible if designs are verifiable. This is not to say that designs are not *correct* unless they are verifiable, only that they are not *verifiably* correct.

Cleanroom designs are written for verification. The stepwise unfolding of specification and design in box structure decompositions ensures traceability of design to specification at every level of the usage hierarchy. Each specification is "distributed" as intended functions for design components during the Increment Design Process, and design components are verified against their intended functions during the Correctness Verification Process.

Identify opportunities for state migration and use of common services.

EXPLANATION: State migration

State migration is a Cleanroom strategy for improving and simplifying designs. It concerns placement of state data at the most effective level of decomposition for its use. State migration implements the software engineering principle of information hiding for limitation of data scope. State migration places data based on its scope of usage at as low a level in a system hierarchy as possible, but at as high a level as necessary. Migration of state data may be possible whenever new black boxes are created in a given clear box. Any state data item used solely by one lower level box can be migrated to it.

EXPLANATION: Common services

Use of common services is another Cleanroom strategy for improving and simplifying designs. Common services are reusable components. They may be newly created for a given system, or drawn from a reuse library. Common services afford economy in system size, effective use of development resources, efficient verification, and increased reliability.

Task 4   **Perform individual correctness verification.**
                   Apply function–theoretic correctness verification on an
                   individual basis to evolving designs, with the objective of
                   entering the Correctness Verification Process with few faults.

Verification

Verification 1   Verification of the correctness of the *Increment Design* is so
                   critical to Cleanroom objectives that an entire process is de-
                   voted to it (see Section 9.3, Correctness Verification Process).

Measurement

                   (See Section 6.3, Common Cleanroom Process Elements.)

Exit

                   The process is complete when the exit criterion is satisfied.

Exit 1   The *Increment Design* has been completed.

9.3 Correctness Verification Process

The purpose of the Correctness Verification Process is to verify the correctness
of a software increment using mathematically based techniques. Correctness
verification is carried out in development team reviews using function-theoretic
reasoning. Black box specifications are verified to be complete, consistent, and
correct. State box specifications are verified with respect to corresponding
black box specifications. Clear box procedures are verified with respect to corresponding state box specifications. Every control structure in every clear box
procedure is verified against its intended function using the Correctness
Conditions of the Correctness Theorem (Linger, Mills, and Witt 1979). Faults
found during verification reviews are documented in the *Increment Verification
Report* and are corrected by the specification and development teams under
engineering change control. The specifications and designs are then reverified.
Written proofs of correctness based on function–theoretic techniques provide
additional rigor if necessary for life-, mission-, and enterprise-critical software.

The Correctness Verification Process is concurrent with the Increment Design Process. Correctness verification is the last intellectual pass at each level of decomposition—the last line of defense against failures encountered during statistical testing and certification. The objective of correctness verification is to enter the testing phase with no faults in the implemented design. Following completion of verification by the development team, the increment is turned over to the certification team for first execution.

Objectives

Objective 1   **The team agrees that the software increment is correct with respect to its specification; in other words, that it contains no remaining faults.**

Objective 2   **Faults and inadequacies found in correctness verification are documented to permit subsequent analysis for process improvement.**

> REFERENCE: CMM Defect Prevention KPA
>
> If compliance with this KPA is an organizational objective, its specific requirements should be reviewed when the Correctness Verification Process is tailored for organizational or project use.

Entry

The process begins when one of the entry criteria is satisfied.

Entry 1   A new *Increment Design* has been completed or is in progress.

Entry 2   A reengineered or corrected *Increment Design* has been completed or is in progress.

Entry work products and the following supporting work products are available.

The *Function Specification* defines the required external behavior of the functions allocated to the increment in the *Increment Construction Plan*.

The *Software Architecture* defines the architectural strategy to be used in the *Increment Design*.

Tasks

Task 1

Verify the correctness of the software increment using mathematically based verification techniques.

Verify the correctness of every specification and design structure in the *Increment Design*.

Carry out verbal proofs of correctness based on function–theoretic techniques in team verification reviews. A consensus of team members is required to establish correctness.

For black box verification, determine the completeness, consistency, and correctness of its specification.

For state box verification, compare state box behavior to corresponding black box behavior for equivalence.

For clear box verification, apply the Correctness Conditions of the Correctness Theorem to determine the correctness of every control structure (including embedded black box specifications) with respect to its intended function.

RECOMMENDATION: Correctness conditions for other recurring constructs

Modern software development environments employ a wide variety of features and constructs that reduce to, but are often not easily recognizable as, standard control structures such as `sequence`, `ifthenelse`, and `whiledo`. Visual programming languages have graphical elements. Real-time facilities have timing mechanisms such as process rendezvous. Application generators have high-level resources such as GUI builders. Multitasking, multiuser, multithreaded applications use such control mechanisms as resource locking, and so on.

A project team should establish the correctness conditions for such recurring constructs using function–theoretic reasoning. The development of standard verification protocols for recurring idioms or patterns is precisely the sort of process tailoring that needs to be done to adapt the Cleanroom process to a given project and environment.

Task 2

Document findings of team verification reviews.

Create an *Increment Verification Report* that documents all faults, problems, and improvements identified in verification reviews, and assign corrective actions.

Task 3   **Create written proofs of correctness as necessary for critical software.**

Develop written proofs of correctness as necessary for life-, mission-, and enterprise-critical software, and verify the proofs in team reviews.

Document the proofs in the *Increment Design* work product.

Task 4   **Reverify all corrections to faults.**

Perform reverification reviews on corrections to faults, including reverification of the full context of corrections to avoid unforeseen side effects.

Verification

Verification 1   **Confirm that every box structure has been verified as correct by team consensus.**

Confirm that each black box, state box, and clear box in the new and changed portions of the *Increment Design* has been verified to be correct.

Measurement

Measurement 1   **Measure the *Increment Design* and the Increment Design Process.**

The Correctness Verification Process is a focused team review of the *Increment Design*. Measure the quality of the *Increment Design* and the effectiveness of the Increment Design Process in terms such as the number, type, and severity of faults found during the verification reviews.

Exit

The process is complete when one of the exit criteria is satisfied.

Exit 1   The increment has been verified with no faults found.

Exit 2   The increment has been verified and contains faults that must be corrected and the engineering changes verified.

Exit 3   The black box, state box, or intended function definitions are insufficient for effective verification, and must be revised before verification can be accomplished.

Exit 4   Initial verification has found faults in sufficient quantity and severity that the process must be terminated and the increment redesigned.

In each case, the *Increment Verification Report* is created. Written proofs, if any, are added to the *Increment Design.* The Correctness Verification Process cannot be completed until the *Increment Design* is completed.

9.4 References

R.C. Linger, H.D. Mills, and B.I. Witt. *Structured Programming: Theory and Practice.* Reading, MA: Addison-Wesley, 1979.

H.D. Mills. "Mathematical Foundations for Structured Programming," in *Software Productivity* (New York: Dorset House, 1988), 115–178.

H.D. Mills. "Structured Programming: Retrospect and Prospect." *IEEE Software* vol. 3 (November 1986): 58–66.

H.D. Mills, M. Dyer, and R.C. Linger. "Cleanroom Software Engineering." *IEEE Software* vol. 4 (November 1987): 19–25.

10

Cleanroom Certification Processes

10.1 Usage Modeling and Test Planning Process

The purpose of the Usage Modeling and Test Planning Process is to refine the *Usage Specification* into usage models for software testing, to define test plans, to obtain customer agreement on the usage models and test plans as the basis for software certification, and to generate statistical test cases and prepare the test environment.

The certification team creates the *Usage Models* and *Increment Test Plan,* and generates the *Statistical Test Cases.* Usage models are used to generate statistical test cases and monitor the progress of testing in the Statistical Testing and Certification Process. A usage model for a software system represents an infinite population of possible uses. It consists of a structure that defines possible traversals of states of use by users, together with probabilities that define the likelihood that particular traversals will occur. In statistical testing, test cases are generated from the usage model based on its transition probabilities. Multiple usage models may be required for multiple classes of users and environments. Models are developed incrementally in accordance with the *Increment Construction Plan,* and accumulate into final form in parallel with increment designs. The customer reviews the usage models and agrees that they will generate all scenarios of use, are correctly weighted, and are appropriate for certification.

Usage model statistics provide a great deal of information about the testing effort that will be required to achieve certification goals given projected failure rates in testing. Usage model analysis provides a basis for test planning and is an effective management tool for reducing the risk of inaccurate resource and schedule estimates.

Objectives

Objective 1   **Valid usage models are defined that represent all possible uses of the software under expected or other usage conditions.**

Objective 2   **A statistical testing plan based on the usage models is defined and validated through model analysis and simulation.**

Objective 3   **The customer agrees to the usage models and statistical test plan as the basis for software certification.**

Entry

The process begins when one of the entry criteria is satisfied.

Entry 1   The *Usage Specification, Function Specification,* and/or *Increment Construction Plan* have been completed or changed. They are the basis for developing the *Usage Models* and *Increment Test Plan,* as well as a source of revisions to them.

Entry 2   The *Usage Models* or *Increment Test Plan* require revision for changes from increment development or certification.

Entry work products and the following supporting work products are available.
The *Software Architecture* and the *Reengineered Software* may also provide information for development of the *Usage Models.*
The *Engineering Change Log* describes proposed changes.

Tasks

Task 1

Define the usage models to be developed.

Use the *Usage Specification* to define the usage models to be elaborated, and the scope and purpose of each.

Include special-purpose models as necessary (e.g., for certification of infrequently used functions with high consequences of failure).

EXPLANATION: Special-purpose models

A usage model represents the conditions under which software is used. In general, expected usage conditions are modeled. In addition, other usage conditions may be of interest as well, and are modeled for special purposes. Hazardous usage conditions, for example, may be of interest for safety-critical software. Malicious usage conditions might be modeled for software with special security requirements. Usage can be characterized in whatever terms are important in the certification context.

Consider use of actual user input when available. Real-time data feeds or the output of automated usage capture facilities can be used as components of usage models.

Task 2

Define the structure of each usage model.

Refine the *Usage Specification* to develop the *Usage Models*. For each model, define all possible usage states and their transitions based on the functions required by the *Increment Construction Plan* and as defined by the *Function Specification*.

Define the structure of each model in the *Usage Models* document.

RECOMMENDATION: Markov chain usage models

The structure of a usage model can be represented as a Markov chain. A Markov chain usage model reflects the stochastic nature of software use, and permits analysis of usage and automation of test activity.

continued

RECOMMENDATION: *continued*

The usage model structure represents all possible uses of the software—expressed in terms of the initial usage state, subsequent sequences of possible usage states, and the terminal usage state. The model can be represented as a directed graph, with nodes (usage states) that are connected by arcs (possible transitions in use). Any usage scenario can be generated from a traversal of the model structure.

Ambiguity, inconsistency, or complexity in the *Function Specification* is often identified during creation of usage model structures.

REFERENCE: Usage modeling

See Whittaker and Poore (1993), and Whittaker and Agrawal (1994).

RECOMMENDATION: Early planning for test automation

It is crucial to anticipate test automation requirements during usage modeling. Linkage with test tools, pre- and postprocessing steps, live data feeds, response capture facilities, and numerous other aspects of automated testing are likely to be simpler if test automation is considered during usage modeling.

Task 3   **Define the transition probabilities of each usage model.**

Determine transition probabilities between usage states based on usage information and certification goals.

Employ user estimates and experience with similar systems and prior versions as sources of information about usage probabilities.

Define transition probabilities for each model in the *Usage Models*.

EXPLANATION: Transition probabilities

While the structure of the usage model defines possible use, the transition probabilities define expected use. The probabilities

continued

EXPLANATION: *continued*

associated with the transitions in the usage model may be known, partially known, or unknown. If they are known, as is often the case with well-instrumented systems in mature domains, the probabilities can be assigned directly. If they are not known, they can be estimated or made uniform. If they are partially known, a combination of these strategies can be used.

Probabilities can also be defined for other than expected use; for example, to emphasize testing of infrequently used functions with high consequences of failure.

The validity of conclusions drawn in statistical testing is entirely related to the usage models employed. Systematic acquisition of knowledge about expected usage is essential for developing accurate usage models.

REFERENCE: Optimization of usage models

Cleanroom practice is evolving toward automatic generation of transition probabilities from usage constraints. Operations research techniques can be applied to optimize usage models for an objective function, such as minimum testing cost, subject to usage constraints that characterize available knowledge about expected use. See Walton (1995).

Task 4

Validate the usage models.

Generate statistics for each usage model. Evaluate the statistics to validate the overall usage profile, and to estimate resources and schedules required to achieve certification goals.

Develop recommendations based on the analysis (e.g., cost-saving simplifications for the user functions defined by the *Function Specification*).

EXPLANATION: Practical interpretation of usage model analysis

Important information is available through standard calculations on a Markov chain usage model; for example,

- The expected length of a usage scenario (i.e., test case length)

continued

EXPLANATION: *continued*

- The expected minimum number of usage scenarios until a given usage state occurs for the first time

- The expected occupancy of each state of use (as a proportion of all states of use) in the long-term use of the software

- The expected minimum number of test cases required to cover all states and all transitions of the model

- The expected number of test cases required to achieve target levels of reliability and confidence

Interpretations of these calculations provide insights about potential hazards in use, allocation of development and testing resources, and other information for management decision making.

REFERENCE: Usage model analysis

See Whittaker and Thomason (1994).

Task 5

Develop a plan for certification testing of the software increment.

Develop a test plan, including schedules, staffing, training, hardware and software environment, certification goals, use of statistical test cases, use of operational input, procedures for verifying correct software performance, and documentation.

Define the test plan to ensure experimental control, including test procedures, test monitoring, results recording, failure evaluation, and engineering change control.

EXPLANATION: Experimental control

Cleanroom testing is conducted as a statistical experiment to permit scientifically valid conclusions about the fitness for use of the software. During a statistical experiment, a series of random trials is performed under specified conditions, the outcomes of the trials are determined according to specified

continued

EXPLANATION: *continued*

criteria, and conclusions about the probabilities of the outcomes are drawn.

In statistical testing, the trials are test cases that are generated randomly from the usage models, the outcomes correspond to the performance of the software, and the conclusions concern the probability of correct and incorrect software performance. Conclusions are used to make informed decisions regarding test management and product release.

Many aspects of statistical testing must be controlled to preserve the properties of the statistical experiment. Performing trials under specified conditions means, for example, that the same software version must be used in each test case; a new software version marks the beginning of a new experiment. Determining the outcomes of the trials according to specified criteria means, for example, that the judgments by the testers and the evaluations by the test oracles must be consistent across all test cases. Explicit policies and operating procedures are required to ensure experimental integrity in statistical testing.

REFERENCE: Experimental control

See Trammell (1995) and Trammell and Poore (1994).

Plan for additional testing techniques to be applied in conjunction with statistical testing as necessary.

EXPLANATION: Other testing strategies

Statistical testing for reliability certification is a form of random testing. Statistical methods for nonrandom testing are often used to accomplish specific objectives as well. Test cases producing the fastest coverage of the usage model, for example, might be generated for use at the beginning of testing to reveal any immediate problems with the software. Some forms of nonstatistical testing may be included in the test plan as well, such as specific tests that are required by the customer, by a standard, or by law.

Document testing plans in the *Increment Test Plan* work product.

Task 6

Generate the statistical test cases.
Use the *Usage Models* to generate the *Statistical Test Cases* to be used during statistical testing.

EXPLANATION: Manual versus automated testing

For manual testing, the generated test cases might be "scripts" of instructions to human testers. For automated testing, the scripts might be command sequences.

Task 7

Prepare the statistical testing environment.
Establish the hardware configuration and software environment required to test the software.

EXPLANATION: Test environment

Preparation of the test environment may be a resource-intensive task. In such cases it will receive special emphasis in the *Schedule and Resource Plan* developed during the Project Planning Process, and in the *Usage Specification* developed in the Usage Specification Process.

Verification

Verification 1

Verify the evolving *Increment Test Plan* and *Usage Models* work products in team reviews.
Conduct frequent certification team reviews of the evolving *Increment Test Plan* and *Usage Models* for completeness, consistency, correctness, and simplicity. Confirm through quantitative analysis of usage model properties, such as the long-run probabilities of state occurrence, that the models are consistent with user estimates and experience.

Verification 2

Verify the completed *Increment Test Plan* and *Usage Models* work products with the customer and the project team.

Review the *Increment Test Plan* and *Usage Models* with the customer, the specification and certification teams, and affected peer groups to obtain agreement on them as the basis for software certification.

Measurement

Measurement 1   **Measure the *Usage Models* work product.**
Measure the size of the *Usage Models* in terms such as the number of usage states, state transitions, and statistically typical paths.

Exit

The process is complete when the exit criterion is satisfied.

Exit 1   The *Increment Test Plan* and the *Usage Models* have been completed and agreed to by the customer as the basis for software certification.

10.2 Statistical Testing and Certification Process

The purpose of the Statistical Testing and Certification Process is to demonstrate the software's fitness for use in a formal statistical experiment. Fitness for use is defined with respect to the usage models and certification goals employed in the testing process. The certification goals, first established in the *Measurement Plan,* and refined in the *Increment Test Plan,* may be expressed in terms such as software reliability, reliability growth rate, and coverage of the usage defined in the usage models.

Software increments undergo first execution in this process. The increments are compiled, the *Executable System* is built, the statistical test cases are executed under experimental control, and the test results are evaluated. The success or failure of test cases is determined by comparison of actual software behavior with the required behavior defined in the *Function Specification.* Failures found during statistical testing are documented in the *Statistical Testing Report.* Intermediate and final test results are evaluated to make informed test management decisions. As testing proceeds, the values of certification measures are compared with certification goals. The results of the comparisons drive decisions on continuing testing, stopping testing for engineering changes, stopping testing for reengineering and reverification, and final software certification.

In addition to measuring software quality and reliability, certification metrics are also used as measures of process control. Cleanroom team performance standards based on historical data, such as failure rates in statistical testing of prior systems, are compared with current metrics to make informed management decisions. Evaluations and decisions regarding product quality and process control are documented in the *Increment Certification Report.*

Objectives

Objective 1   **Software testing is conducted using a formal statistical design under experimental control.**

Objective 2   **The software is demonstrated to perform correctly with respect to its specification.**

Objective 3   **Statistically valid estimates of the properties addressed by the certification goals are derived for the software.**

Objective 4   **Management decisions regarding continuation of testing and certification of the software are based on statistical estimates of software quality.**

Entry

The process begins when the entry criteria are satisfied.

Entry 1   The *Increment Test Plan* has been completed, the *Statistical Test Cases* have been generated, and the test environment has been prepared.

A new or corrected *Increment Design* is available for compilation.

The *Function Specification* and *Usage Models* are available for use in evaluating observed behavior against specified behavior.

Tasks

Task 1   **Prepare the software increment for testing.**

Compile the software increment. If corrections are necessary, initiate the Engineering Change Process. After successful compilation, create the *Executable System* containing the load modules required for execution.

Task 2   **Perform other types of testing if necessary.**

Perform other types of testing if necessary prior to statistical testing. For example, special testing may be required to demonstrate specific scenarios of use or to achieve complete usage model coverage with the minimum number of test cases.

EXPLANATION: Order of statistical and other testing

The key consideration in determining whether to perform other types of tests before or after statistical testing is the effect on certification. When a reliability estimate is made at the conclusion of statistical testing, it applies to the specific version of the software that was tested. If changes are made as a result of subsequent testing, the reliability estimate may require revision. It is generally preferable to perform any nonstatistical tests prior to statistical testing. Nonstatistical tests performed after statistical testing may complicate the reliability certification if the software is changed.

Task 3   **Execute the statistical test cases in the test environment.**

Execute the *Statistical Test Cases* according to the procedures defined in the *Increment Test Plan.*

Task 4   **Evaluate the statistical test case results.**

Evaluate the correctness of the software responses with respect to the behavior defined in the *Function Specification.*

If failures are observed, evaluate their impact on the continuation of testing, experimental control, and the validity of certification results. If corrections are necessary, initiate the Engineering Change Process.

> EXPLANATION: Independent trials
>
> A key requirement in a statistical experiment is that the trials be independent—that is, the outcome of one trial must have no effect on the outcome of any other trial. Although randomly generated test cases may ensure independent trials in statistical testing, the requirement for independence can still be undermined by failures in testing. For example, if a failure on a test case "blocks" access to functions required by a subsequent test case, testing should be stopped and the problem fixed.

Document test results in the *Statistical Testing Report.* Record data for each failure, including the test environment, test case, test results, failure type and severity, and any other information that will assist in determining its cause.

Task 5

Derive certification measures.

Use the *Usage Models, Statistical Test Cases, Statistical Testing Report,* and results of other testing to derive measures of the fitness for use of the software with respect to certification goals.

Measures can include reliability and confidence, reliability growth rate, MTTF, representativeness of the test case sample, and other measures derived from comparison of expected and observed software performance.

Use statistical methods such as hypothesis testing, interval analysis, and analysis of failure data with reliability models.

> EXPLANATION: Reliability measurement
>
> Software reliability measurement is a hallmark of Cleanroom. Reliability estimation based on Markov chain usage models is a prominent approach to reliability measurement in Cleanroom practice. The Markov chain approach provides measures of reliability, confidence, and other stopping criteria.
>
> Classic statistical hypothesis testing is also used in Cleanroom for reliability estimation. Models of reliability growth can be used when their underlying assumptions are justified.

REFERENCE: Certification measures

See Whittaker and Thomason (1994).

Document certification measures in the *Increment Certification Report.*

Task 6

Compare certification measures with certification goals.

Compare the values of trends in the certification measures with project goals for product quality and process control.

If appropriate, combine certification measures from the current statistical testing experiment with measures from other experiments.

EXPLANATION: Conditions for combining test information

If test conditions (e.g., software version, usage model, execution environment) are the same, data from various statistical testing experiments can simply be combined. If testing conditions are not the same, more complex approaches to combining information must be used to ensure the validity of conclusions.

Document evaluations in the *Increment Certification Report.*

Task 7

Decide whether to stop testing.

Positive case: Testing can be stopped and the software certified as fit for use if the current values of the certification measures satisfy certification goals and if no failures have been observed during testing of the current software version (or none worth the cost and risk of correction).

Negative case: Testing should be stopped and the software reengineered and reverified if process control standards have been violated. Violation of process control standards occurs when certification goals cannot be achieved given current values of the certification measures and the remaining schedule and resources for testing.

EXPLANATION: Certification goals and process control standards

Certification goals are targets for final results. *Process control standards* are gauges of intermediate progress toward certification goals. The certification goals answer the question: Is the software currently fit for its intended use? Process control standards answer the question: Is the software likely to be certified as fit for use on the expected schedule? In general, certification goals are defined by the customer, process control standards are defined by the developer, and both exist within the context of the predefined certification protocol in the test plan.

Document decisions in the *Increment Certification Report.*

Verification

Verification 1   **Verify that the tests were executed according to the test plan.**

Verification 2   **Verify the correctness of statistical calculations.**

Measurement

Measurement 1   **Measure the *Statistical Test Cases* and the results of their execution.**
Measure the *Statistical Test Cases* in terms such as the number and size of the test cases, and the execution times for each.
Measure the number and severity of failures reported.

Measurement 2   **Measure the Statistical Testing and Certification Process.**
Measure the sufficiency of testing in terms such as the coverage of the usage models employed and the statistical similarity between expected usage and tested usage.

Exit

The process is complete when one of the exit criteria is satisfied.

Exit 1   The software increment satisfies certification goals.

Exit 2   The software increment has failed to satisfy certification goals and must be reengineered and reverified before testing can resume.

In either case, the *Statistical Testing Report* and *Increment Certification Report* are completed.

10.3 References

C.J. Trammell. "Quantifying the Reliability of Software: Statistical Testing Based on a Usage Model," in *Proceedings of the Second IEEE International Symposium on Software Engineering Standards* (Los Alamitos, CA: IEEE Computer Society Press, 1995), 208–218.

C.J. Trammell and J.H. Poore. "Experimental Control in Software Reliability Certification," in *Proceedings of the Seventeenth Annual NASA/Goddard Software Engineering Workshop* (Greenbelt, Maryland: NASA, November 30–December 1, 1994).

G.H. Walton. *Generating Transition Probabilities for Markov Chain Usage Models.* Ph.D. diss. University of Tennessee, 1995.

G.H. Walton and J.H. Poore. *Measuring Complexity and Coverage of Software Specifications.* Technical report. Knoxville, TN: Department of Computer Science, University of Tennessee, 1995.

J.A. Whittaker and K.K. Agrawal. "A Case Study in Software Reliability Measurement," in *Proceedings of the 7th International Quality Week,* ed. (San Francisco: Software Research, Inc., 1994).

J.A. Whittaker and J.H. Poore. "Markov Analysis of Software Specifications." *ACM Transactions on Software Engineering and Methodology,* vol. 2, no. 1 (January 1993): 93–106.

J.A. Whittaker and M.G. Thomason. "A Markov Chain Model for Statistical Software Testing." *IEEE Transactions on Software Engineering,* vol. 20, no. 10 (October 1994): 812–824.

11

Cleanroom and the Capability Maturity Model for Software

11.1 The CMM for Software

As use of Cleanroom software engineering becomes more widespread, interest in its relationship to the Software Engineering Institute's Capability Maturity Model (CMM) for Software (Paulk, Weber, Curtis, and Chrissis 1995) has increased. The CMM provides a well-defined paradigm for software process improvement that has experienced successful application in many organizations. Cleanroom software engineering provides well-defined theoretical foundations and practices for software specification, development, testing, and certification. The principal focus of the CMM is on management and organization; the principal focus of Cleanroom is on technology and engineering practices. Effective management processes are an essential prerequisite for successful software development. However, technology-based solutions to problems of software development can often produce results that no amount of good management can achieve in their absence. For example, the introduction of structured programming technology in the 1970s swept away a sea of complexity in software development that had made management of large-scale projects a risky proposition indeed. It is for this reason that the integration of technology and management in software development is so important and so effective. The right technology has the potential to improve and often reshape management processes while reducing software development risks and uncertainties.

Table 11.1 CMM maturity levels

Level	Description
Level 1: Initial	The software process is characterized as ad hoc, and occasionally even chaotic. Few processes are defined, and success depends on individual effort and heroics.
Level 2: Repeatable	Basic project management processes are established to track cost, schedule, and functionality. The necessary process discipline is in place to repeat earlier successes on projects with similar applications.
Level 3: Defined	The software processes for both management and engineering activities are documented, standardized, and integrated into a standard software process for the organization. All projects use an approved, tailored version of the organization's standard software process for developing and maintaining software.
Level 4: Managed	Detailed measures of the software process and product quality are collected. Both the software process and products are quantitatively understood and controlled.
Level 5: Optimizing	Continuous process improvement is enabled by quantitative feedback from the process and from piloting innovative ideas and technologies.

Table 11.1 characterizes the five CMM maturity levels and highlights the primary process changes made at each level. Except for level 1, each maturity level is decomposed into several KPAs that indicate the areas on which an organization should focus to improve its software process. KPAs identify the issues that must be addressed to achieve a maturity level. Each KPA identifies a cluster of related activities that, when performed collectively, achieve a set of goals considered important for enhancing process capability. The six level 2 KPAs focus on basic project management controls, as summarized in Table 11.2. The seven KPAs at level 3 address both project and organizational issues, as the organization establishes an infrastructure for institutionalizing software engineering and management processes across all projects, as summarized in Table 11.3.

The two KPAs at level 4 focus on establishing a quantitative understanding of both the software process and the software work products being built, as summarized in Table 11.4. The three KPAs at level 5 cover the issues that both the organization and the projects must address to implement continuous and measurable software process improvement, as summarized in Table 11.5.

Table 11.2 CMM level 2 KPAs

Key Process Area	Description
Requirements Management	Establish a common understanding between the customer and the software project of the customer's requirements that will be addressed by the software project.
Software Project Planning	Establish reasonable plans for performing the software engineering and for managing the software project.
Software Project Tracking and Oversight	Establish adequate visibility into actual progress so that managers can take effective actions when the software project's performance deviates significantly from the software plans.
Software Subcontract Management	Select qualified software subcontractors and manage them effectively.
Software Quality Assurance	Provide management with appropriate visibility into the process being used by the software project and the products being built.
Software Configuration Management	Establish and maintain the integrity of the products of the software project throughout the project's software life cycle.

Table 11.3 CMM level 3 KPAs

Key Process Area	Description
Organization Process Focus	Establish the organizational responsibility for software process activities that improve the organization's overall software process capability.
Organization Process Definition	Develop and maintain a usable set of software process assets that improve process performance across the projects and provide a basis for cumulative, long-term benefits to the organization.
Training Program	Develop the skills and knowledge of individuals so they can perform their roles effectively and efficiently.
Integrated Software Management	Integrate the software engineering and management activities into a coherent, defined project software process that is tailored from the organization's standard software process and related process assets.
Software Product Engineering	Consistently perform a well-defined engineering process that integrates all the software engineering activities to produce correct, consistent software products effectively and efficiently.
Intergroup Coordination	Establish a means for the software engineering group to participate actively with the other engineering groups so the project is better able to satisfy the customer's needs effectively and efficiently.

continued

Table 11.3 *continued*

Key Process Area	Description
Peer Reviews	Remove defects from the software work products early and efficiently. An important corollary effect is to develop a better understanding of the software work products and of the defects that can be prevented.

Table 11.4   CMM level 4 KPAs

Key Process Area	Description
Quantitative Process Management	Control the process performance of the software project quantitatively.
Software Quality Management	Develop a quantitative understanding of the quality of the project's software products and achieve specific quality goals.

Table 11.5   CMM level 5 KPAs

Key Process Area	Description
Defect Prevention	Identify the root causes of defects and prevent them from recurring.
Technology Change Management	Identify beneficial new technologies (e.g., tools, methods, and processes) and transfer them into the organization in an orderly manner.
Process Change Management	Continually improve the software processes used in the organization with the intent of improving software quality, increasing productivity, and decreasing the cycle time for product development.

11.2 Cleanroom Process Mappings to CMM KPAs

A number of general process management attributes cut across the KPAs. The coverage of these attributes by the Cleanroom processes and work products is summarized in Table 11.6. The left column lists the KPA process management attributes and the right column lists their location in terms of Cleanroom process names, sections, and work products (in italics).

Tables 11.8 through 11.11 describe the overall mapping of the Cleanroom processes, defined in Chapters 7 through 10, to each of the CMM KPAs. Descriptions and references to the CMM can be found in Paulk, Weber, Curtis, and Chrissis (1995), and details of the mapping can be found in Linger, Paulk, and Trammell (1996). The tables list the KPAs in the left column, principal Cleanroom processes in the middle column, and an assessment of the overall correspondence in the right column, based on the categories identified in Table 11.7.

There is a scope consideration in mapping Cleanroom to the organizational KPAs (i.e., Organizational Process Focus, Organizational Process Definition,

Table 11.6 Process attribute coverage

Key Process Area Process Management Attribute	Location in Cleanroom Processes
A written policy to do the work exists.	Organization's *Cleanroom Engineering Guide*
A documented procedure for doing the work exists.	Project Planning: *Cleanroom Engineering Guide* tailored to the specific project
Responsibility for doing the work has been established.	Project Planning: *Project Organization Plan*
Affected groups agree to their roles.	Project Planning: Verification section
Resources and funding for the work exist.	Project Planning: *Schedule and Resource Plan*; Project Management
People are trained to perform the work.	Project Planning: *Training Plan*; Project Management
Work products documenting the work are created.	Project Planning: *Work Product Plan*; all processes: Exit sections
Baselines for data and work products are established.	Project Planning: *Configuration Management Plan*
Changes to work products occur in a controlled fashion.	Project Planning: *Configuration Management Plan*; Project Management; Engineering Change
The status of work is measured.	All processes: Measurement section
The status of work is reviewed by senior management.	All processes: Verification section
The status of work is reviewed by the project manager.	All processes: Verification section
The status of work is reviewed by the software quality assurance (SQA) group.	Intent is addressed by the Verification and Exit sections of all processes, and independent statistical testing and certification

Training Program, Technology Change Management, and Process Change Management). If Cleanroom is the only process standardized by an organization, it could fully address the concerns of an organizational KPA, and the correspondence would be high. The case is more likely, however, that multiple methodologies are supported by an organization, one of which is Cleanroom. In that case, the implementation of the organizational KPAs goes beyond the Cleanroom processes, and the Cleanroom mapping to these KPAs cannot be more than partial. This latter case is reflected in the following tables.

Table 11.7   Cleanroom/CMM correspondence definitions

Correspondence Category	Rating
The KPA is consistent with Cleanroom, and implementation by Cleanroom processes is high.	High
The KPA is consistent with Cleanroom, and implementation by Cleanroom processes is partial.	Partial
The KPA is consistent with Cleanroom, and implementation by Cleanroom processes is low.	Low
The KPA is consistent with Cleanroom, but is not implemented in the Cleanroom processes, or is implemented in an indirect way.	Consistent

Table 11.8   Cleanroom/CMM level 2 correspondence

Key Process Area	Principal Cleanroom Processes	Rating
Requirements Management	Requirements Analysis	High
Software Project Planning	Project Planning	High
Software Project Tracking and Oversight	Project Management	High
Software Subcontract Management	Project Management	Consistent
Software Quality Assurance	Project Planning, Project Management	Partial
Software Configuration Management	All processes, especially Project Planning, Project Management, and Engineering Change	Partial

Table 11.9 Cleanroom/CMM level 3 correspondence

Key Process Area	Principal Cleanroom Processes	Rating
Organization Process Focus	Project Planning, Project Management, Performance Improvement	Consistent
Organization Process Definition	Project Planning, Project Management, Performance Improvement	Partial
Training Program	Project Planning, Project Management	Partial
Integrated Software Management	Project Planning, Project Management	High
Software Product Engineering	Requirements Analysis, Function Specification, Usage Specification, Architecture Specification, Increment Planning, Increment Design, Correctness Verification, Software Reengineering, Engineering Change, Usage Modeling and Test Planning, Statistical Testing and Certification	High
Intergroup Coordination	Project Planning, Project Management	High
Peer Reviews	All processes, especially Correctness Verification	High

Table 11.10 Cleanroom/CMM level 4 correspondence

Key Process Area	Principal Cleanroom Processes	Rating
Quantitative Process Management	Project Planning, Project Management, Statistical Testing and Certification, Performance Improvement	High
Software Quality Management	Project Planning, Project Management, Statistical Testing and Certification, Performance Improvement	High

Table 11.11 Cleanroom/CMM level 5 correspondence

Key Process Area	Principal Cleanroom Processes	Rating
Defect Prevention	Correctness Verification, Performance Improvement	High
Technology Change Management	Performance Improvement	Partial
Process Change Management	Performance Improvement	Partial

As these tables illustrate, Cleanroom and the CMM are compatible and mutually supportive. The technology-based practices of Cleanroom provide much of the "how" for the "what" defined by the CMM.

11.3 Integrating CRM Technology and CMM Management

As noted earlier, technology-based solutions to problems of software development can often produce results that no amount of good management can achieve in their absence. A principle objective of CMM management processes is informed decision making based on measurements of software products and processes. Quantitative management is particularly important at higher levels of the CMM. The technical basis and validity of the measurements is thus very important. For example, quality and reliability measurements are vital to effective and timely management decisions, such as whether to release a software product for customer use. Cleanroom testing and certification technologies provide a scientific basis for such decisions, for which no amount of good management based on anecdotal information can substitute.

As described earlier, Cleanroom statistical usage-based testing is conducted as a formal statistical experiment. The infinite population of possible executions is sampled by generating test cases randomized against usage distributions, the quality and reliability of the software are measured by executing the test cases, and the results are interpreted at a defined level of confidence to the entire population of possible executions. In effect, statistical testing provides a means of estimating system performance for all the usage scenarios in the population that could not be executed (which field use will be sampling throughout the life of the system). The two Cleanroom processes involved in statistical testing and certification are the Usage Modeling and Test Planning Process and the Statistical Testing and Certification Process.

The Usage Modeling and Test Planning Process requires that the system usage environment be modeled as a basis for deriving statistical test cases. The usage models can represent a variety of conditions, including nominal and expected usage, stress situations, and use of infrequently invoked functions with high consequences of failure. The Statistical Testing and Certification Process requires that testing proceed under experimental control in a formal statistical design to produce valid statistical measures of software performance with respect to certification goals.

The scientific measurements of quality and reliability produced by these processes provide a rigorous basis for informed decision making, and can literally transform the technical basis of management action. Decision makers can move from nagging uncertainty (which may force additional and perhaps unnecessary resource expenditures in testing in an effort to reduce risk) to confidence that software quality and reliability have been measured scientifically and that decisions based on these measurements are indeed supported by the evidence. Cleanroom technology can provide a useful foundation for the CMM management objective of measurement-based decision making.

11.4 References

R.C. Linger, M.C. Paulk, and C.J. Trammell. *Cleanroom Software Engineering Implementation of the CMM for Software.* CMU/SEI-96-TR-023. Pittsburgh: Software Engineering Institute, Carnegie Mellon University, 1996.

M.C. Paulk, C.V. Weber, B. Curtis, and M.B. Chrissis. *The Capability Maturity Model: Guidelines for Improving the Software Process.* Reading, MA: Addison-Wesley, 1995.

PART III

A Case Study in Cleanroom Software Engineering

12

Satellite Control System Requirements

12.1 The Satellite Control System Case Study

A case study is presented in Part III for a sufficiently large system to illustrate scalability of Cleanroom processes and their associated work products. The case study involves development of embedded software for a Satellite Control System (SCS), and is based on requirements and specifications included in the *Object-Orientation/Cleanroom Integration Study* by Ett and Trammell (1996). The case study includes:

- Black box specification, Chapter 13
- State box specification, Chapter 14
- Clear box design, Chapter 15
- Statistical testing plans and models, Chapter 16

The case study does not contain examples of all work products from Part II, due to space limitations.

The SCS consists of four components:

1. The ground control system (GCS) initiates and terminates connections, and monitors satellite health.

2. The space vehicle (SV) processes commands from the GCS and supplies half-duplex communications between two other ground sites.

3. The uplink site (UL) transmits data to the SV when connected.

4. The downlink site (DL) receives data from the UL through the half-duplex connection supplied by the SV.

The following requirements address only the software component of the SV, known as the Satellite Operations Software (SOS), which is used during normal operation. Launch, orbital insertion, and deployment are not addressed in these requirements.

12.2 Satellite Operations Software Requirements

The requirements are initially described here in natural language, a form in which requirements often first appear. They are subsequently restated in more precise terms to support further study and analysis.

The SOS is initialized by the initialization (IN) command from the GCS. On receiving the IN command, the SOS replies with an initialization acknowledgment (INA). The GCS must next command the SOS to enter maintenance mode with the maintenance time-slot go (MG) command, and then request the SV health with a health request (HR). If a successful health check (HS) is reported, the GCS will then send any bandwidth/location (B/L) table update requests (BR) and firing requests (FR).

After successfully completing SV maintenance, the GCS may put the SOS into transmit mode by sending UL and DL information in a transmit time-slot go (TG) message. The SOS forwards the TG (TGF) to both the UL and DL. The two sites complete connection by sending uplink go (UG) and downlink go (DG) messages. When both sites have connected, the SOS sends a start data transmit (SDT) command to the UL, which then starts sending packets (data packet in, or DI).

The SOS forwards all data packets from the UL (i.e., DI) to the DL (i.e., data out, or DO). If the DL detects a corrupted packet, it sends a packet bad (PB) message with the packet identifier to the SOS. The SOS forwards the packet bad message (PBF) to the UL. The UL and DL are responsible for negotiating packet transmit failures.

When the UL has sent all packets, it sends the transmit-end (TE) message to the SOS, which forwards the TE (TEF) to the DL. When the DL site has received the TEF and all packets (including any re-sent due to PB messages), it sends downlink transmit-end (DTE) to the SOS, which forwards this to the UL site as TEF. The connection is then closed, and the SOS informs the GCS of this by sending it a TEF.

During transmit mode, the GCS may send a time-slot cancel (TC) to the SOS to indicate that the transmit window has expired or the GCS operator has requested that the SOS exit transmit mode. The SOS immediately forwards the time-slot cancel (TCF) to the UL and the DL, and then replies to the GCS with TEF and exits transmit mode.

Protocol errors detected by the SOS should be reported to the GCS using an error report (ERR). The SOS should always attempt recovery if possible. If the SOS cannot recover, it should exit the mode in which it is currently working and send a fatal error (FE) report to the GCS (and the UL and DL if connected).

Natural language statements such as these must be analyzed and refined by systems engineers in consultation with customers to produce a complete set of requirements expressed in traceable form. Such a requirements analysis is provided in Table 12.1 for the SOS, subject to revision as development proceeds. Mnemonics are introduced as work progresses, and each requirement is numbered for tracing purposes. Many of these requirements were not in the original natural language specification, but were derived during analysis. The natural language specification could be updated, if desired.

This statement of requirements is employed in the sequence-based specification process used in Chapter 13. A summary of acronyms used is presented in Chapter 13.

Table 12.1   SOS requirements

Requirement No.	Requirement
1	SOS inputs
1.1	GCS commands
1.1.1	The SOS shall accept the IN (initialize) command from the GCS.
1.1.2	The SOS shall accept the HR (health request) command from the GCS.
1.1.3	The SOS shall accept the MG (maintenance time-slot go) command from the GCS.
1.1.4	The SOS shall accept the BR (bandwidth/location table update request) command from the GCS.
1.1.5	The SOS shall accept the FR (firing request) command from the GCS.
1.1.6	The SOS shall accept the TG (transmit time-slot go) command from the GCS.
1.1.7	The SOS shall accept the TC (time-slot cancel) command from the GCS.
1.2	On-board system signals

continued

Table 12.1 *continued*

Requirement No.	Requirement
1.2.1	The SOS shall accept the OTE (on-board timer expired) signal from the on-board countdown timer.
1.2.2	The SOS shall accept firing report signals from the reaction control subsystem (RCS).
1.2.3	The SOS shall accept ISF (internal/subsystem failure) and ISN (internal/subsystem nominal) reports from all internal subsystems.
1.3	Uplink inputs
1.3.1	The SOS shall accept inputs from the UL only after a successful TG from the GCS.
1.3.2	The SOS shall accept the UG (uplink go) message from the UL.
1.3.3	The SOS shall accept the DI (data packet in) message from the UL.
1.3.4	The SOS shall accept the TE (transmit end) message from the UL.
1.3.5	The SOS shall accept the UB (uplink site fail) message from the UL.
1.4	Downlink inputs
1.4.1	The SOS shall accept inputs from the DL only after a successful TG from the GCS.
1.4.2	The SOS shall accept the DG (downlink go) message from the DL.
1.4.3	The SOS shall accept the PB (data packet bad) message from the DL.
1.4.4	The SOS shall accept the DTE (downlink transmit end) message from the DL.
1.4.5	The SOS shall accept the DB (downlink site fail) message from the DL.
2	SOS outputs
2.1	GCS messages
2.1.1	The SOS shall output the INA (initialization acknowledgment) message.
2.1.2	The SOS shall output the HF (health check fail) message.
2.1.3	The SOS shall output the HS (health check success) message.
2.1.4	The SOS shall output the FF (firing failure) message.
2.1.5	The SOS shall output the FS (firing success) message.
2.1.6	The SOS shall output the TSCAN (time-slot canceled) message.
2.1.7	The SOS shall output the TEF (transmit end forwarded) message.
2.1.8	The SOS shall output the ERR (error report) message.
2.1.9	The SOS shall output the FE (fatal error) message.

Requirement No.	Requirement
2.2	Internal hardware interface
2.2.1	The SOS shall output the CDI (countdown timer initialize) command.
2.2.2	The SOS shall output the HT (hardware test) command.
2.2.3	The SOS shall output the FRF (firing request forwarded) command.
2.3	Uplink messages
2.3.1	The SOS shall output the TGF (time-slot go forwarded) message.
2.3.2	The SOS shall output the SDT (start data transmit) message.
2.3.3	The SOS shall output the TCF (time-slot cancel forwarded) message.
2.3.4	The SOS shall output the TEF (transmit end forwarded) message.
2.3.5	The SOS shall output the PBF (packet bad forwarded) message.
2.3.6	The SOS shall output the FE (fatal error) message.
2.4	Downlink messages
2.4.1	The SOS shall output the TGF (time-slot go forwarded) message.
2.4.2	The SOS shall output the TCF (time-slot cancel forwarded) message.
2.4.3	The SOS shall output the TEF (transmit end forwarded) message.
2.4.4	The SOS shall output the DO (data out) message.
2.4.5	The SOS shall output the FE (fatal error) message.
3	System initialization
3.1	During system initialization the SOS shall process the IN command from the GCS.
3.2	The SOS shall respond to the IN command within TBD seconds.
4	System maintenance
4.1	The SOS shall enter maintenance mode when it receives the MG command from the GCS.
4.2	The SOS shall require the HR as the first command after entering maintenance mode.
4.3	Health request
4.3.1	The SOS shall process the HR command from the GCS only during maintenance mode.
4.3.2	On receiving the HR command from the GCS, the SOS shall query its internal hardware systems (i.e., HT).

continued

Table 12.1   *continued*

Requirement No.	Requirement
4.3.3	If the SOS detects a problem during processing of a HR command, or if a component does not respond within TBD seconds of the query, the SOS shall report an HF to the GCS.
4.3.4	If the SOS does not detect any problems during processing of an HR command, the SOS shall report an HS to the GCS.
4.4	BL table update
4.4.1	The SOS shall process the BR command from the GCS only during maintenance mode.
4.4.2	The BR command will specify an index in the SOS B/L table and information to overwrite the specified index of the table.
4.4.3	On receiving a BR command, the SOS shall update its internal B/L table with the information specified in the command, overwriting any previous information for the specified index.
4.4.4	B/L table size shall be chosen such that all indices are a fixed number of bits and none are illegal (the B/L table size shall be an integer power of 2).
4.5	Thruster firing request
4.5.1	The SOS shall process the FR command from the GCS only during maintenance mode.
4.5.2	The FR command will specify pitch, yaw, and roll information for the SOS.
4.5.3	On receiving an FR command, the SOS shall initiate the firing by passing an FRF message to the RCS.
4.5.4	If the RCS reports a successful firing, the SOS shall send an FS report to the GCS.
4.5.5	If the RCS reports a failed firing, the SOS shall send an FF report to the GCS.
4.5.6	If the RCS fails to report firing information to the SOS within TBD seconds of the FRF message, then the SOS shall send an FF report to the GCS.
5.	Transmit mode
5.1	The SOS shall only enter transmit mode from maintenance mode.
5.2	The following commands are transmit mode commands and shall only be accepted by the SOS during transmit mode: TC, UG, DI, TE, UB, DG, PB, DTE, and DB.
5.3	A site is considered valid only if its information is present in the B/L table.

Requirement No.	Requirement
5.4	The SOS shall enter transmit mode on receiving a TG with valid UL and DL sites.
5.5	On entering transmit mode, the SOS shall send a TGF to both the UL and DL.
5.6	The SOS shall send the TSCAN(1) failure message to the GCS if it receives a TG with an invalid UL and a valid DL.
5.7	The SOS shall send the TSCAN(2) failure message to the GCS if it receives a TG with a valid UL and an invalid DL.
5.8	The SOS shall send the TSCAN(3) failure message to the GCS if it receives a TG with an invalid UL and DL.
5.9	Connecting
5.9.1	As soon as both the UL and DL are connected, the connection is considered fully open and the GCS shall send the SDT command to the UL.
5.9.2	Uplink connection
5.9.2.1	If the SOS does not receive a UG or UB message from the UL within TBD seconds of sending the TGF to the UL and DL, it shall send the TSCAN(1) failure message to the GCS and send TCF to both the UL and the DL. The SOS shall then exit transmit mode.
5.9.2.2	If the SOS receives a UB message from the UL within TBD seconds of sending the TGF to the UL and the DL, it shall send the TSCAN(1) failure message to the GCS and send TCF to both the UL and the DL. The SOS shall then exit transmit mode.
5.9.2.3	If the SOS receives a UG message from the UL within TBD seconds of sending the TGF to the UL and the DL, the UL is considered connected.
5.9.3	Downlink connection
5.9.3.1	If the SOS does not receive a DG or DB message from the DL within TBD seconds of sending the TGF to the UL and the DL, it shall send the TSCAN(2) failure message to the GCS and send TCF to both the UL and the DL. The SOS shall then exit transmit mode.
5.9.3.2	If the SOS receives a DB message from the DL within TBD seconds of sending the TGF to the UL and the DL, it shall send TSCAN(2) failure message to the GCS and send the TCF to both the UL and the DL. The SOS shall then exit transmit mode.
5.9.3.3	If the SOS receives a DG message from the DL within TBD seconds of sending the TGF to the UL and the DL, the DL shall be considered connected.

continued

Table 12.1 *continued*

Requirement No.	Requirement
5.10	Data transmit
5.10.1	If both the UL and the DL are connected, the SOS shall accept DI messages from the UL.
5.10.2	Within TBD seconds of receiving a DI message from the UL, the SOS shall forward the data in a DO message to the DL.
5.10.3	If the SOS receives a PB message from the DL, the SOS shall forward the message (i.e., PBF) to the UL for packet repeat.
5.11	Disconnecting
5.11.1	On exiting transmit mode, the SOS shall send the TEF message to the GCS.
5.11.2	The SOS shall ignore messages from the UL and the DL if not in transmit mode.
5.11.3	Transmit end
5.11.3.1	On receiving a TE message from the UL, the SOS shall forward the message to the DL as a TEF message.
5.11.3.2	The SOS shall continue to process DI and PB messages from the UL and the DL after receiving a TE message from the UL.
5.11.3.3	On receiving a DTE message from the DL, the SOS shall forward the message to the UL as a TEF message. The SOS shall then exit transmit mode.
5.11.4	Transmit cancel
5.11.4.1	On receiving the TC message from the GCS, the SOS shall send TCF messages to the UL and the DL, and immediately exit transmit mode.
6	Protocol errors
6.1	If the SOS detects a protocol error due to an unexpected message, it shall immediately send an ERR to the GCS.
6.2	If recovery from a protocol error is not possible, the SOS shall send an FE to the GCS and exit any mode in which it is operating.
6.3	Recovery from a protocol error is declared not possible if the SOS is unable to determine how to proceed.
6.4	The SOS shall attempt recovery from a protocol error by ignoring the packet that resulted in the protocol error.

Requirement No.	Requirement
6.5	If the UL and/or the DL are connected and a protocol error occurs from which recovery is not possible, the SOS shall send an FE to the connected sites.

12.3 Reference

W. Ett and C. Trammell. *Object-Orientation/Cleanroom Integration Study.* 1996. http://source.asset.com/stars/loral/cleanroom/oo/study.htm

13

Satellite Control System Black Box Specification

13.1 Black Box Sequence-Based Specification

The basic work flow for the sequence-based specification process was presented in Chapter 3 and referenced in the function specification process defined in Chapter 8. The instantiation of that work flow used to produce the SOS black box specification is summarized in the following steps.

Step 1: Define the system boundary.

1. Identify all components of the system to be developed and then identify all other components in the environment with which the system communicates directly.

2. Identify each interface between a system component and an environment component, and define the stimuli and responses associated with the interface.

3. Identify any assumptions about each interface.

Step 2: Enumerate stimulus sequences.

1. Enumerate sequences in order by length.

2. Document and trace each sequence (legal and illegal) in the enumeration to the requirements that define its expected response and equivalence (if any).

3. If there is no requirement associated with a sequence, document a derived requirement subject to confirmation.

4. Invent and use abstractions as needed to keep the work at a productive level.

5. Stop when every sequence of the longest length is either illegal or equivalent to a previous sequence.

Step 3: Analyze canonical sequences.

1. Extract all canonical sequences from the enumeration.

2. Identify and name the system properties and values that will make all canonical sequences pairwise distinguishable.

Step 4: Define specification functions.

Step 5: Construct the black box tables.

1. Create one table for each stimulus that contains one row for each response in the enumeration.

2. Enter canonical sequence conditions based on the enumeration and canonical sequence analysis.

With the tagged system requirements from Chapter 12 in hand, development of the black box specification can begin. It will be necessary to revise the requirements during the specification process; this is natural and desirable. Conflicts among requirements and omissions may be identified early in a project through development of complete, consistent, and traceably correct black box specifications. This emphasis on up-front specification and resolution of conflicts and omissions helps to eliminate later requirements changes. The black box derivation provides feedback to revise requirements in a controlled and documented fashion.

Two techniques are mentioned earlier in the list of process steps for the SCS black box derivation that are used to maintain a productive level of abstraction in the work flow. First, black box specification functions are mappings from the domain of the black box to a co-domain of convenience. The co-domain is often {true, false} for specification functions that answer a question about the sequences. Specification functions may, but need not, map to a subset of the black box responses. It is critical that an effective process for actually evaluating each specification function be known that could be written if necessary. Some specification functions will be displaced later by state data, others will be transformed into state box specification functions, and some might actually be implemented in code.

Second, black box abstractions are many-to-one mappings from the domain of atomic sequences to a co-domain of convenience. The co-domain often consolidates atomic stimuli or represents specific strings to reduce the number of items active in an enumeration.

The case study is large and necessarily table and acronym intensive. The following acronyms are used in the tables and code throughout the remaining chapters in Part III.

ASN	all subsystems nominal
B/L	bandwidth/location
BR	B/L table update request
BRA	B/L table update request acknowledge
CDI	countdown timer initialize
DB	downlink bad
DG	downlink go
DI	data packet in
DL	downlink site
DO	data packet out
DTE	downlink transmit end
ERR	error report
FE	fatal error
FF	firing failure
FFR	firing failure report
FR	firing request
FRF	firing request forwarded
FS	firing success
FSR	firing success report
GCS	ground control system
HF	health check fail
HR	health request
HS	health check success
HT	hardware test
IH	interrupt handler
IN	initialization
INA	initialization acknowledgment
ISF	internal subsystem failure
ISN	internal subsystem nominal
MG	maintenance time-slot go
OTE	on-board timer expired
PB	packet bad

PBF	packet bad forwarded
RCS	reaction control subsystem
SDT	start data transfer
SF	subsystem failure
SOS	satellite operations software
TC	time-slot cancel
TCF	time-slot cancel forwarded
TE	transmit end
TEF	transmit end forwarded
TG	transmit time-slot go
TGF	time-slot go forwarded
TSCAN	time-slot canceled
UB	uplink bad
UG	uplink go
UL	uplink site

13.2 Step 1: Define the System Boundary

The system consists of only the SOS. The environment consists of the GCS, the hardware controllers (which contain the RCS), the UL, and the DL.

The stimuli and responses for each of the interfaces are listed in Tables 13.1 through 13.8. The mnemonics for stimulus and response names in the SOS requirements defined in Table 12.1 are used here with the exception of responses FE, TEF, and TCF, which may have multiple destinations. It is necessary to distinguish among the different possible destinations of these responses, so an additional letter (u for UL, d for DL, and g for GCS) will be appended to these responses. On-board signals FSR (firing successful report) and FFR (firing failure report) are introduced to allow on-board communication to be specified in more detail than given in the requirements.

Even this rudimentary requirements analysis identifies potential problems. In this case, requirements 5.11.2 and 5.2 are found to be redundant. This is a problem because if one is changed and not the other, the requirements may be contradictory. To resolve this problem, requirement 5.11.2 is dropped (the requirements are not renumbered).

Requirements concerning exiting transmit mode (e.g., 5.11.1 and 6.2) are in conflict. The following modification is introduced to resolve this: 5.11.1, On exiting transmit mode, the SOS shall send the TEF message to the GCS unless there is another message (FE, TSCAN, or INA) pending for the GCS, which indicates exit of transmit mode.

Table 13.1 SOS stimuli from the GCS

Stimulus Name	Description	Associated Requirements
IN	Initialization command	1.1.1, 3.1, 3.2
HR	Health request command	1.1.2, 4.2, 4.3.1, 4.3.2, 4.3.3, 4.3.4
MG	Maintenance time-slot go command	1.1.3, 4.1

BR	B/L table update request command
	Two parameters:
	  i. Table index (0–8191)
	  ii. Site information
		1.1.4,
		4.4.1, 4.4.2, 4.4.3, 4.4.4

FR	Firing request command
	Three parameters:
	  i. Pitch
	  ii. Yaw
	  iii. Roll
		1.1.5,
		4.5.1, 4.5.2, 4.5.3

TG	Transmit time-slot go command
	Two parameters:
	  i. Uplink site identifier
	  ii. Downlink site identifier
		1.1.6,
		5.1, 5.3, 5.4, 5.5, 5.6, 5.7, 5.8

TC	Transmit time-slot cancel command	1.1.7, 5.11.1, 5.11.4.1, 5.2

Table 13.2 SOS stimuli from on-board subsystems

Stimulus Name	Description	Associated Requirements
OTE	On-board timer expired (from on-board timer)	1.2.1, 4.3.3, 4.5.6, 5.9.2.1, 5.9.3.1
FSR	Firing successful report (from RCS)	1.2.2, 4.5.4
FFR	Firing failure report (from RCS)	1.2.2, 4.5.5
ISN	Internal subsystem nominal (from any subsystem) One parameter: i. Subsystem identifier	1.2.3, 4.3.4
ISF	Internal subsystem failure (from any subsystem) One parameter: i. Subsystem identifier	1.2.3, 4.3.3

Table 13.3   SOS stimuli from UL

Stimulus Name	Description	Associated Requirements
UG	Uplink go message	1.3.1, 1.3.2, 5.2, 5.9.2.1, 5.9.2.3, 5.10.1, 6.5

DI	Data packet in message
	Two parameters:
	  i. Packet identifier
	  ii. Packet payload
		1.3.1, 1.3.3, 5.2, 5.10.1, 5.10.2, 5.11.3.2

TE	Transmit end message	1.3.1, 1.3.4, 5.2, 5.11.3.1, 5.11.3.2
UB	Uplink bad message	1.3.1, 1.3.5, 5.2, 5.9.2.1, 5.9.2.2

Table 13.4   SOS stimuli from DL

Stimulus Name	Description	Associated Requirements
DG	Downlink go message	1.4.1, 1.4.2, 5.1.1, 5.2, 5.9.3.1, 5.9.3.3, 6.5
PB	Packet bad message One parameter: i. Packet identifier	1.4.1, 1.4.3, 5.2, 5.10.3, 5.11.3.2
DTE	Downlink transmit end message	1.4.1, 1.4.4, 5.2, 5.11.3.3
DB	Downlink bad message	1.4.1, 1.4.5, 5.2, 5.9.3.1, 5.9.3.2

Requirements 6.3 and 6.4 do not appear in the table because they are currently too ill-defined to map unambiguously to stimuli or responses. They will be properly defined during the process of sequence enumeration.

The following assumption is made. In the SOS system, the B/L table is maintained by an external subsystem, but the subsystem's responses are completely predictable from the point of view of the system (the system's stimulus sequence completely determines the behavior of the B/L table subsystem). The subsystem is very simple and highly reliable, so it will be treated as part of the system. Treating this component as internal to the system eliminates the interface and consequently reduces the complexity of the specification.

Table 13.5   SOS responses to the GCS

Stimulus Name	Description	Associated Requirements
INA	Initialization acknowledgment message	2.1.1, 3.2
HF	Health check fail message	2.1.2, 4.3.3
HS	Health check success message	2.1.3, 4.3.4
FF	Firing failure message	2.1.4, 4.5.5, 4.5.6
FS	Firing success message	2.1.5, 4.5.4
TSCAN	Time-slot canceled message One parameter: 　i. Reason (1 = invalid UL) (2 = invalid DL) (3 = invalid UL and DL)	2.1.6, 5.6, 5.7, 5.8, 5.9.2.1, 5.9.2.2, 5.9.3.1, 5.9.3.2
TEFg	Transmit-end forwarded message to GCS	2.1.7, 5.11.1
ERR	Error report message	2.1.8, 6.1
FEg	Fatal error message	2.1.9, 6.2

Table 13.6   Responses to on-board subsystems

Stimulus Name	Description	Associated Requirements
CDI	Countdown timer initialize command (to on-board timer) One parameter: 　i. Duration	2.2.1
HT	Hardware test command (to all subsystems)	2.2.2, 4.3.2
FRF	Firing request forwarded command (to RCS) Three parameters: 　i. Pitch 　ii. Yaw 　iii. Roll	2.2.3, 4.5.3, 4.5.6

Table 13.7   Responses to the UL

Stimulus Name	Description	Associated Requirements
TGFu	Time-slot go forwarded command to uplink	2.3.1, 5.5, 5.9.2.1, 5.9.2.2, 5.9.2.3, 5.9.3.1, 5.9.3.2, 5.9.3.3
SDT	Start data transmit command	2.3.2, 5.9.1
TCFu	Time-slot cancel forwarded command to uplink	2.3.3, 5.9.2.1, 5.9.2.2, 5.9.3.1, 5.9.3.2, 5.11.4.1
TEFu	Transmit end forwarded command to uplink	2.3.4, 5.11.3.3, 5.11.1
PBF	Packet bad forwarded command One parameter: i. Packet identifier	2.3.5, 5.10.3
FEu	Fatal error message	2.3.6, 6.5

Table 13.8   Responses to the DL

Stimulus Name	Description	Associated Requirements
TGFd	Time-slot go forwarded command to downlink	2.4.1, 5.5, 5.9.2.1, 5.9.2.2, 5.9.2.3, 5.9.3.1, 5.9.3.2, 5.9.3.3
TCFd	Time-slot cancel forwarded command to downlink	2.4.2, 5.9.2.1, 5.9.2.2, 5.9.3.1, 5.9.3.2, 5.11.4.1
TEFd	Transmit end forwarded command to downlink	2.4.3, 5.11.3.1
DO	Data packet out command Two parameters: i. Packet identifier ii. Packet payload	2.4.4, 5.10.2
FEd	Fatal error message	2.4.5, 6.5

13.3 Step 2: Enumerate Stimulus Sequences

The organization of the SV functionality into subsystems is likely to change because future versions of the SV are likely to have additional subsystems. The specification can be made independent of the final decision about the subsystem list by using abstract stimuli. Specifically, two abstract stimuli are required:

1. *All subsystems nominal* (ASN). This abstract stimulus corresponds to one ISN from every subsystem (and no ISFs from any subsystem) following the most recent HR that led to an HT not followed by an OTE.

2. *Subsystem failure* (SF). This stimulus corresponds to either an ISN or an ISF from every subsystem (with at least one ISF following the most recent HR that led to an HT) or an OTE with at least one subsystem not responding following the most recent HR that led to an HT.

The first part of the sequence enumeration is provided in Table 13.9. Derived requirements are assigned numbers and explained in the Derived Requirements and Notes column.

During the enumeration of Table 13.9, a potential problem is discovered. All BR stimuli must be kept in the enumeration so that the UL and the DL can be validated for a TG (in accordance with requirement 5.3). However, keeping these stimuli in the enumeration will make it very long. There are really only four cases for a TG:

1. Neither the UL nor the DL is valid.
2. The UL is valid but the DL is not.
3. The DL is valid but the UL is not.
4. Both the UL and the DL are valid.

If abstract stimuli could be introduced to capture these four cases, the enumeration could be shortened substantially. For the purpose of illustration, these abstract stimuli are defined formally, hiding any unknowns in as-yet undefined specification functions. Given a sequence, it is possible to determine if a particular site has been added (and not overwritten) with a BR stimulus.

All specification functions will be given in prefix recursive form; that is, they will be written as recursive functions computed on prefixes of sequences. This is a very natural way to write functions over sequences, and has valuable theoretical properties. In the following function definitions, h will always be a stimulus sequence. The variable p denotes the prefix of h, up to but not including the last stimulus. The variable s denotes the last (most recent) stimulus. Thus $h = ps$. The tables can be read as follows: Given that *prefix conditions*

Table 13.9 Initial enumeration

Sequence	Response	Equivalence	Trace	Derived Requirements and Notes
IN	INA		3.1, 3.2, 3.3	3.3 The SOS shall respond to the IN command with the INA message.
...	illegal		3.4	3.4 Power-on is observed by the SOS as an IN message. Note: All other length-one sequences are illegal because power must be on before the SOS can observe messages.
IN IN	INA	IN	3.1, 3.2, 3.3, 3.5	3.5 IN messages subsequent to the first shall cause the SOS to exit immediately any mode it might be in without issuing any messages other than an INA.
IN HR	ERR	IN	3.6, 4.3.1, 6.1, 6.4	3.6 Initially the SOS shall not be considered to be in any mode.
IN MG	null		4.1, 4.1.1	4.1.1 The system shall issue no response for an MG.
IN BR	ERR	IN	4.4.1, 6.1, 6.4	
IN FR	ERR	IN	4.5.1 6.1, 6.4	
IN TG	ERR	IN	5.1, 6.1, 6.4	

Table 13.10 Specification function B/L*(h, n)*

Stimulus	Prefix Conditions	Value	Trace
	h = empty	empty	4.4.5 The B/L table is initially empty.
BR(*n, s*)	Mode(*p*) = maintenance	*s*	4.4.2, 4.4.3
s	otherwise (*h* = *ps*)	B/L(*p, n*)	Method

hold, then for *stimulus* the function evaluates to *value*. Table 13.10 presents a specification function to determine the site information at a particular index in the B/L table.

Note that the function of Table 13.10 references another specification function, "Mode," which has not been defined. This is because there is not yet enough information to determine precisely the current mode of the SOS.

Now the abstract stimuli can be defined:

1. TG will denote both the UL and the DL invalid. Let TG denote TG(*u, d*) when there are no indices *m* and *n* in the table such that B/L(*h, m*) = *u* and B/L(*h, n*) = *d* for current stimulus sequence *h*.

2. TGu will denote a valid UL and an invalid DL. Let TGu denote TG(*u, d*) when there exists index *m* such that B/L(*h, m*) = *u* and there is no index *n* such that B/L(*h, n*) = *d* for current stimulus sequence *h*.

3. TGd will denote an invalid UL and a valid DL. Let TGd denote TG(*u, d*) when there exists index *m* such that B/L(*h, m*) = *d* and there is no index *n* such that B/L(*h, n*) = *u* for current stimulus sequence *h*.

4. TGud will denote both the UL and the DL valid. Let TGud denote TG(*u, d*) when there exists indices *m* and *n* in the table such that B/L(*h, m*) = *u* and B/L(*h, n*) = *d* for current stimulus sequence *h*.

Using these four abstract stimuli, there is no longer a need to keep the BR stimuli in the abstract enumeration. Note that none of the omitted atomic stimuli are used in Table 13.9, so there is no need to restart enumeration.

The enumeration proceeds in Table 13.11, completing the extensions of IN. A new derived requirement (1.2.4) is required to deal with unexpected signals from the internal subsystems.

Only one sequence of Table 13.9 must be extended. Sequence IN MG is canonical and is extended in Table 13.12. The sequence IN MG OTE presents a problem. When the SOS has received MG, it expects to receive an HR. However, it instead receives OTE. Although this is an on-board signal and not (strictly speaking) a protocol error, it does illustrate the problem. It is better in this case to ignore the signal, in keeping with requirement 1.2.4, than to

Table 13.11 Remaining extensions of IN (continued from Table 13.9)

Sequence	Response	Equivalence	Trace	Derived Requirements and Notes
IN TGu	ERR	IN	5.1 6.1, 6.4	
IN TGd	ERR	IN	5.1, 6.1, 6.4	
IN TGud	ERR	IN	5.1, 6.1, 6.4	
IN TC	ERR	IN	5.2, 6.1, 6.4	
IN OTE	null	IN	1.2.4	1.2.4 The SOS shall ignore any unexpected interrupts or signals from internal subsystems.
IN FSR	null	IN	1.2.4	
IN FFR	null	IN	1.2.4	
IN ASN	illegal		Definition of ASN	Note: The definition of the abstract stimulus cannot be satisfied because no HR has occurred. The situation is impossible.
IN SF	illegal		Definition of SF	Note: The definition of the abstract stimulus cannot be satisfied because no HR has occurred. The situation is impossible.
IN UG	null	IN	5.2	Policy: Ignoring a command is preferable to generating a protocol error.
IN DI	null	IN	5.2	

Sequence	Response	Equivalence	Trace	Derived Requirements and Notes
IN TE	null	IN	5.2	
IN UB	null	IN	5.2	
IN DG	null	IN	5.2	
IN PB	null	IN	5.2	
IN DTE	null	IN	5.2	
IN DB	null	IN	5.2	

Table 13.12 Extensions of IN MG

Sequence	Response	Equivalence	Trace	Derived Requirements and Notes
IN MG IN	INA	IN	3.5	
IN MG HR	CDI, HT		4.3.2, 4.3.3	
IN MG MG	ERR	IN MG	4.2, 4.2.1, 6.1, 6.4	4.2.1 MG commands issued in maintenance mode shall be treated as protocol errors.
IN MG BR	ERR	IN MG	4.2, 6.1, 6.4	
IN MG FR	ERR	IN MG	4.2, 6.1, 6.4	
IN MG TG	ERR	IN MG	4.2, 6.1, 6.4	
IN MG TGu	ERR	IN MG	4.2, 6.1, 6.4	
IN MG TGd	ERR	IN MG	4.2, 6.1, 6.4	
IN MG TGud	ERR	IN MG	4.2, 6.1, 6.4	
IN MG TC	ERR	IN MG	4.2, 6.1, 6.4	
IN MG OTE	null	IN MG	1.2.4	
IN MG FSR	null	IN MG	1.2.4	
IN MG FFR	null	IN MG	1.2.4	
IN MG ASN	illegal		Definition of ASN	Note: The definition of the abstract stimulus cannot be satisfied because no HR has occurred. The situation is impossible.

Sequence	Response	Equivalence	Trace	Derived Requirements and Notes
IN MG SF	illegal		Definition of SF	Note: The definition of the abstract stimulus cannot be satisfied because no HR has occurred. The situation is impossible.
IN MG UG	null	IN MG	5.2	
IN MG DI	null	IN MG	5.2	
IN MG TE	null	IN MG	5.2	
IN MG UB	null	IN MG	5.2	
IN MG DG	null	IN MG	5.2	
IN MG PB	null	IN MG	5.2	
IN MG DTE	null	IN MG	5.2	
IN MG DB	null	IN MG	5.2	

generate a protocol error, in keeping with requirement 6.1. This is a policy decision and it is documented in the enumeration.

Again, only one sequence of Table 13.12 must be extended. IN MG HR is extended in Table 13.13. A number of new cases of behavior are encountered in Table 13.13; specifically, the interruption of commands (such as FR), which require time to execute. Derived requirements and a new policy are documented to resolve this.

Only IN MG HR ASN of Table 13.13 is canonical. It is extended in Table 13.14. On reaching the sequence IN MG HR ASN BR, a question arises: How will the GCS know if the BR was received and processed by the SOS? This is resolved by adding the new response BRA.

The enumeration continues with extensions of IN MG HR ASN FR in Table 13.15, and extensions of IN MG HR ASN TGud in Table 13.16. Significant new behavior is discovered in Table 13.16, including information about when the mode of the SOS changes and when it does not. Without this information, attempts to define precisely many of the abstractions presented earlier could not proceed. There are two canonical sequences to be extended: IN MG HR ASN TGud UG and IN MG HR ASN TGud DG. These are shown in Tables 13.17 and 13.18 respectively.

More missing but important requirements are discovered when IN MG HR ASN TGud UG DG is extended in Table 13.19. What happens if UB or DB is sent on a fully open connection? These situations are handled with derived requirements, and the single canonical sequence IN MG HR ASN TGud UG DG TE is extended in Table 13.20, completing the enumeration. The complete enumeration denotes a complete, consistent, and traceably correct specification of system behavior at the given level of abstraction.

Table 13.13 Extensions of IN MG HR

Sequence	Response	Equivalence	Trace	Derived Requirements and Notes
IN MG HR IN	INA	IN	3.5	
IN MG HR HR	ERR	IN MG HR	4.3.5, 6.1, 6.4	4.3.5 If the SOS receives a command (other than IN) from the GCS during processing of a previous command, a protocol error shall be generated and processing of the previous command shall continue. Policy: Avoid interrupting commands that require processing (such as thruster firings).
IN MG HR MG	ERR	IN MG HR	4.3.5, 4.3.6, 6.1, 6.4	4.3.6 MG commands issued during maintenance mode that otherwise would be ignored shall generate a protocol error if they interrupt a command.
IN MG HR BR	ERR	IN MG HR	4.3.5, 6.1, 6.4	
IN MG HR FR	ERR	IN MG HR	4.3.5, 6.1, 6.4	
IN MG HR TG	ERR	IN MG HR	4.3.5, 6.1, 6.4	
IN MG HR TGu	ERR	IN MG HR	4.3.5, 6.1, 6.4	

continued

Table 13.13 *continued*

Sequence	Response	Equivalence	Trace	Derived Requirements and Notes
IN MG HR TGd	ERR	IN MG HR	4.3.5, 6.1, 6.4	
IN MG HR TGud	ERR	IN MG HR	4.3.5, 6.1, 6.4	
IN MG HR TC	ERR	IN MG HR	4.3.5, 6.1, 6.4	
IN MG HR OTE	HF	IN MG HR ASN	4.3.3, 4.3.7	4.3.7 The outcome of an HT shall be reported by the SOS but shall not affect subsequent SOS functionality.
IN MG HR FSR	null	IN MG HR	1.2.4	
IN MG HR FFR	null	IN MG HR	1.2.4	
IN MG HR ASN	HS		4.3.4	
IN MG HR SF	HF	IN MG HR ASN	4.3.3, 4.3.7	
IN MG HR UG	null	IN MG HR	5.2	
IN MG HR DI	null	IN MG HR	5.2	
IN MG HR TE	null	IN MG HR	5.2	
IN MG HR UB	null	IN MG HR	5.2	
IN MG HR DG	null	IN MG HR	5.2	
IN MG HR PB	null	IN MG HR	5.2	
IN MG HR DTE	null	IN MG HR	5.2	
IN MG HR DB	null	IN MG HR	5.2	

Table 13.14 Extensions of IN MG HR ASN

Sequence	Response	Equivalence	Trace	Derived Requirements and Notes
IN MG HR ASN IN	INA	IN	3.5	
IN MG HR ASN HR	CDI, HT	IN MG HR	4.3.2, 4.3.3	
IN MG HR ASN MG	ERR	IN MG HR ASN	4.2.1, 6.1, 6.4	
IN MG HR ASN BR	BRA	IN MG HR ASN	4.4.6	4.4.6 The SOS shall respond to the BR with an acknowledgment message (i.e., BRA).
IN MG HR ASN FR	CDI, FRF		4.5.3, 4.5.6	
IN MG HR ASN TG	TSCAN(3)	IN MG HR ASN	5.8, 5.6.1	5.6.1 The SOS shall not enter transmit mode on receipt of a TG with an invalid UL or DL.
IN MG HR ASN TGu	TSCAN(2)	IN MG HR ASN	5.7, 5.6.1	
IN MG HR ASN TGd	TSCAN(1)	IN MG HR ASN	5.6, 5.6.1	
IN MG HR ASN TGud	CDI, TGFu, TGFd		5.4, 5.5, 5.9.2.1, 5.9.2.2, 5.9.3.1, 5.9.3.2	
IN MG HR ASN TC	ERR	IN MG HR ASN	5.2, 6.1, 6.4	
IN MG HR ASN OTE	null	IN MG HR ASN	1.2.4	

continued

Table 13.14 *continued*

Sequence	Response	Equivalence	Trace	Derived Requirements and Notes
IN MG HR ASN FSR	null	IN MG HR ASN	1.2.4	
IN MG HR ASN FFR	null	IN MG HR ASN	1.2.4	
IN MG HR ASN ASN	illegal		Definition of ASN	Note: The definition of the abstract stimulus cannot be satisfied because all subsystems have already reported. The situation is impossible.
IN MG HR ASN SF	illegal		Definition of SF	Note: The definition of the abstract stimulus cannot be satisfied because all subsystems have already reported. The situation is impossible.
IN MG HR ASN UG	null	IN MG HR ASN	5.2	
IN MG HR ASN DI	null	IN MG HR ASN	5.2	
IN MG HR ASN TE	null	IN MG HR ASN	5.2	
IN MG HR ASN UB	null	IN MG HR ASN	5.2	
IN MG HR ASN DG	null	IN MG HR ASN	5.2	
IN MG HR ASN PB	null	IN MG HR ASN	5.2	
IN MG HR ASN DTE	null	IN MG HR ASN	5.2	
IN MG HR ASN DB	null	IN MG HR ASN	5.2	

Table 13.15 Extensions of IN MG HR ASN FR

Sequence	Response	Equivalence	Trace	Derived Requirements and Notes
IN MG HR ASN FR IN	INA	IN	3.5	
IN MG HR ASN FR HR	ERR	IN MG HR ASN FR	4.3.5, 6.1, 6.4	
IN MG HR ASN FR MG	ERR	IN MG HR ASN FR	4.3.5, 6.1, 6.4	
IN MG HR ASN FR BR	ERR	IN MG HR ASN FR	4.3.5, 6.1, 6.4	
IN MG HR ASN FR FR	ERR	IN MG HR ASN FR	4.3.5, 6.1, 6.4	
IN MG HR ASN FR TG	ERR	IN MG HR ASN FR	4.3.5, 6.1, 6.4	
IN MG HR ASN FR TGu	ERR	IN MG HR ASN FR	4.3.5, 6.1, 6.4	
IN MG HR ASN FR TGd	ERR	IN MG HR ASN FR	4.3.5, 6.1, 6.4	
IN MG HR ASN FR TGud	ERR	IN MG HR ASN FR	4.3.5, 6.1, 6.4	
IN MG HR ASN FR TC	ERR	IN MG HR ASN FR	4.3.5, 6.1, 6.4	
IN MG HR ASN FR OTE	FF	IN MG HR ASN	4.5.6	
IN MG HR ASN FR FSR	FS	IN MG HR ASN	4.5.4	
IN MG HR ASN FR FFR	FF	IN MG HR ASN	4.5.5	
IN MG HR ASN FR ASN	illegal		Definition of ASN	Note: The definition of the abstract stimulus cannot be satisfied because all subsystems have already reported. The situation is impossible.

continued

Table 13.15 *continued*

Sequence	Response	Equivalence	Trace	Derived Requirements and Notes
IN MG HR ASN FR SF	illegal		Definition of SF	Note: The definition of the abstract stimulus cannot be satisfied because all subsystems have already reported. The situation is impossible.
IN MG HR ASN FR UG	null	IN MG HR ASN FR	5.2	
IN MG HR ASN FR DI	null	IN MG HR ASN FR	5.2	
IN MG HR ASN FR TE	null	IN MG HR ASN FR	5.2	
IN MG HR ASN FR UB	null	IN MG HR ASN FR	5.2	
IN MG HR ASN FR DG	null	IN MG HR ASN FR	5.2	
IN MG HR ASN FR PB	null	IN MG HR ASN FR	5.2	
IN MG HR ASN FR DTE	null	IN MG HR ASN FR	5.2	
IN MG HR ASN FR DB	null	IN MG HR ASN FR	5.2	

Table 13.16 Extensions of IN MG HR ASN TGud

Sequence	Response	Equivalence	Trace	Derived Requirements and Notes
IN MG HR ASN TGud IN	INA	IN	3.5	
IN MG HR ASN TGud HR	ERR	IN MG HR ASN TGud	4.3.1, 6.1, 6.4	
IN MG HR ASN TGud MG	ERR	IN MG HR ASN TGud	4.1.2, 6.1, 6.4	4.1.2 The SOS shall not enter maintenance mode from transmit mode.
IN MG HR ASN TGud BR	ERR	IN MG HR ASN TGud	4.4.1, 6.1, 6.4	
IN MG HR ASN TGud FR	ERR	IN MG HR ASN TGud	4.5.1, 6.1, 6.4	
IN MG HR ASN TGud TG	ERR	IN MG HR ASN TGud	5.1, 6.1, 6.4	
IN MG HR ASN TGud TGu	ERR	IN MG HR ASN TGud	5.1, 6.1, 6.4	
IN MG HR ASN TGud TGd	ERR	IN MG HR ASN TGud	5.1, 6.1, 6.4	
IN MG HR ASN TGud TGud	ERR	IN MG HR ASN TGud	5.1, 6.1, 6.4	
IN MG HR ASN TGud TC	TCFu, TCFd, TEFg	IN	5.11.1, 5.11.4.1	
IN MG HR ASN TGud OTE	TSCAN(3), TCFu, TCFd	IN	5.9.1.1	5.9.1.1 If the UL fails to respond with UB or UG within TBD seconds of sending TGFu, and the DL also fails to respond with DB or DG within TBD seconds of sending TGFd, the SOS shall send the TSCAN(3) failure message to the GCS and send TCF to both the UL and the DL. The SOS shall then exit transmit mode.

continued

Table 13.16 *continued*

Sequence	Response	Equivalence	Trace	Derived Requirements and Notes
IN MG HR ASN TGud FSR	null	IN MG HR ASN TGud	1.2.4	
IN MG HR ASN TGud FFR	null	IN MG HR ASN TGud	1.2.4	
IN MG HR ASN TGud ASN	illegal		Definition of ASN	Note: The definition of the abstract stimulus cannot be satisfied because all subsystems have already reported. The situation is impossible.
IN MG HR ASN TGud SF	illegal		Definition of SF	Note: The definition of the abstract stimulus cannot be satisfied because all subsystems have already reported. The situation is impossible.
IN MG HR ASN TGud UG	null		5.9.2.3	
IN MG HR ASN TGud DI	ERR	IN MG HR ASN TGud	5.10.1.1, 6.1, 6.4	5.10.1.1 If either the UL or the DL is not connected, DI and PB messages will result in a protocol error.
IN MG HR ASN TGud TE	FEg	IN	5.11.3.4, 6.2	5.11.3.4 Unexpected TE and DTE messages shall be declared unrecoverable protocol errors.
IN MG HR ASN TGud UB	TSCAN(1), TCFu, TCFd	IN	5.9.2.2	

Sequence	Response	Equivalence	Trace	Derived Requirements and Notes
IN MG HR ASN TGud DG	null	IN MG HR ASN TGud	5.9.3.3	
IN MG HR ASN TGud PB	ERR		5.10.1.1, 6.1, 6.4	
IN MG HR ASN TGud DTE	FEg	IN	5.11.3.4, 6.2	
IN MG HR ASN TGud DB	TSCAN(2), TCFu, TCFd	IN	5.9.3.2	

Table 13.17 Extensions of IN MG HR ASN TGud UG

Sequence	Response	Equivalence	Trace	Derived Requirements and Notes
IN MG HR ASN TGud UG IN	INA	IN	3.5	
IN MG HR ASN TGud UG HR	ERR	IN MG HR ASN TGud UG	4.3 1, 6.1, 6.4	
IN MG HR ASN TGud UG MG	ERR	IN MG HR ASN TGud UG	4.1 2, 6.1, 6.4	
IN MG HR ASN TGud UG BR	ERR	IN MG HR ASN TGud UG	4.4.1, 6.1, 6.4	
IN MG HR ASN TGud UG FR	ERR	IN MG HR ASN TGud UG	4.5.1, 6.1, 6.4	
IN MG HR ASN TGud UG TG	ERR	IN MG HR ASN TGud UG	5.1, 6.1, 6.4	
IN MG HR ASN TGud UG TGu	ERR	IN MG HR ASN TGud UG	5.1, 6.1, 6.4	
IN MG HR ASN TGud UG TGd	ERR	IN MG HR ASN TGud UG	5.1, 6.1, 6.4	
IN MG HR ASN TGud UG TGud	ERR	IN MG HR ASN TGud UG	5.1, 6.1, 6.4	
IN MG HR ASN TGud UG TC	TCFu, TCFd, TEFg	IN	5.11.1, 5.11.4.1	
IN MG HR ASN TGud UG OTE	TSCAN(2), TCFu, TCFd	IN	5.9.3.1	
IN MG HR ASN TGud UG FSR	null	IN MG HR ASN TGud UG	1.2.4	
IN MG HR ASN TGud UG FFR	null	IN MG HR ASN TGud UG	1.2.4	
IN MG HR ASN TGud UG ASN	illegal		Definition of ASN	Note: The definition of the abstract stimulus cannot be satisfied because all subsystems have already reported. The situation is impossible.

Sequence	Response	Equivalence	Trace	Derived Requirements and Notes
IN MG HR ASN TGud UG SF	illegal		Definition of SF	Note: The definition of the abstract stimulus cannot be satisfied because all subsystems have already reported. The situation is impossible.
IN MG HR ASN TGud UG UG	null	IN MG HR ASN TGud UG	5.9.2.4	5.9.2.4 Any UG subsequent to an initial UG shall be ignored.
IN MG HR ASN TGud UG DI	ERR	IN MG HR ASN TGud UG	5.10.1.1, 6.1, 6.4	
IN MG HR ASN TGud UG TE	FEg, FEu	IN	5.11.3.4, 6.2, 6.5	
IN MG HR ASN TGud UG UB	TSCAN(1), TCFu, TCFd	IN	5.9.2.2	
IN MG HR ASN TGud UG DG	SDT		5.9.1, 5.9.2.3, 5.9.3.3	
IN MG HR ASN TGud UG PB	ERR	IN MG HR ASN TGud UG	5.10.1.1, 6.1, 6.4	
IN MG HR ASN TGud UG DTE	FEg, FEu	IN	5.11.3.4, 6.2, 6.5	
IN MG HR ASN TGud UG DB	TSCAN(2), TCFu, TCFd	IN	5.9.3.2	

Table 13.18 Extensions of IN MG HR ASN TGud DG

Sequence	Response	Equivalence	Trace	Derived Requirements and Notes
IN MG HR ASN TGud DG IN	INA	IN	3.5	
IN MG HR ASN TGud DG HR	ERR	IN MG HR ASN TGud DG	4.3 1, 6.1, 6.4	
IN MG HR ASN TGud DG MG	ERR	IN MG HR ASN TGud DG	4.1 2, 6.1, 6.4	
IN MG HR ASN TGud DG BR	ERR	IN MG HR ASN TGud DG	4.4 1, 6.1, 6.4	
IN MG HR ASN TGud DG FR	ERR	IN MG HR ASN TGud DG	4.5 1, 6.1, 6.4	
IN MG HR ASN TGud DG TG	ERR	IN MG HR ASN TGud DG	5.1 6.1, 6.4	
IN MG HR ASN TGud DG TGu	ERR	IN MG HR ASN TGud DG	5.1 6.1, 6.4	
IN MG HR ASN TGud DG TGd	ERR	IN MG HR ASN TGud DG	5.1 6.1, 6.4	
IN MG HR ASN TGud DG TGud	ERR	IN MG HR ASN TGud DG	5.1 6.1, 6.4	
IN MG HR ASN TGud DG TC	TCFu, TCFd, TEFg	IN	5.11.1, 5.11.4.1	
IN MG HR ASN TGud DG OTE	TSCAN(1), TCFu, TCFd	IN	5.9 3.1	
IN MG HR ASN TGud DG FSR	null	IN MG HR ASN TGud DG	1.2 4	
IN MG HR ASN TGud DG FFR	null	IN MG HR ASN TGud DG	1.2 4	
IN MG HR ASN TGud DG ASN	illegal		Definition of ASN	Note: The definition of the abstract stimulus cannot be satisfied because all subsystems have already reported. The situation is impossible.

Sequence	Response	Equivalence	Trace	Derived Requirements and Notes
IN MG HR ASN TGud DG SF	illegal		Definition of SF	Note: The definition of the abstract stimulus cannot be satisfied because all subsystems have already reported. The situation is impossible.
IN MG HR ASN TGud DG UG	SDT	IN MG HR ASN TGud UG DG	5.9.1, 5.9.2.3, 5.9.3.3	
IN MG HR ASN TGud DG DI	ERR	IN MG HR ASN TGud DG	5.10.1.1, 6.1, 6.4	
IN MG HR ASN TGud DG TE	FEg, FEd	IN	5.11.3.4, 6.2, 6.5	
IN MG HR ASN TGud DG UB	TSCAN(1), TCFu, TCFd	IN	5.9.2.2	
IN MG HR ASN TGud DG DG	null	IN MG HR ASN TGud DG	5.9.3.4	5.9.3.4 Any DG subsequent to an initial DG shall be ignored.
IN MG HR ASN TGud DG PB	ERR	IN MG HR ASN TGud DG	5.10.1.1, 6.1, 6.4	
IN MG HR ASN TGud DG DTE	FEg, FEd	IN	5.11.3.4, 6.2, 6.5	
IN MG HR ASN TGud DG DB	TSCAN(2), TCFu, TCFd	IN	5.9.3.2	

Table 13.19 Extensions of IN MG HR ASN TGud UG DG

Sequence	Response	Equivalence	Trace	Derived Requirements and Notes
IN MG HR ASN TGud UG DG IN	INA	IN	3.5	
IN MG HR ASN TGud UG DG HR	ERR	IN MG HR ASN TGud UG DG	4.3.-, 6.1, 6.4	
IN MG HR ASN TGud UG DG MG	ERR	IN MG HR ASN TGud UG DG	4.1.2, 6.1, 6.4	
IN MG HR ASN TGud UG DG BR	ERR	IN MG HR ASN TGud UG DG	4.4.1, 6.1, 6.4	
IN MG HR ASN TGud UG DG FR	ERR	IN MG HR ASN TGud UG DG	4.5.1, 6.1, 6.4	
IN MG HR ASN TGud UG DG TG	ERR	IN MG HR ASN TGud UG DG	5.1, 6.1, 6.4	
IN MG HR ASN TGud UG DG TGu	ERR	IN MG HR ASN TGud UG DG	5.1, 6.1, 6.4	
IN MG HR ASN TGud UG DG TGd	ERR	IN MG HR ASN TGud UG DG	5.1, 6.1, 6.4	
IN MG HR ASN TGud UG DG TGud	ERR	IN MG HR ASN TGud UG DG	5.1 6.1, 6.4	
IN MG HR ASN TGud UG DG TC	TCFu, TCFd, TEFg	IN	5.11.1, 5.11.4.1	
IN MG HR ASN TGud UG DG OTE	null	IN MG HR ASN TGud UG DG	1.2.4	

Sequence	Response	Equivalence	Trace	Derived Requirements and Notes
IN MG HR ASN TGud UG DG FSR	null	IN MG HR ASN TGud UG DG	1.2.4	
IN MG HR ASN TGud UG DG FFR	null	IN MG HR ASN TGud UG DG	1.2.4	
IN MG HR ASN TGud UG DG ASN	illegal		Definition of ASN	Note: The definition of the abstract stimulus cannot be satisfied because all subsystems have already reported. The situation is impossible.
IN MG HR ASN TGud UG DG SF	illegal		Definition of SF	Note: The definition of the abstract stimulus cannot be satisfied because all subsystems have already reported. The situation is impossible.
IN MG HR ASN TGud UG DG UG	null	IN MG HR ASN TGud UG DG	5.9.2.4	
IN MG HR ASN TGud UG DG DI	DO	IN MG HR ASN TGud UG DG	5.10.2, 5.10.1	
IN MG HR ASN TGud UG DG TE	TEFd		5.11.3.1	

continued

Table 13.19 *continued*

Sequence	Response	Equivalence	Trace	Derived Requirements and Notes
IN MG HR ASN TGud UG DG UB	TSCAN(1), TCFu, TCFd	IN	5.9.2.5	5.9.2.5 If the UL reports UB during transmit mode on a fully open connection, the SOS shall send TCF messages to the UL and the DL, shall send TSCAN(1) to the GCS, and shall exit transmit mode.
IN MG HR ASN TGud UG DG DG	null	IN MG HR ASN TGud UG DG	5.9.3.4	
IN MG HR ASN TGud UG DG PB	PBF	IN MG HR ASN TGud UG DG	5.10.3	
IN MG HR ASN TGud UG DG DTE	FEg, FEu, FEd	IN	5.11.3.4, 6.2, 6.5	
IN MG HR ASN TGud UG DG DB	TSCAN(2), TCFu, TCFd	IN	5.9.3.5	5.9.3.5 If the DL reports DB during transmit mode on a fully open connection, the SOS shall send TCF messages to the UL and the DL, shall send TSCAN(2) to the GCS, and shall exit transmit mode.

Table 13.20 Extensions of IN MG HR ASN TGud UG DG TE

Sequence	Response	Equivalence	Trace	Derived Requirements and Notes
IN MG HR ASN TGud UG DG TE IN	INA	IN	3.5	
IN MG HR ASN TGud UG DG TE HR	ERR	IN MG HR ASN TGud UG DG TE	4.3.1, 6.1, 6.4	
IN MG HR ASN TGud UG DG TE MG	ERR	IN MG HR ASN TGud UG DG TE	4.1.2, 6.1, 6.4	
IN MG HR ASN TGud UG DG TE BR	ERR	IN MG HR ASN TGud UG DG TE	4.4.1, 6.1, 6.4	
IN MG HR ASN TGud UG DG TE FR	ERR	IN MG HR ASN TGud UG DG TE	4.5.1, 6.1, 6.4	
IN MG HR ASN TGud UG DG TE TG	ERR	IN MG HR ASN TGud UG DG TE	5.1, 6.1, 6.4	
IN MG HR ASN TGud UG DG TE TGu	ERR	IN MG HR ASN TGud UG DG TE	5.1, 6.1, 6.4	
IN MG HR ASN TGud UG DG TE TGd	ERR	IN MG HR ASN TGud UG DG TE	5.1, 6.1, 6.4	
IN MG HR ASN TGud UG DG TE TGud	ERR	IN MG HR ASN TGud UG DG TE	5.1, 6.1, 6.4	
IN MG HR ASN TGud UG DG TE TC	TCFu, TCFd, TEFg	IN	5.11.1, 5.11.4.1	

continued

Table 13.20 *continued*

Sequence	Response	Equivalence	Trace	Derived Requirements and Notes
IN MG HR ASN TGud UG DG TE OTE	null	IN MG HR ASN TGud UG DG TE	1.2.4	
IN MG HR ASN TGud UG DG TE FSR	null	IN MG HR ASN TGud UG DG TE	1.2.4	
IN MG HR ASN TGud UG DG TE FFR	null	IN MG HR ASN TGud UG DG TE	1.2.4	
IN MG HR ASN TGud UG DG TE ASN	illegal		Definition of ASN	Note: The definition of the abstract stimulus cannot be satisfied because all subsystems have already reported. The situation is impossible.
IN MG HR ASN TGud UG DG TE SF	illegal		Definition of SF	Note: The definition of the abstract stimulus cannot be satisfied because all subsystems have already reported. The situation is impossible.
IN MG HR ASN TGud UG DG TE UG	null	IN MG HR ASN TGud UG DG TE	5.9.2.4	
IN MG HR ASN TGud UG DG TE DI	DO	IN MG HR ASN TGud UG DG TE	5.10.2, 5.11.3.2	
IN MG HR ASN TGud UG DG TE TE	TEFd	IN MG HR ASN TGud UG DG TE	5.11.3.1	

254

Sequence	Response	Equivalence	Trace	Derived Requirements and Notes
IN MG HR ASN TGud UG DG TE UB	TSCAN(1), TCFu, TCFd	IN	5.9.2.5	
IN MG HR ASN TGud UG DG TE DG	null	IN MG HR ASN TGud UG DG TE	5.9.3.4	
IN MG HR ASN TGud UG DG TE PB	PBF	IN MG HR ASN TGud UG DG TE	5.10.3, 5.11.3.2	
IN MG HR ASN TGud UG DG TE DTE	TEFu, TEFg	IN	5.11.1, 5.11.3.3	
IN MG HR ASN TGud UG DG TE DB	TSCAN(2), TCFu, TCFd	IN	5.9.3.5	

13.4 Step 3: Analyze Canonical Sequences

Canonical sequence analysis is an iterative process for identifying and naming important system properties. During analysis of the SOS enumeration's canonical sequences, the following properties are chosen. Other choices are possible. The choice made will depend on domain architectures and how designers view the importance of various aspects of the system.

1. Has the system been initialized for the first time? Call this "Initialized" and assign values of true (the system has been initialized) and false (the system has not been initialized).

2. In what mode is the system currently operating? Call this "Mode" and assign it values of transmit, maintenance, and none.

3. Has the initial health check required on entry to maintenance mode been performed? Call this "HealthCheck" and assign it values of done

Table 13.21   Sequence analysis

Sequence	Initialized	Mode	Processing	Health Check	Connected
Empty	false				
IN	true	none			
IN MG	true	maintenance	idle	pending	
IN MG HR	true	maintenance	health	pending	
IN MG HR ASN	true	maintenance	idle	done	
IN MG HR ASN FR	true	maintenance	firing	done	
IN MG HR ASN TGud	true	transmit			none
IN MG HR ASN TGud UG	true	transmit			uplink
IN MG HR ASN TGud DG	true	transmit			downlink
IN MG HR ASN TGud UG DG	true	transmit			full
IN MG HR ASN TGud UG DG TE	true	transmit			half

(the health check has been performed) and pending (a health check is in progress or has not been performed).

4. Is the system currently processing a GCS command (i.e., waiting for internal signals before replying to the GCS)? Call this "Processing" and assign it values of idle (not processing), firing (waiting for a reply from the RCS), and health (waiting for replies to an HT from internal subsystems).

5. Is the system partially or completely connected? Call this "Connected" and assign it values of none (no connection), uplink (the uplink is connected but not the downlink), downlink (the downlink is connected but not the uplink), full (both uplink and downlink are connected), and half (the connection is half-closed because the uplink has sent TE).

The complete analysis is provided in Table 13.21.

13.5 Step 4: Define Specification Functions

Additional specification functions identified during canonical sequence analysis are defined in this step. All information necessary for this step is provided by the canonical sequence analysis and the sequence enumeration. The resulting specification functions are given in Tables 13.22 through 13.26.

Table 13.22 Specification function: Initialized(h)

Stimulus	Prefix Conditions	Value
	h = empty	false
IN	any	true
s	otherwise ($h = ps$)	Initialized(p)

Table 13.23   Specification function: Mode(*h*)

Stimulus	Prefix Conditions	Value
	h = empty	none
MG	Initialized(*p*) = true Mode(*p*) = none	maintenance
IN	Any	none
TGud	Initialized(*p*) = true Mode(*p*) = maintenance Processing(*p*) = idle HealthCheck(*p*) = done	transmit
OTE	Initialized(*p*) = true Mode(*p*) = transmit (Connected(*p*) = none *or* Connected(*p*) = downlink *or* Connected(*p*) = uplink)	none
TC, UB, DTE, DB	Initialized(*p*) = true Mode(*p*) = transmit	none
TE	Initialized(*p*) = true Mode(*p*) = transmit (Connected(*p*) = none *or* Connected(*p*) = downlink *or* Connected(*p*) = uplink)	none
s	otherwise (*h* = *ps*)	Mode(*p*)

Table 13.24   Specification function: Processing(*h*)

Stimulus	Prefix Conditions	Value
	h = empty	idle
HR	Initialized(*p*) = true Mode(*p*) = maintenance Processing(*p*) = idle	health
IN, OTE, ASN, SF	Initialized(*p*) = true Mode(*p*) = maintenance Processing(*p*) = health HealthCheck(*p*) = pending	idle
FR	Initialized(*p*) = true Mode(*p*) = maintenance Processing(*p*) = idle HealthCheck(*p*) = done	firing
IN, OTE, FSR, FFR	Initialized(*p*) = true Mode(*p*) = maintenance Processing(*p*) = firing HealthCheck(*p*) = done	idle
s	otherwise (*h* = *ps*)	Processing(*p*)

Table 13.25   Specification function: HealthCheck(*h*)

Stimulus	Prefix Conditions	Value
	h = empty	pending
OTE, ASN, SF	Initialized(*p*) = true Mode(*p*) = maintenance Processing(*p*) = health HealthCheck(*p*) = pending	done
HR	Initialized(*p*) = true Mode(*p*) = maintenance Processing(*p*) = idle HealthCheck(*p*) = done	pending
IN	Any	pending
TE, OTE	Initialized(*p*) = true Mode(*p*) = transmit (Connected(*p*) = none *or* Connected(*p*) = uplink *or* Connected(*p*) = downlink)	pending
TC, UB, DTE, DB	Initialized(*p*) = true Mode(*p*) = transmit	pending
s	otherwise (*h* = *ps*)	HealthCheck(*p*)

Table 13.26   Specification function: Connected(*h*)

Stimulus	Prefix Conditions	Value
	h = empty	none
UG	Initialized(*p*) = true Mode(*p*) = transmit Connected(*p*) = none	uplink
DG	Initialized(*p*) = true Mode(*p*) = transmit Connected(*p*) = none	downlink
IN, TC, UB, DTE, DB	Initialized(*p*) = true Mode(*p*) = transmit (Connected(*p*) = uplink *or* Connected(*p*) = downlink *or* Connected(*p*) = full *or* Connected(*p*) = half)	none
OTE, TE	Initialized(*p*) = true Mode(*p*) = transmit (Connected(*p*) = uplink *or* Connected(*p*) = downlink)	none

continued

Table 13.26   *continued*

Stimulus	Prefix Conditions	Value
DG	Initialized(p) = true Mode(p) = transmit Connected(p) = uplink	full
UG	Initialized(p) = true Mode(p) = transmit Connected(p) = downlink	full
TE	Initialized(p) = true Mode(p) = transmit Connected(p) = full	half
s	otherwise ($h = ps$)	Connected(p)

13.6 Step 5: Construct the Black Box Tables

All information necessary to construct the black box tables is provided by the canonical sequence analysis and the sequence enumeration. The resulting tables make reference to the specification function tables generated in the previous step.

First, a black box table is defined for each abstract stimulus. Second, the table rows are defined directly from the enumeration and canonical sequence analysis as a mechanical process; no other information is necessary. The resulting tables are included here as Tables 13.27 through 13.49. These tables define the intended software response for each of the stimuli. As with the specification function tables, p denotes the prefix up to but not including the current stimulus (which is fixed for a given table).

Note that every property has been replaced with a reference to the corresponding specification function. The black box tables are now complete.

Table 13.27   Current stimulus: IN

Prefix Conditions	Response	Trace
any	INA	3.1, 3.2, 3.3, 3.5

Table 13.28   Current stimulus: HR

Prefix Conditions	Response	Trace
Initialized(p) = false	illegal	3.4
Initialized(p) = true (Mode(p) $\neq$ maintenance *or* Processing(p) $\neq$ idle)	ERR	3.6, 4.3.1, 4.3.5, 6.1, 6.4
Initialized(p) = true Mode(p) = maintenance Processing(p) = idle	CDI, HT	4.3.2, 4.3.3, 4.3.1

Table 13.29   Current stimulus: MG

Prefix Conditions	Response	Trace
Initialized(p) = false	illegal	3.4
Initialized(p) = true Mode(p) = none	null	4.1, 4.1.1
Initialized(p) = true Mode(p) $\neq$ none	ERR	4.1.2, 4.2, 4.2.1, 4.3.5, 4.3.6, 6.1, 6.4

Table 13.30   Current stimulus: BR

Prefix Conditions	Response	Trace
Initialized(p) = false	illegal	3.4
Initialized(p) = true (Mode(p) = none *or* Mode(p) = transmit)	ERR	4.4.1, 6.1, 6.4
Initialized(p) = true Mode(p) = maintenance (Processing(p) $\neq$ idle *or* HealthCheck(p) $\neq$ done)	ERR	4.2, 4.3.5, 6.1, 6.4
Initialized(p) = true Mode(p) = maintenance Processing(p) = idle HealthCheck(p) = done	BRA	4.4.6

Table 13.31 Current stimulus: FR

Prefix Conditions	Response	Trace
Initialized(p) = false	illegal	3.4
Initialized(p) = true (Mode(p) = none or Mode(p) = transmit)	ERR	4.5.1, 6.1, 6.4
Initialized(p) = true Mode(p) = maintenance (Processing(p) ≠ idle or HealthCheck(p) ≠ done)	ERR	4.2, 4.3.5, 6.1, 6.4
Initialized(p) = true Mode(p) = maintenance Processing(p) = idle HealthCheck(p) = done	CDI, FRF	4.5.3, 4.5.6

Table 13.32 Current stimulus: TG

Prefix Conditions	Response	Trace
Initialized(p) = false	illegal	3.4
Initialized(p) = true (Mode(p) = none or Mode(p) = transmit)	ERR	5.1, 6.1, 6.4
Initialized(p) = true Mode(p) = maintenance (Processing(p) ≠ idle or HealthCheck(p) ≠ done)	ERR	4.2, 4.3.5, 6.1, 6.4
Initialized(p) = true Mode(p) = maintenance Processing(p) = idle HealthCheck(p) = done	TSCAN(3)	5.8, 5.6.1

Table 13.33   Current stimulus: TGu

Prefix Conditions	Response	Trace
Initialized(*p*) = false	illegal	3.4
Initialized(*p*) = true (Mode(*p*) = none *or* Mode(*p*) = transmit)	ERR	5.1, 6.1, 6.4
Initialized(*p*) = true Mode(*p*) = maintenance (Processing(*p*) ≠ idle *or* HealthCheck(*p*) ≠ done)	ERR	4.2, 4.3.5, 6.1, 6.4
Initialized(*p*) = true Mode(*p*) = maintenance Processing(*p*) = idle HealthCheck(*p*) = done	TSCAN(2)	5.7, 5.6.1

Table 13.34   Current Stimulus: TGd

Prefix Conditions	Response	Trace
Initialized(*p*) = false	illegal	3.4
Initialized(*p*) = true (Mode(*p*) = none *or* Mode(*p*) = transmit)	ERR	5.1, 6.1, 6.4
Initialized(*p*) = true Mode(*p*) = maintenance (Processing(*p*) ≠ idle *or* HealthCheck(*p*) ≠ done)	ERR	4.2, 4.3.5, 6.1, 6.4
Initialized(*p*) = true Mode(*p*) = maintenance Processing(*p*) = idle HealthCheck(*p*) = done	TSCAN(1)	5.6, 5.6.1

Table 13.35 Current stimulus: TGud

Prefix Conditions	Response	Trace
Initialized(p) = false	illegal	3.4
Initialized(p) = true (Mode(p) = none *or* Mode(p) = transmit)	ERR	5.1, 6.1, 6.4
Initialized(p) = true Mode(p) = maintenance (Processing(p) $\neq$ idle *or* HealthCheck(p) $\neq$ done)	ERR	4.2, 4.3.5, 6.1, 6.4
Initialized(p) = true Mode(p) = maintenance Processing(p) = idle HealthCheck(p) = done	CDI, TGFu, TGFd	5.4, 5.5, 5.9.2.1, 5.9.2.2, 5.9.3.1, 5.9.3.2

Table 13.36 Current stimulus: TC

Prefix Conditions	Response	Trace
Initialized(p) = false	illegal	3.4
Initialized(p) = true Mode(p) $\neq$ transmit	ERR	4.2, 4.3.5, 5.2, 6.1, 6.4
Initialized(p) = true Mode(p) = transmit	TCFu, TCFd, TEFg	5.11.1, 5.11.4.1

Table 13.37 Current stimulus: OTE

Prefix Conditions	Response	Trace
Initialized(p) = false	illegal	3.4
Initialized(p) = true Mode(p) = none	null	1.2.4
Initialized(p) = true Mode(p) = maintenance Processing(p) = idle	null	1.2.4, 4.2, 6.1, 6.4
Initialized(p) = true Mode(p) = maintenance Processing(p) = health HealthCheck(p) = pending	HF	4.3.3, 4.3.7
Initialized(p) = true Mode(p) = maintenance Processing(p) = firing HealthCheck(p) = done	FF	4.5.6

Prefix Conditions	Response	Trace
Initialized(p) = true Mode(p) = transmit Connected(p) = none	TSCAN(3), TCFu, TCFd	5.9.1.1
Initialized(p) = true Mode(p) = transmit Connected(p) = uplink	TSCAN(2), TCFu, TCFd	5.9.3.1
Initialized(p) = true Mode(p) = transmit Connected(p) = downlink	TSCAN(1), TCFu, TCFd	5.9.3.1
Initialized(p) = true Mode(p) = transmit (Connected(p) = full *or* Connected(p) = half)	null	1.2.4

Table 13.38 Current stimulus: FSR

Prefix Conditions	Response	Trace
Initialized(p) = false	illegal	3.4
Initialized(p) = true (Mode(p) = none *or* Mode(p) = transmit)	null	1.2.4
Initialized(p) = true Mode(p) = maintenance Processing(p) $\neq$ firing	null	1.2.4
Initialized(p) = true Mode(p) = maintenance Processing(p) = firing	FS	4.5.4

Table 13.39 Current stimulus: FFR

Prefix Conditions	Response	Trace
Initialized(p) = false	illegal	3.4
Initialized(p) = true (Mode(p) = none *or* Mode(p) = transmit)	null	1.2.4
Initialized(p) = true Mode(p) = maintenance Processing(p) $\neq$ firing	null	1.2.4
Initialized(p) = true Mode(p) = maintenance Processing(p) = firing	FF	4.5.5

Table 13.40   Current stimulus: ASN

Prefix Conditions	Response	Trace
Initialized(p) = false	illegal	3.4
Initialized(p) = true (Mode(p) = none *or* Mode(p) = transmit)	illegal	Definition of ASN
Initialized(p) = true Mode(p) = maintenance Processing(p) $\neq$ health	illegal	Definition of ASN
Initialized(p) = true Mode(p) = maintenance Processing(p) = health	HS	4.3.4

Table 13.41   Current stimulus: SF

Prefix Conditions	Response	Trace
Initialized(p) = false	illegal	3.4
Initialized(p) = true (Mode(p) = none *or* Mode(p) = transmit)	illegal	Definition of SF
Initialized(p) = true Mode(p) = maintenance Processing(p) $\neq$ health	illegal	Definition of SF
Initialized(p) = true Mode(p) = maintenance Processing(p) = health	HF	4.3.3, 4.3.7

Table 13.42   Current stimulus: UG

Prefix Conditions	Response	Trace
Initialized(p) = false	illegal	3.4
Initialized(p)= true (Mode(p) = none *or* Mode(p) = maintenance)	null	5.2
Initialized(p) = true Mode(p) = transmit Connected(p) $\neq$ downlink	null	5.9.2.3, 5.9.2.4
Initialized(p) = true Mode(p) = transmit Connected(p) = downlink	SDT	5.9.1, 5.9.2.3, 5.9.3.3

Table 13.43   Current stimulus: DI

Prefix Conditions	Response	Trace
Initialized(*p*) = false	illegal	3.4
Initialized(*p*)= true (Mode(*p*) = none *or* Mode(*p*) = maintenance)	null	5.2
Initialized(*p*) = true Mode(*p*) = transmit (Connected(*p*) ≠ full *and* Connected(*p*) ≠ half)	ERR	5.10.1.1, 6.1, 6.4
Initialized(*p*) = true Mode(*p*) = transmit (Connected(*p*) = full *or* Connected(*p*) = half)	DO	5.10.1, 5.10.2

Table 13.44   Current stimulus: TE

Prefix Conditions	Response	Trace
Initialized(*p*) = false	illegal	3.4
Initialized(*p*)= true (Mode(*p*) = none *or* Mode(*p*) = maintenance)	null	5.2
Initialized(*p*) = true Mode(*p*) = transmit Connected(*p*) = none	FEg	5.11.3.4, 6.2
Initialized(*p*) = true Mode(*p*) = transmit Connected(*p*) = uplink	FEg, FEu	5.11.3.4, 6.2, 6.5
Initialized(*p*) = true Mode(*p*) = transmit Connected(*p*) = downlink	FEg, FEd	5.11.3.4, 6.2, 6.5
Initialized(*p*) = true Mode(*p*) = transmit (Connected(*p*) = full *or* Connected(*p*) = half)	TEFd	5.11.3.1

Table 13.45   Current stimulus: UB

Prefix Conditions	Response	Trace
Initialized(*p*) = false	illegal	3.4
Initialized(*p*)= true (Mode(*p*) = none *or* Mode(*p*) = maintenance)	null	5.2
Initialized(*p*) = true Mode(*p*) = transmit	TSCAN(1), TCFu, TCFd	5.9.2.2, 5.9.2.5

Table 13.46   Current stimulus: DG

Prefix Conditions	Response	Trace
Initialized(p) = false	illegal	3.4
Initialized(p)= true (Mode(p) = none *or* Mode(p) = maintenance)	null	5.2
Initialized(p) = true Mode(p) = transmit Connected(p) ≠ uplink	null	5.9.3.3, 5.9.3.4
Initialized(p) = true Mode(p) = transmit Connected(p) = uplink	SDT	5.9.1, 5.9.2.3, 5.9.3.3

Table 13.47   Current stimulus: PB

Prefix Conditions	Response	Trace
Initialized(p) = false	illegal	3.4
Initialized(p)= true (Mode(p) = none *or* Mode(p) = maintenance)	null	5.2
Initialized(p) = true Mode(p) = transmit Connected(p) ≠ full Connected(p) ≠ half	ERR	5.10.1.1, 6.1, 6.4
Initialized(p) = true Mode(p) = transmit (Connected(p) = full *or* Connected(p) = half)	PBF	5.10.3, 5.11.3.2

Table 13.48   Current stimulus: DTE

Prefix Conditions	Response	Trace
Initialized(p) = false	illegal	3.4
Initialized(p)= true (Mode(p) = none *or* Mode(p) = maintenance)	null	5.2
Initialized(p) = true Mode(p) = transmit Connected(p) = none	FEg	5.11.3.4, 6.2
Initialized(p) = true Mode(p) = transmit Connected(p) = uplink	FEg, FEu	5.11.3.4, 6.2, 6.5
Initialized(p) = true Mode(p) = transmit Connected(p) = downlink	FEg, FEd	5.11.3.4, 6.2, 6.5

Prefix Conditions	Response	Trace
Initialized(p) = true Mode(p) = transmit Connected(p) = full	FEg, FEu, FEd	5.11.3.4, 6.2, 6.5
Initialized(p) = true Mode(p) = transmit Connected(p) = half	TEFu, TEFg	5.11.1, 5.11.3.3

Table 13.49   Current stimulus: DB

Prefix Conditions	Response	Trace
Initialized(p) = false	illegal	3.4
Initialized(p)= true (Mode(p) = none *or* Mode(p) = maintenance)	null	5.2
Initialized(p) = true Mode(p) = transmit	TSCAN(2), TCFu, TCFd	5.9.3.2, 5.9.3.5

13.7 Removing Abstractions

Although the black box is finished, it contains abstractions. As noted earlier, formal definitions could be created for abstractions after a system's function is understood. Although this is seldom necessary, it will be done in this case to illustrate the technique.

Recall that the definition of specification function B/L required a specification function Mode to determine whether the system was in maintenance mode. A specification function Mode was defined earlier, but is at the wrong level of abstraction (it mentions TGud, which depends on B/L, which depends on Mode, etc.). Fortunately, all recursion is to prefixes, and the abstraction definitions can be composed with the specification function definition (a benefit of the referential transparency of abstractions and specification functions) by simple substitution. The changes are shown in bold type in Table 13.50.

This leaves abstract stimuli ASN and SF. Formal definitions for these are now very simple. Let *Sys* denote the set of all SV subsystems. Let p denote the previous stimulus sequence in the following definitions. Let Good_Systems(p) and Bad_Systems(p) be the sets consisting of systems that have passed their health check and that have failed their health check respectively for history p (these will be defined as specification functions later).

Let ASN denote ISN(x) when x is in *Sys*, Good_Systems(p) = *Sys* − {x}, Bad_Systems(p) = { }, and Processing(p) = health. Thus the SOS has just received a positive health report from every subsystem.

Table 13.50   Specification function revisited: Mode(*h*)

Stimulus	Prefix Conditions	Value
	h = empty	none
MG	Initialized(*p*) = true Mode(*p*) = none	maintenance
IN	any	none
TG(*u*, *d*)	Initialized(*p*) = true Mode(*p*) = maintenance Processing(*p*) = idle HealthCheck(*p*) = done **There exist indices *m* and *n* such that** **B/L(*p, m*) = *u* and B/L(*p, n*) = *d***	transmit
OTE	Initialized(*p*) = true Mode(*p*) = transmit (Connected(*p*) = none *or* Connected(*p*) = downlink *or* Connected(*p*) = uplink)	none
TC, UB, DTE, DB	Initialized(*p*) = true Mode(*p*) = transmit	none
TE	Initialized(*p*) = true Mode(*p*) = transmit (Connected(*p*) = none *or* Connected(*p*) = downlink *or* Connected(*p*) = uplink)	none
s	otherwise (*h* = *ps*)	Mode(*p*)

Let SF denote any of the following conditions:

1. ISN(*x*) when *x* is in *Sys*, Good_Systems(*p*) ∪ Bad_Systems(*p*) = *Sys* – {*x*}, Bad_Systems(*p*) ≠ { }, and Processing(*p*) = health. Thus the SOS has just received a success or failure report from every subsystem, and at least one failed.

2. ISF(*x*) when *x* is in *Sys*, Good_Systems(*p*) ∪ Bad_Systems(*p*) = *Sys* – {*x*}, and Processing(*p*) = health. Thus the SOS has just received a success or failure report from every subsystem, and at least one failed.

3. OTE when Processing(*p*) = health. Thus the timer has expired prior to completion of a health check.

These definitions make use of the Processing specification function, which is written in terms of abstract stimuli ASN and SF. Again, the recursion is always to proper prefixes, and the specification function can be rewritten by substitution. The result is shown in Table 13.51.

Table 13.51   Specification function: Processing(*h*)

Stimulus	Prefix Conditions	Value
	h = empty	idle
HR	Initialized(*p*) = true Mode(*p*) = maintenance Processing(*p*) = idle	health
ISF(*x*), ISN(*x*)	Initialized(*p*) = true Mode(*p*) = maintenance Processing(*p*) = health HealthCheck(*p*) = pending ***x* is in *Sys*** **Good_Systems(*p*) ∪ Bad_Systems(*p*)** **= *Sys* − {*x*}**	idle
IN, OTE	Initialized(*p*) = true Mode(*p*) = maintenance Processing(*p*) = health HealthCheck(*p*) = pending	idle
FR	Initialized(*p*) = true Mode(*p*) = maintenance Processing(*p*) = idle HealthCheck(*p*) = done	firing
IN, OTE, FSR, FFR	Initialized(*p*) = true Mode(*p*) = maintenance Processing(*p*) = firing HealthCheck(*p*) = done	idle
s	otherwise (*h* = *ps*)	Processing(*p*)

Finally, there are two new specification functions mentioned: Good_Systems and Bad_Systems. They must return the sets of subsystems reporting good health and bad health respectively. Their definitions are very simple, given what is now known. The specification function for Good_Systems is defined in Table 13.52, and the function for Bad_Systems is defined in Table 13.53.

Every specification function and every black box table could be easily rewritten in terms of the atomic stimuli. This would give a black box at the atomic level and would reveal any details that might have been overlooked because of the abstraction. In short, it is always possible to remove all abstractions at the black box level, but this requires formally defining all abstractions. The abstractions will be left in for this case study so that removal at a later stage can be illustrated.

Table 13.52 Specification function: Good_Systems(*h*)

Stimulus	Prefix Conditions	Value
	h = empty	{ }
ISN(*x*)	Processing(*p*) = health	Good_Systems(*p*) ∪ {*x*}
any	Processing(*p*) ≠ health	{ }
s	otherwise (*h* = *ps*)	Good_Systems(*p*)

Table 13.53 Specification function: Bad_Systems(*h*)

Stimulus	Prefix Conditions	Value
	h = empty	{ }
ISF(*x*)	Processing(*p*) = health	Bad_Systems(*p*) ∪ {*x*}
any	Processing(*p*) ≠ health	{ }
s	otherwise (*h* = *ps*)	Bad_Systems(*p*)

This completes the black box development, and work continues with state box specification in Chapter 14. This chapter concludes with comments on abstraction techniques.

13.8 Common Sequence Abstraction Techniques

Sequence abstraction is a fundamental technique in sequence-based specification. There are many different ways to define abstract stimuli to solve problems. Practitioners should use the abstract stimuli that seem, to them, most natural, and then document their choices. This section describes common forms of abstract stimuli that are often used in sequence-based specification. It also provides guidance for constructing informal abstract stimulus definitions.

13.8.1 Informal Abstract Stimulus Definitions

When an informal abstract stimulus definition is constructed, it is important to ensure that it is in fact a proper abstract stimulus. A proper abstract stimulus must satisfy three properties:

1. The abstract stimulus definition must depend only on stimulus sequences. If an abstraction needs information that cannot be obtained from the atomic stimulus sequence, the system boundary must be revisited.

2. The abstract stimulus definition must depend only on stimulus history, never future stimuli, and must be computable.

3. All abstract stimuli used simultaneously must be disjoint. That is, two abstract stimuli can never apply at the same time because this gives a one-to-many relation, and not a many-to-one mapping as required. If it must be decided whether two or more conditions apply simultaneously, invent a single abstract stimulus for that case, or use an abstract stimulus along with specification functions.

Any informal definition used must be sufficiently precise to show that these criteria are satisfied. (Obviously, it must also be defined precisely enough to communicate its meaning unambiguously.) Condition 3 is the easiest to miss. Here is an example of two abstract stimuli that fail to be disjoint:

1. Let V denote every fifth clock pulse.

2. Let X denote every tenth clock pulse.

Which abstract stimulus corresponds to the tenth clock pulse, X or V? Given the definitions, both do. The definitions provide the opportunity to introduce inconsistency into the enumeration. If this error is missed, the sequences "a b c V V" and "a b c V X" might be mapped to different responses, resulting in an inconsistent enumeration. This can be resolved by changing the definitions:

1. Every tenth clock pulse is denoted X.

2. Every fifth clock pulse which is not also a tenth clock pulse is denoted V.

13.8.2 Stimulus-Based Abstractions

Stimulus-based abstractions are commonly used early in the process, often before enumeration has even started. There are three common forms:

1. A *bundle abstraction* replaces ("bundles") several atomic stimuli under a single abstract stimulus. For example, a program may provide several ways to save a file. A user might choose Save from a File menu, click an icon of a disk, type Control+S, or press F6. These may be very different events from the point of view of the software, but all are intended to have the same result. These could be "bundled" together, replacing them with the abstract stimulus Save. This reduces the number of stimuli to be enumerated.

2. A *partition abstraction* partitions a collection of stimuli into one of several abstract stimuli. For example, there are many different possibilities for file names, but for the purposes of specification only valid (properly constructed) and invalid file names need be considered. Each file name is really a different stimulus, however these can be partitioned into valid and invalid, replacing the many different stimuli with only two abstract stimuli. This can reduce significantly the number of stimuli to be enumerated.

3. A *deletion abstraction* deletes all but a particular collection of distinguished stimuli. There are two primary forms: indexed and nonindexed. A nonindexed deletion abstraction allows developers to focus on one interface or aspect of system behavior. For example, there may be a particular dialog with an operation that is largely independent of all other dialogs. The stimuli for only that dialog may be enumerated to determine its behavior independently of the rest of the system or to identify those instances in which its behavior depends on the rest of the system.

    An indexed deletion is used when a software system has a large number of identical interfaces. For example, a disk array might have several identical small computer systems interfaces (SCSIs). To determine the behavior for the system, enumerate stimuli for a single instance of the interface, with the knowledge that the results will apply equally to all interfaces.

13.8.3   Sequence-Based Abstractions

Sequence-based abstractions are commonly invented during enumeration. A useful heuristic is to observe when practitioners invent a name for a particular sequence of events (just opened a valid project, just closed the last open file, just completed entering the number, just entered the correct combination). In such a case, an abstract stimulus can be invented for that event sequence, and referenced as work proceeds. This makes an abstraction that practitioners were already using an explicit part of the specification. Sequence-based abstractions are primarily introduced to allow equivalences to be created and thus allow the enumeration to be completed. There are three common forms of sequence-based abstraction:

1. A *counting abstraction* is invented whenever the nth occurrence of an event is significant. The simplest example is a time-out, when the behavior is directly tied to some large number of clock pulses.

2. A *history-encapsulating abstraction* eliminates the need to keep certain events in the sequence by encapsulating those events into other

stimuli. For example, a request for a network connection might generate an error message if there are already, say, 16 open connections. To map a request for a network connection to a response, therefore, all network connection information must be kept in the sequence. This results in very long sequences before the behavior is revealed. Alternately, an abstraction can be invented that breaks the network connection request stimulus into two abstract stimuli (one for which there are fewer than 16 open connections, and one for which there are 16). The network connection events can then be discarded from the abstract sequence. The TG, TGu, TGd, and TGud abstract stimuli used earlier are examples of this.

3. An *accumulating abstraction* is one that collects information from the sequence into a single abstract stimulus. For example, a software system might deal with entering a phone number. The atomic sequence would then contain single-digit presses, although the primary concern is the phone number dialed. An abstract stimulus might be constructed that replaces history "Off-hook 4 clock_pulse clock_pulse 4 clock_pulse 2 clock_pulse clock_pulse clock_pulse 1 clock_pulse 2 7" with abstract stimulus "Dial(442–127)."

14

Satellite Control System State Box Specification

14.1 State Box Specification

With the black box completed in Chapter 13, development of the state box specification can begin. The state box progresses toward the implementation by moving from an external, sequence-based view of the system to a state-based view. The state box is derived from the black box. Completeness and consistency were established at the black box and need only be preserved.

The basic work flow for creating a state-based specification from a sequence-based specification is given in Chapter 4 and in the Cleanroom Specification Process defined in Chapter 8. The instantiation used to produce the SOS state box is summarized in the following list:

Step 1: Invent the state data.

1. Invent an item of state data for each specification function used in the black box.

2. Invent any additional state required to compute each abstraction.

3. Invent any additional state required to compute the black box mapping rule.

4. Invent any additional state required to compute responses.

Step 2: Construct the state box tables.

1. Replace every reference to previous stimuli with a reference to state data.

2. Introduce additional information required for state update.

Step 3: Verify the state box to the black box.

1. Transform each state-based entity into a sequence-based function.

2. Compare the derived sequenced-based function to the corresponding black box function.

(Because of space considerations and because the verification artifacts add no new information for the reader, verification of the state box is not presented for the case study.)

14.2 Step 1: Invent the State Data

The black box sources of state data are the following:

1. Each specification function can be transformed into an item of state data, although all may not be required. This transformation will be direct if the specification functions are written in prefix-recursive form.

2. Abstractions may also reference stimulus histories and may require state data to remove the dependency on prior stimuli.

3. The mapping rule may also reference stimulus histories, and these references must be replaced with state data references.

4. If abstract responses were used, these can be removed at this stage by adding any necessary state data to compute the response.

It is not necessary to remove all abstractions at this stage. Abstractions may be left until later in the process, especially if they have a natural, well-established representation as a procedure. For example, algorithms are known to exist for determining whether or not a number is prime, and thus an abstraction into prime and composite numbers can be left in until code is written. An abstraction from individual bits or bytes to packets might even be left in the clear box to be removed in a lower level black box.

14.2.1 Specification Functions

Tables 14.1 through 14.4 are derived directly from the specification function tables presented in Chapter 13. The initial state value is given in the first row of each table.

Note that the original specification functions with the abstract stimuli were used because not all specification functions were converted to atomic stimuli in the previous section.

These tables reveal how the state data items must be updated. They may be integrated into the state box tables or they may remain separate. The primary

Table 14.1 State data item: Mode

Stimulus	Current State	New Value
	initial value = none	
MG	Mode = none	maintenance
IN	any	none
TGud	Mode = maintenance Processing = idle HealthCheck = done	transmit
OTE TE	Mode = transmit (Connected = none *or* Connected = uplink *or* Connected = downlink)	none
TC UB DTE DB	Mode = transmit	none

Table 14.2 State data item: Processing

Stimulus	Current State	New Value
	initial value = idle	
HR	Mode = maintenance Processing = idle	health
IN, OTE, ASN, SF	Mode = maintenance Processing = health HealthCheck = pending	idle
FR	Mode = maintenance Processing = idle HealthCheck = done	firing
IN, OTE, FSR, FFR	Mode = maintenance Processing = firing HealthCheck = done	idle

benefit of integrating them is that the state box tables are more representative of the final code. The primary benefits of leaving them separate is that the tables more closely resemble the black box tables.

14.2.2 Abstractions

Abstractions may also be a source of state data if they are to be removed. At this step, the TG, TGu, TGd, and TGud abstract stimuli will be removed as an illustration. (Note that this illustration will duplicate some of the work done in the black box.)

Table 14.3   State data item: HealthCheck

Stimulus	Current State	New Value
	initial value = pending	
OTE, ASN, SF	Mode = maintenance Processing = health HealthCheck = pending	done
HR	Mode = maintenance Processing = idle HealthCheck = done	pending
IN	any	pending
TE, OTE	Mode = transmit (Connected = none *or* Connected = uplink *or* Connected = downlink)	pending
TC, UB, DTE, DB	Mode = transmit	pending

Table 14.4   State data item: Connected

Stimulus	Current State	New Value
	initial value = none	
UG	Mode = transmit Connected = none	uplink
DG	Mode = transmit Connected = none	downlink
IN, TC, UB, DTE, DB	Mode = transmit (Connected = uplink *or* Connected = downlink *or* Connected = full *or* Connected = half)	none
OTE, TE	Mode = transmit (Connected = uplink *or* Connected = downlink)	none
DG	Mode = transmit Connected = uplink	full
UG	Mode = transmit Connected = downlink	full
TE	Mode = transmit Connected = full	half

The definitions of the TG abstract stimuli could be rewritten using only state data if the B/L specification function were converted to state data. This has been done in Table 14.5. (This is only required if the abstraction is to be removed.)

The state data item definition for B/L says nothing about how the data are to be stored. It simply reports the initial value of a given index n, and records that the value is changed by BR(n, s). At the state box level one should say what must be stored, but avoid saying how. Although it may seem obvious that B/L should be implemented as an array, there may be time constraints on determining whether a site is stored in B/L. In this case the item might be implemented as a hash table, tree, or some other structure to optimize the look-up. There is seldom enough information at the state box level to determine the exact implementation of each state data item, and this decision should be deferred.

This definition makes use of the state data item Mode, which has an update table that is based on abstract stimuli. The definition for state data item Mode is rewritten in Table 14.6.

Table 14.5   State data item: B/L[n]

Stimulus	Current State	New Value
	initial value = empty	
BR(n, s)	Mode = maintenance Processing = idle HealthCheck = done	s

Table 14.6   State data item: Mode (revisited)

Stimulus	Current State	New Value
	initial value = none	
MG	Mode = none	maintenance
IN	any	none
TG(u, d)	Mode = maintenance Processing = idle HealthCheck = done **There are indices *m* and *n* such that B/L[*m*] = *u* and B/L[*n*] = *d***	transmit
OTE, TE	Mode = transmit (Connected = none *or* Connected = uplink *or* Connected = downlink)	none
TC, UB, DTE, DB	Mode = transmit	none

The abstract stimuli ASN and SF may also be removed at this stage by introducing state data. To do this, the specification functions Processing, Good_Systems, and Bad_Systems must be rewritten to use state data and atomic stimuli. Processing is rewritten in Table 14.7, Good_Systems is rewritten in Table 14.8, and Bad_Systems is rewritten in Table 14.9.

Table 14.7   State data item: Processing (revisited)

Stimulus	Current State	New Value
	initial value = idle	
HR	Mode = maintenance Processing = idle	health
IN, OTE	Mode = maintenance Processing = health HealthCheck = pending	idle
ISN(x)	Mode = maintenance Processing = health HealthCheck = pending ***x* is in *Sys*** **Good_Systems ∪ Bad_Systems = *Sys* – {*x*}**	idle
ISF(x)	Mode = maintenance Processing = health HealthCheck = pending ***x* is in *Sys*** **Good_Systems ∪ Bad_Systems = *Sys* – {*x*}**	idle
FR	Mode = maintenance Processing = idle HealthCheck = done	firing
IN, OTE, FSR, FFR	Mode = maintenance Processing = firing HealthCheck = done	idle

Table 14.8   State data item: Good_Systems

Stimulus	Current State	New Value
	initial value = { }	
ISN(x)	Processing = health	Good_System ∪ {x}
any	Processing ≠ health	{ }

Table 14.9 State data item: Bad_Systems

Stimulus	Current State	New Value
	initial value = { }	
ISF(*x*)	Processing = health	Bad_Systems ∪ {*x*}
any	Processing ≠ health	{ }

It is now possible to remove the ASN and SF abstract stimuli from the specification, and this will be done in the next section when the state box tables are constructed.

14.2.3 Responses

Other state data may be associated with responses. For example, an HF may include a list of all subsystems that reported their health to allow the ground crew to diagnose the problem. The necessary state data are already available; Good_Systems and Bad_Systems capture these data.

14.3 Step 2: Construct the State Box Tables

State box construction involves rewriting each black box table to eliminate stimulus history references:

1. Replace every reference to previous stimuli with a reference to state data. In the case of specification functions, this is often direct, as illustrated in the previous section. There may be other references. It is not uncommon to use expressions such as "there has been an *X* stimulus more recently than all *Y* stimuli" or "the argument of the most recent *A* stimulus." Such expressions are references to previous stimuli and must be replaced with references to state data items.

2. Introduce additional information for state update. Under what conditions must the value of the state data item change? This additional information most often comes directly from the specification function tables, as illustrated in the previous section.

Several specification function tables were transformed into state data item tables in the previous section. HealthCheck and Connected are transformed here as Tables 14.10 and 14.11 respectively.

Table 14.10   State data item: HealthCheck

Stimulus	Current State	New Value
	initial value = pending	
OTE	Mode = maintenance Processing = health HealthCheck = pending	done
ISN(*x*)	Mode = maintenance Processing = health HealthCheck − pending *x* is in *Sys* **Good_Systems** ∪ **Bad_Systems = *Sys* − {*x*}**	done
ISF(*x*)	Mode = maintenance Processing = health HealthCheck = pending *x* is in *Sys* **Good_Systems** ∪ **Bad_Systems = *Sys* − {*x*}**	done
HR	Mode = maintenance Processing = idle HealthCheck = done	pending
IN	any	pending
TE, OTE	Mode = transmit (Connected = none *or* Connected = uplink *or* Connected = downlink)	pending
TC, UB, DTE, DB	Mode = transmit	pending

Table 14.11   State data item: Connected

Stimulus	Current State	New Value
	initial value = none	
UG	Mode = transmit Connected = none	uplink
DG	Mode = transmit Connected = none	downlink
IN, TC, UB, DTE, DB	Mode = transmit (Connected = uplink *or* Connected = downlink *or* Connected = full *or* Connected = half)	none
OTE, TE	Mode = transmit (Connected = uplink *or* Connected = downlink)	none

Stimulus	Current state	New value
DG	Mode = transmit Connected = uplink	full
UG	Mode = transmit Connected = downlink	full
TE	Mode = transmit Connected = full	half

Next the black box tables are transformed into state box tables. Note that it is now possible to construct state box tables for the atomic stimulus TG(u, d). The response information will be integrated with the state update information from the state data item tables because this helps advance the specification toward code. The state data item tables should still be kept, however, because they will be useful in correctness verification of the clear box. The resulting state box tables, one per stimulus, appear in Tables 14.12 through 14.31. Note that several rows had to be split to accommodate the state data changes, and that rows for illegal behavior have been dropped. Because of the strong correspondence between state box rows and black box rows, the trace information is the same as for the black box and is not repeated here.

In the following tables, an asterisk in the New State column indicates that a state data item may already have the indicated value (in other words, two or more rows of the table have been combined to reduce the table length).

Table 14.12   Current stimulus: IN

Current State	Response	New State
any	INA	Mode := none Processing := idle HealthCheck := pending Connected := none Good_Systems := { } Bad_Systems := { }

Table 14.13   Current stimulus: HR

Current State	Response	New State
(Mode ≠ maintenance *or* Processing ≠ idle)	ERR	no change
Mode = maintenance Processing = idle	CDI, HT	Processing := health HealthCheck := pending* Good_Systems := { }* Bad_Systems := { }*

Table 14.14 Current stimulus: MG

Current State	Response	New State
Mode = none	null	Mode := maintenance
Mode ≠ none	ERR	no change

Table 14.15 Current stimulus: BR(*n*, *s*)

Current State	Response	New State
(Mode = none *or* Mode = transmit)	ERR	no change
Mode = maintenance (Processing ≠ idle *or* HealthCheck ≠ done)	ERR	no change
Mode = maintenance Processing = idle HealthCheck = done	BRA	B/L[*n*] = *s**

Table 14.16 Current stimulus: FR

Current State	Response	New State
(Mode = none *or* Mode = transmit)	ERR	no change
Mode = maintenance (Processing ≠ idle *or* HealthCheck ≠ done)	ERR	no change
Mode = maintenance Processing = idle HealthCheck = done	CDI, FRF	Processing := firing Good_Systems := { }* Bad_Systems := { }*

Table 14.17 Current stimulus: TG(*u*, *d*)

Current State	Response	New State
(Mode = none *or* Mode = transmit)	ERR	no change
Mode = maintenance (Processing ≠ idle *or* HealthCheck ≠ done)	ERR	no change
Mode = maintenance Processing = idle HealthCheck = done There is no index *m* such that B/L[*m*] = *u* There is no index *n* such that B/L[*n*] = *d*	TSCAN(3)	no change

Current State	Response	New State
Mode = maintenance Processing = idle HealthCheck = done There is an index *m* such that B/L[*m*] = *u* There is no index *n* such that B/L[*n*] = *d*	TSCAN(2)	no change
Mode = maintenance Processing = idle HealthCheck = done There is no index *m* such that B/L[*m*] = *u* There is an index *n* such that B/L[*n*] = *d*	TSCAN(1)	no change
Mode = maintenance Processing = idle HealthCheck = done There is an index *m* such that B/L[*m*] = *u* There is an index *n* such that B/L[*n*] = *d*	CDI, TGFu, TGFd	Mode := transmit

Table 14.18   Current stimulus: TC

Current State	Response	New State
Mode ≠ transmit	ERR	no change
Mode = transmit	TCFu, TCFd, TEFg	Mode := none HealthCheck := pending Connected := none*

Table 14.19   Current stimulus: OTE

Current State	Response	New State
Mode = none	null	no change
Mode = maintenance Processing = idle	null	no change
Mode = maintenance Processing = health HealthCheck = pending	HF	Processing := idle HealthCheck := done Good_Systems := { } Bad_Systems := { }

continued

Table 14.19 *continued*

Current State	Response	New State
Mode = maintenance Processing = firing HealthCheck = done	FF	Processing := idle Good_Systems := { } Bad_Systems := { }
Mode = transmit Connected = none	TSCAN(3), TCFu, TCFd	Mode := none HealthCheck := pending
Mode = transmit Connected = uplink	TSCAN(2), TCFu, TCΓd	Mode := none HealthCheck := pending Connected := none
Mode = transmit Connected = downlink	TSCAN(1), TCFu, TCFd	Mode := none HealthCheck := pending Connected := none
Mode – transmit (Connected = full *or* Connected = half)	null	no change

Table 14.20   Current stimulus: FSR

Current State	Response	New State
(Mode = none *or* Mode = transmit)	null	no change
Mode = maintenance Processing ≠ firing	null	no change
Mode = maintenance Processing = firing	FS	Processing := idle Good_Systems := { }* Bad_Systems := { }*

Table 14.21   Current stimulus: FFR

Current State	Response	New State
(Mode = none *or* Mode = transmit)	null	No change
Mode = maintenance Processing ≠ firing	null	No change
Mode = maintenance Processing = firing	FF	Processing := idle Good_Systems := { }* Bad_Systems := { }*

Table 14.22 Current stimulus: ISN(*x*)

Current State	Response	New State
Mode = none *or* Mode = transmit	null	no change
Mode = maintenance Processing ≠ health	null	no change
Mode = maintenance Processing = health Good_Systems ∪ Bad_Systems ≠ *Sys* – {*x*}	null	Good_Systems := Good_Systems ∪ {*x*}
Mode = maintenance Processing = health Good_Systems ∪ Bad_Systems = *Sys* – {*x*} Bad_Systems ≠ { }	HF	Processing := idle HealthCheck := done Good_Systems := { } Bad_Systems := { }
Mode = maintenance Processing = health Good_Systems = *Sys* – {*x*}	HS	Processing := idle HealthCheck := done Good_Systems := { } Bad_Systems := { }*

Table 14.23 Current stimulus: ISF(*x*)

Current State	Response	New State
Mode = none *or* Mode = transmit	null	no change
Mode = maintenance Processing ≠ health	null	no change
Mode = maintenance Processing = health Good_Systems ∪ Bad_Systems ≠ *Sys* – {*x*}	null	Bad_Systems := Bad_Systems ∪ {*x*}
Mode = maintenance Processing = health Good_Systems ∪ Bad_Systems = *Sys* – {*x*}	HF	Processing := idle HealthCheck := done Good_Systems := { } Bad_Systems := { }

Table 14.24   Current stimulus: UG

Current State	Response	New State
(Mode = none *or* Mode = maintenance)	null	no change
Mode = transmit Connected = none	null	Connected := uplink
Mode = transmit Connected ≠ none Connected ≠ downlink	null	no change
Mode = transmit Connected = downlink	SDT	Connected := full

Table 14.25   Current stimulus: DI

Current State	Response	New State
(Mode = none *or* Mode = maintenance)	null	no change
Mode = transmit Connected ≠ full Connected ≠ half	ERR	no change
Mode = transmit (Connected = full *or* Connected = half)	DO	no change

Table 14.26   Current stimulus: TE

Current State	Response	New State
(Mode = none *or* Mode = maintenance)	null	no change
Mode = transmit Connected = none	FEg	Mode := none HealthCheck := pending
Mode = transmit Connected = uplink	FEg, FEu	Mode := none HealthCheck := pending Connected := none
Mode = transmit Connected = downlink	FEg, FEd	Mode := none HealthCheck := pending Connected := none

Current State	Response	New State
Mode = transmit Connected = full	TEFd	Connected := half
Mode = transmit Connected = half	TEFd	no change

Table 14.27   Current stimulus: UB

Current State	Response	New State
(Mode = none *or* Mode = maintenance)	null	no change
Mode = transmit	TSCAN(1), TCFu, TCFd	Mode := none HealthCheck := pending Connected := none*

Table 14.28   Current stimulus: DG

Current State	Response	New State
(Mode = none *or* Mode = maintenance)	null	no change
Mode = transmit Connected = none	null	Connected := downlink
Mode = transmit Connected ≠ none Connected ≠ uplink	null	no change
Mode = transmit Connected = uplink	SDT	Connected := full

Table 14.29   Current stimulus: PB

Current State	Response	New State
(Mode = none *or* Mode = maintenance)	null	no change
Mode = transmit Connected ≠ full Connected ≠ half	ERR	no change
Mode = transmit (Connected = full *or* Connected = half)	PBF	no change

Table 14.30   Current stimulus: DTE

Current State	Response	New State
(Mode = none *or* Mode = maintenance)	null	no change
Mode = transmit Connected = none	FEg	Mode := none HealthCheck := pending
Mode = transmit Connected = uplink	FEg, FEu	Mode := none HealthCheck := pending Connected := none
Mode = transmit Connected = downlink	FEg, FEd	Mode := none HealthCheck := pending Connected := none
Mode = transmit Connected = full	FEg, FEu, FEd	Mode := none HealthCheck := pending Connected := none
Mode = transmit Connected = half	TEFu, TEFd	Mode := none HealthCheck := pending Connected := none

Table 14.31   Current stimulus: DB

Current State	Response	New State
(Mode = none *or* Mode = maintenance)	null	no change
Mode = transmit	TSCAN(2), TCFu, TCFd	Mode := none HealthCheck := pending Connected := none*

15

Satellite Control System Clear Box Design

15.1 Clear Box Implementation

Following the completion of the state-based specification, clear box procedures and algorithms can be developed to implement the state box. The fundamentals of clear box design were provided in Chapter 4.

A summary of the work flow used in the portion of the SOS implementation presented in this chapter is provided in the following list:

Step 1: Select a high-level software architecture.

Step 2: Select an implementation for stimulus gathering.

1. For each stimulus, elaborate specifically how the running software will obtain the stimulus.

2. Plan for interrupt handlers, callbacks, or other mechanisms required to get stimuli.

Step 3: Select an implementation for response generation.

1. For each response, elaborate specifically how the running software will generate the response.

Step 4: Select an implementation for the state data items.

Step 5: Select an implementation for each entry in the state box table.

1. Rewrite each cell of the state box tables using the chosen state implementations.

Step 6: Reorganize the implementations into executable code.

15.2 Step 1: Select a High-Level Software Architecture

15.2.1   Invocation and Termination

All software systems must deal with invocation; however, some software systems may be intended never to terminate. In the case of the SOS, termination of the embedded software is unacceptable.

Software invocation of the SOS happens whenever the system receives power. The B/L table need not be initialized because it will be stored in non-volatile memory, which is initialized prior to satellite launch. All other state data items will be reset to their initial values on invocation.

Because software termination is unacceptable, practitioners must consider each potential source of termination and exclude it. This includes ensuring that all software exceptions are caught, that power supplies are adequate and sufficiently responsive to changes in power demands, and that no execution path exists that exits or returns from the main program.

15.2.2   Target Hardware Architecture

The SOS will execute on a single processor on a Java virtual machine, and will be driven by hardware and software interrupts.

On software invocation, a Java virtual machine is started and the `main()` method of the Control object is invoked. The `main()` method first instantiates the interrupt handler (IH), then all other objects. Each object that is to process an interrupt registers itself during construction with the IH by invoking the `IH.addObserver()` method, telling it which interrupt it is interested in. When all objects are instantiated, the processor enters power save mode until an interrupt occurs. This start-up sequence is shown in Figure 15.1.

When an interrupt is generated by internal hardware (possibly in response to a signal from ground, uplink, or downlink) the processor is switched on and the `irqNotify()` method of the IH is invoked. The IH then invokes the `notify()` method of each object registered for the interrupt, in sequence. These objects may emit responses, invoke methods of other objects, and so on. When all registered objects have been notified and have completed execution, the IH returns and, if no further events are pending, the processor enters power save mode. The execution sequence is shown in Figure 15.2.

15.2.3   Hardware Interface

The hardware interfaces will be implemented by classes consisting only of static native methods (i.e., they need not be instantiated and are implemented in

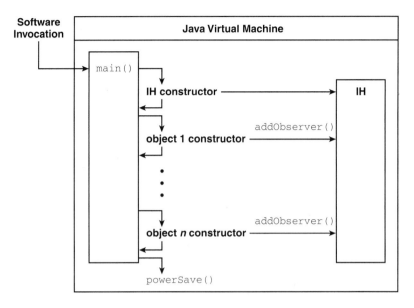

Figure 15.1   SOS start-up

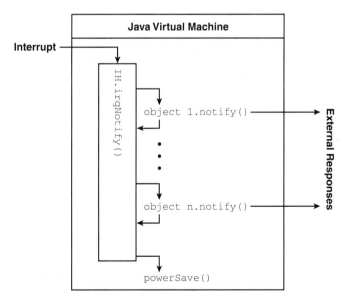

Figure 15.2   SOS execution

firmware). Only the classes, methods, variables, and constants required for the discussion are presented. All classes presented here are part of the `scs.kernel` package, and constitute the "operating system" for the satellite hardware. The reader may skip the class definitions here and return only as necessary to understand the software implementation.

Kernel Interface to the Impulse Control Subsystem (ICS).   The ICS is accessed through the methods of the ICS class.

```
// Impulse control subsystem interface.

package scs.kernel;

/** This class encapsulates the low-level interface to the impulse
    control subsystem. */
public final class ICS {
    // This class has no constructor.
    // All methods are class methods.

    /** Request firing. The controller hardware must have been armed
        first. Success or failure is reported through a hardware
        interrupt after the firing is completed.
        @param pitch The change in pitch (wrt SV body).
        @param yaw The change in yaw (wrt SV body).
        @param roll The change in roll (wrt SV body). */
    public static native void fire(double pitch, double yaw, double roll);

    /** Arm the reaction control hardware for a firing. The hardware
        is disarmed at the end of the firing. */
    public static native void arm();

    /** Return current status. See the constants defined in this class
        for the various possible return values.
        @return Current status of impulse control system. */
    public static native int getStatus();
    // The following are public class constants that define
    // the various possible statuses of the impulse control
    // subsystem, as reported by the getStatus() method.
    // These must be the same as the native code.
    public static final int SUCCESS = 0;
    public static final int FAILURE = 1;
    public static final int NOT_READY = 2;
    public static final int IN_PROGRESS = 3;
}
```

Kernel Interrupt Controller Interface.   The Interrupt class encapsulates all low-level interrupt handling.

```
// Interrupt handler.

package scs.kernel;

import java.util.Vector;

/** This class encapsulates the low-level interrupt controller
    interface. */
public final class Interrupt {
    // This class has no constructors.
    // All methods are class methods.

    /** Set the interrupt vector to the irqNotify() method
        of an object. The object must implement the IRQObserver
        interface.
        @param o The object to notify.
        @return The previously stored vector as a long. */
    public static native long setIRQVector(IRQObserver o);

    /** This interface must be implemented by any object that wishes
        to have interrupt events vectored to it. */
    public interface IRQObserver {
        /** Notify an object that an interrupt has occurred. */
        public void irqNotify();
    }

    /** Push the specified value onto the return stack so that
        the next return directs control to the address specified
        by the argument.
        @param v The address as a long. */
    public static native long redirectStack(long v);

    /** Get the type of the most recent IRQ event.
        @return The most recent IRQ event type. */
    public static native int getIRQID();

    /** Get any arguments for the most recent IRQ event. These
        will be stored in a Java vector.
        @return A Java Vector that holds the arguments, or null
        if there are no arguments. */
    public static native Vector getIRQArguments();
```

```
/** Return true if the most recent interrupt is a maskable hardware
    interrupt. Return false if the most recent interrupt is a
    nonmaskable interrupt (NMI) or a software interrupt (SWI).
    @return True if the last interrupt is a hardware interrupt. */
public static native boolean isHWI();

/** Return true if the most recent interrupt is a software
    interrupt.
    @return True if the last interrupt is a software interrupt. */
public static native boolean isSWI();

/** Schedule a timer event.
    @param o The object requesting the timer event. The object must
    implement the TimerObserver interface.
    @param c The number of milliseconds from now to generate the
    timer event. */
public static native void scheduleTimer(TimerObserver o, long c);

/** This interface must be implemented by any object that wishes
    to receive timer events. */
public interface TimerObserver {
    /** Notify the caller that a requested timer has expired. */
    public void timerNotify();
}

/** Clear any scheduled timer events. */
public static native void resetTimer();

// The following are public class constants that define
// the various types of interrupt events. These values
// should be used for the irqid.
public static final int HWI_TRANSMIT_GROUND = 0x00010001;
public static final int HWI_TRANSMIT_UPLINK = 0x00010002;
public static final int HWI_TRANSMIT_DOWNLINK = 0x00010003;
public static final int HWI_DATA_RECEIVED = 0x00020001;
public static final int HWI_FIRING_COMPLETE = 0x00030005;
public static final int HWI_ONBOARD_TIMER_EXPIRED = 0x00050001;
public static final int HWI_INTERNAL_SUBSYSTEM_NOMINAL = 0x00000001;
public static final int HWI_INTERNAL_SUBSYSTEM_FAILURE = 0x00000002;
}
```

Kernel Interface to the System Data Bus for Internal Messaging

```
// Handle internal messaging.

package scs.kernel;

import java.util.Vector;

/** This class encapsulates access to the internal data bus. */
public final class Message {
    // This class has no constructor.
    // All methods are class methods.

    /** Set all lines high to signal system initialization to all
        devices on the bus. This method may only be used if the
        bus has been captured; otherwise it will be ignored. */
    public static native void initialize();

    /** Capture the bus. Other devices are forbidden to send signals on
        the bus during a capture. */
    public static native void capture();

    /** Release the bus. Devices may resume signaling on the bus. */
    public static native void release();

    /** Send a message on the bus. No capture is required.
        @param id The id of the device or group to which the message
        is being sent.
        @param message The message to be sent. */
    public static native void send(long id, long message);

    // The following are public class constants that define
    // the various destinations for messages and the messages
    // themselves.
    public static final long BROADCAST = 0x80000000;// Send to everyone.
    public static final long HEALTH_TEST = 0x00000001;
}
```

Kernel Nonvolatile Memory Manager

```
// Nonvolatile Memory Manager Interface

package scs.kernel;

import java.util.Vector;
```

```
/** This class encapsulates the nonvolatile memory manager. */
public final class NVMM {
    // This class has no constructor.
    // All methods are class methods.

    /** Put information into nonvolatile memory, associating it with
        both a string and an integer. The integer must be unique; if
        there is already an item associated with the integer, it will
        be overwritten.
        @param id The unique integer identifying this item.
        @param name A (possibly nonunique) name for this item.
        @param o The data to store. */
    public static native void put(long id, String name, Object o);

    /** Get the data item for a given id. If the id does not exist,
        null is returned.
        @param id The unique integer identifying the item.
        @return The item, if found, and null if not. */
    public static native Object getData(long id);

    /** Get the name for a given data item. If no matching item is
        found, null is returned.
        @param id The unique integer identifying the item.
        @return The item's name, if found, and null if not. */
    public static native String getName(long id);

    /** Get a data item for a given string. The id of the first matching
        item is returned. If no matching item is found, null is
        returned.
        @param name The name to find.
        @return The unique id of a data item with the specified name,
        or a negative value if none can be found. */
    public static native long search(String name);
}
```

Kernel Interface to Transmitter Hardware

```
// Transmitter hardware interface.

package scs.kernel;

import java.util.Vector;

/** This class encapsulates the low-level transmitter hardware
    interface. */
```

```java
public final class Transmit {
    // This class has no constructor.
    // All methods are class methods.

    /** Transmit a stream of bytes to the selected destination.
        An interrupt will be generated when transmit is completed.
        @see scs.kernel.Interrupt for interrupt information.
        @param data The data to send.
        @param count The number of bytes in the data. */
    public static native void transmit(byte[] data, long count);

    /** Select a particular destination for future transmit requests.
        @param i The destination, provided by one of the constants
        defined in this class. */
    public static native void select(int i);

    /** Specify uplink site information. The transmit hardware will
        attempt to locate and establish communication with the uplink
        site, which should then send either UG or UB.
        @param si The site information. */
    public static native void setUplink(SiteInfo si);

    /** Specify downlink site information. The transmit hardware will
        attempt to locate and establish communication with the downlink
        site, which should then send either DG or DB.
        @param si The site information. */
    public static native void setDownlink(SiteInfo si);

    /** A class for encapsulating all necessary site information. */
    public final class SiteInfo;

    /** Forget the uplink site connection. */
    public static native void detachUplink();

    /** Forget the downlink site connection. */
    public static native void detachDownlink();

    // The following are public class constants that define the
    // various destinations for transmit. These values should be
    // used with the select() method.
    public static final int GROUND = 0;
    public static final int UPLINK = 1;
    public static final int DOWNLINK = 2;
}
```

15.2.4   Software Architecture

The software implementation will be a Java application. It is assumed that sufficient prototyping work has been done to ensure that all processing speed, response time, capacity, and precision requirements can be met. All data flow will be push, based on the observer design pattern, with only a few exceptions for state-encapsulating objects such as Mode.

The SOS will be implemented using a single-threaded architecture. Object creation will be tightly constrained so that memory management issues are minimized. The incoming data stream is read by hardware decoders, which queue their input until it can be processed. This is not expected to be a problem because processor speeds far outstrip maximum transmission bandwidth.

The state machine represented by the state box will be allocated to several top-level classes. These are described in Table 15.1. Following the table is the Java code for each class. Most of these classes are incomplete. The behavioral information from the state box tables will be merged with the architectural information to complete the definitions by implementing each of the methods.

Table 15.1   Top-level classes

Object Name	Description
IH	Handles all interrupts and dispatches events to registered callers.
Control	Manages invocation and sets up interrupt handling.
Mode	Preserves the mode globally. This class maintains the mode in a class variable accessible everywhere through class accessor and mutator methods.
HealthCheck	The HealthCheck object administers the health check via the interrupts passed to it from the IH.
BLTable	The BLTable object handles all updates to the B/L table stored in nonvolatile memory.
FiringControl	The FiringControl object handles all firing requests.
Connection	The Connection class handles construction of a new connection as well as shutdown of an existing connection. In addition, the Connection class will handle events that change mode (such as IN and MG).
PacketParser	The PacketParser object transforms information from the receiver hardware into packets for consumption by the other classes. It receives hardware interrupts from the IH and generates software interrupts.
PacketScheduler	The PacketScheduler object handles sending of packets to uplink, downlink, and ground sites.

Class: scs.sos.IH

```
// Interrupt handler.

package scs.sos;

import java.util.Vector;
import java.util.Hashtable;
import java.util.Enumeration;
import scs.kernel.Interrupt;

/** This class is the "top level" of the SOS. Interrupt events (stimuli)
    arrive here and are dispatched to the appropriate class. */
public final class IH implements Interrupt.IRQObserver {
    /** Construct a new interrupt handler and install it as a "wedge." */
    public IH() {
        // Install the interrupt handler, saving the previous vector.
        oldvector = Interrupt.setIRQVector(this);
    }


    /** Register an object to receive forwarded interrupt events.
        @param o The object wishing to receive event notification.
        This object must implement the InterruptObserver interface.
        @param irqid The event (from constants defined in the
        Interrupt class or here). */
    public void addObserver(InterruptObserver o, int irqid) {
        // Change the irqid into a Java object so we can get its
        // hash code.
        Integer Irqid = new Integer(irqid);

        // Get the list of registered observers from the hash table.
        Vector obs = (Vector)registry.get(Irqid);
        if(obs == null) {
            // The list of observers is empty. Create a new list.
            obs = new Vector();
            registry.put(Irqid, obs);
        }

        // Add this object to the list of observers.
        obs.addElement(o);
    }


    /** This interface must be implemented by any object wishing to
        receive interrupt notification. */
```

```java
public interface InterruptObserver {
    /** This method is invoked to notify an object that an event
        has occurred.
        @param irqid The event type (from the constants defined
        in the Interrupt class or here).
        @param args A Vector of any additional arguments for the
        event, or null if none. */
    public void notify(int irqid, Vector args);
}

/** Interrupts are directed here. This code then dispatches the
    event to the appropriate object(s). */
public void irqNotify() {
    // Get the interrupt id.
    int irqid = Interrupt.getIRQID();

    // Get any arguments for the interrupt.
    Vector args = Interrupt.getIRQArguments();

    // Now get the list of observers for this event.
    Integer Irqid = new Integer(irqid);
    Vector obs = (Vector)registry.get(Irqid);
    if(obs != null) {
        // There are observers for this event. Notify all
        // of them.
        Enumeration e = obs.elements();
        while(e.hasMoreElements()) {
            // Notify an observer.
            InterruptObserver o = (InterruptObserver)e.nextElement();
            o.notify(irqid, args);
        }
    }

    // Now return control to the previously installed interrupt
    // handler.
    Interrupt.redirectStack(oldvector);
}

// Private data.
private long oldvector = 0;
private Hashtable registry = new Hashtable();

// The following are public class constants that define
// the various types of software interrupts. These values
```

```
    // are defined here because the kernel doesn't know about
    // software interrupts.
    public static final int SWI_IN = 0x0001F001;
    public static final int SWI_HR = 0x0001F002;
    public static final int SWI_MG = 0x0001F003;
    public static final int SWI_BR = 0x0001F004;
    public static final int SWI_FR = 0x0001F005;
    public static final int SWI_TG = 0x0001F006;
    public static final int SWI_TC = 0x0001F007;
    public static final int SWI_UG = 0x0002F001;
    public static final int SWI_DI = 0x0002F002;
    public static final int SWI_TE = 0x0002F003;
    public static final int SWI_UB = 0x0002F004;
    public static final int SWI_DG = 0x0003F001;
    public static final int SWI_PB = 0x0003F002;
    public static final int SWI_DTE = 0x0003F003;
    public static final int SWI_DB = 0x0003F004;
}
```

Class: scs.sos.Control

```
// Start-up for SOS.

package scs.sos;

/** This class starts execution of the SOS by installing the
    interrupt handler. */
public final class Control {
    // This class has no constructor.
    // All methods are class methods.

    /** This is the main method, which executes on start-up. It
        creates and installs the interrupt handler, then creates
        all other required objects. */
    public static void main() {
        // Create a new interrupt handler. The constructor installs
        // the interrupt handler.
        IH ih = new IH();
    }
}
```

Class: scs.sos.Mode

```
// The systemwide mode.
```

```
package scs.sos;

/** This class encapsulates the state data item Mode. */
public final class Mode {
    // This class has no constructor.
    // All methods are class methods.

    /** Set the system mode.
        @param m The new mode, from the constants defined in this class. */
    public static void setMode(int m) {
        mode = m;
    }

    /** Get the system mode.
        @return One of the constants defined in this class. */
    public static int getMode() {
        return mode;
    }

    // The following are public class constants that define the
    // various system modes.
    public static final int NONE = 0;
    public static final int MAINTENANCE = 1;
    public static final int TRANSMIT = 2;

    // A private class variable that holds the current mode.
    private static int mode = NONE;
}
```

Class: scs.sos.HealthCheck

```
// Administer the health check.

package scs.sos;

/** This class administers the health check through
    interrupts. */
public final class HealthCheck
  implements IH.InterruptObserver {

  /** Interrupt notification arrives here.
      @param irqid The interrupt id.
      @param args Any arguments associated with the interrupt. */
```

```
public void notify(long irqid, Vector args);
// Will be implemented later.

/** Force the health check object to reset its state and halt
    any current checks. */
public void reset(); // Will be implemented later.

/** Return the current status of the health check.
    @return The current status as one of the class constants. */
public int getStatus(); // Will be implemented later.

// These are public class constants that define the statuses for
// the HealthCheck object.
public static final int PENDING = 0;
public static final int PROCESSING = 1;
public static final int COMPLETE = 2;
}
```

Class: scs.sos.BLTable

```
// Manage the B/L table.

package scs.sos;

/** This class manages the B/L table updates and accesses. */
public final class BLTable
  implements IH.InterruptObserver {
  /** Interrupt notification arrives here.
      @param irqid The interrupt id.
      @param args Any arguments associated with the interrupt. */
  public void notify(long irqid, Vector args);
  // Will be implemented later.

  /** Request for a B/L entry for a site. If there is an entry, the
      site data is returned. Otherwise, null is returned. */
  public Transmit.SiteInfo findSite(String name) {
    // Look for the site.
    long id = NVMM.search(name);
    if(id < 0) return null;

    // Return the site information.
    return (Transmit.SiteInfo)NVMM.getData(id);
  }
}
```

Class: scs.sos.FiringControl

```
// Handle thruster firings.

package scs.sos;

/** This class handles thruster firing requests. */
public final class FiringControl
  implements IH.InterruptObserver {
  /** Interrupt notification arrives here.
      @param irqid The interrupt id.
      @param args Any arguments associated with the interrupt. */
  public void notify(long irqid, Vector args);
  // Will be implemented later.
  /** Force the firing control object to reset its state and halt
      any firings. */
  public void reset(); // Will be implemented later.
}
```

Class: scs.sos.Connection

```
// Manage the connection.

package scs.sos;

/** This class manages the connection. */
public final class Connection
  implements IH.InterruptObserver {
  /** Interrupt notification arrives here.
      @param irqid The interrupt id.
      @param args Any arguments associated with the interrupt. */
  public void notify(long irqid, Vector args);
  // Will be implemented later.
}
```

Class: scs.sos.PacketParser

```
// Parse incoming packets.

package scs.sos;

/** This class parses the incoming data streams into packets, and
    then generates appropriate software interrupts. */
public final class PacketParser
  implements IH.InterruptObserver {
```

```
    /** Interrupt notification arrives here.
        @param irqid The interrupt id.
        @param args Any arguments associated with the interrupt. */
    public void notify(long irqid, Vector args);
    // Will be implemented later.
}
```

Class: scs.sos.PacketScheduler

```
// Schedule packets to be sent.

package scs.sos;

import scs.kernel.Transmit;
import scs.kernel.Interrupt;
import scs.kernel.Queue;
import java.io.ByteArrayOutputStream;
import java.io.ObjectOutputStream;
import java.util.Vector;

/** This class handles construction and transmit of packages to
    the uplink / downlink / ground. */
public final class PacketScheduler implements IH.InterruptObserver {
    // This class uses the default constructor.

    /** Interrupt notification arrives here.
        @param irqid The interrupt id.
        @param args Any arguments associated with the interrupt. */
    public void notify(int irqid, Vector args) {
        // See what happenned.
        Queue q = null;
        int destination = 0;
        if(irqid == Interrupt.HWI_TRANSMIT_DOWNLINK) {
            q = downlink;
            destination = Transmit.DOWNLINK;
        }
        else if(irqid == Interrupt.HWI_TRANSMIT_UPLINK) {
            q = uplink;
            destination = Transmit.UPLINK;
        }
        else if(irqid == Interrupt.HWI_TRANSMIT_GROUND) {
            q = ground;
            destination = Transmit.GROUND;
        }
```

```
        else return;

        // A packet was just sent. See if another
        // packet is waiting to be sent to the same
        // destination.
        q.pop();
        if(!q.isEmpty()) {
            // Another packet is waiting to be sent. Send it now.
            Transmit.select(destination);
            Transmit.transmit(
                ((ByteArrayOutputStream)q.next()).toByteArray(),
                ((ByteArrayOutputStream)q.next()).size());
        }
    }

/** Construct and queue a packet for transmit.
    @param destination The destination of the packet, from
    the constants defined in Transmit.
    @param type The type of packet to send, from the constants
    defined in this class.
    @param args Any additional arguments to include in the packet. */
public void send(long destination, long type, Vector args) {
        // Figure out the destination.
        Queue q = null;
        if(destination == Transmit.DOWNLINK) q = downlink;
        else if(destination == Transmit.UPLINK) q = uplink;
        else if(destination == Transmit.GROUND) q = ground;
        else // Can't send; ignore request.
            return;

        // This serializes each of the objects to a byte output stream.
        // This will be correctly handled by the kernel transmit method.
        ByteArrayOutputStream baos = new ByteArrayOutputStream();

        // Wrap the stream in an object output stream.
        ObjectOutputStream oos = null;
        try {
            oos = new ObjectOutputStream(baos);

            // Write the packet type.
            oos.writeLong(type);

            // Now write the arguments.
```

```
                oos.writeObject(args);
        }
        catch(Exception e) {
            // If there is an exception, then just ignore the packet.
            return;
        }

        // If the appropriate queue is empty, this data can be
        // sent now.
        // Otherwise, just queue it. Packets are dequeued only
        // after being sent.
        if(q.isEmpty()) {
            q.push(baos);
            Transmit.transmit(baos.toByteArray(), baos.size());
        }
        else {
            q.push(baos);
        }
    }

    // Private queues.
    Queue downlink = new Queue();
    Queue uplink = new Queue();
    Queue ground = new Queue();

    // The following are public class constants that define the
    // various types of packets that can be sent.
    public static final long INA   = 0x00010000;
    public static final long HF    = 0x00010001;
    public static final long HS    = 0x00010002;
    public static final long FF    = 0x00010003;
    public static final long FS    = 0x00010004;
    public static final long TSCAN = 0x00010005;
    public static final long TEF   = 0x00070001;
    public static final long ERR   = 0x00010006;
    public static final long FE    = 0x00010007;
    public static final long TGF   = 0x00070002;
    public static final long SDT   = 0x00020001;
    public static final long TCF   = 0x00060001;
    public static final long PBF   = 0x00020002;
    public static final long DO    = 0x00040001;
}
```

15.3 Step 2: Select an Implementation for Stimulus Gathering

The list of stimuli to the SOS is provided in Table 15.2, along with the mechanism by which the stimulus will be collected. Each stimulus from the GCS, UL, or DL is actually a packet that contains security information (to avoid unauthorized access to the satellite), and any required parameters. The design of the packet parser is beyond the scope of this case study, but is a well-studied problem (there are many powerful parser generators available, including JavaCC for developing Java parsers—it is seldom necessary to create such a parser from scratch). The packet parser will be driven by hardware interrupts from the decoders.

Table 15.2   Stimuli and stimulus gathering

Stimulus	Stimulus-Gathering Mechanism
Stimuli received from GCS	
IN	Processor power-on vector stored in read-only memory, and message from ground site decoded through the PacketParser and made available as software interrupt `IH.SWI_IN`.
HR	Message from ground decoded through PacketParser and made available as software interrupt `IH.SWI_HR`.
MG	Message from ground decoded through PacketParser and made available as software interrupt `IH.SWI_MG`.
BR(*i, s*)	Message from ground decoded through PacketParser and made available as software interrupt `IH.SWI_BR` with arguments *i* and *s*.
FR(*p, y, r*)	Message from ground decoded through PacketParser and made available as software interrupt `IH.SWI_FR` with arguments *p, y,* and *r*.
TG(*u, d*)	Message from ground decoded through PacketParser and made available as software interrupt `IH.SWI_TG` with arguments *u* and *d*.
TC	Message from ground decoded through PacketParser and made available as software interrupt `IH.SWI_TC`.
Stimuli received from on-board subsystems	
OTE	Implemented by internal hardware interrupt `Interrupt.HWI_ONBOARD_TIMER_EXPIRED`. When the timer interrupt occurs, the kernel IH will pass control to the requesting object. If no object has requested the timer, the kernel IH will ignore the event per requirement 1.2.4.

Stimulus	Stimulus-Gathering Mechanism
Stimuli received from on-board subsystems	
FSR FFR	Implemented by internal hardware interrupt `Interrupt.HWI_FIRING_COMPLETE.` If `ICS.getStatus()` returns `SUCCESS`, FSR is intended; if `ICS.getStatus()` does not return `SUCCESS`, FFR is intended.
ISN(*id*)	Implemented by internal hardware interrupt `Interrupt.HWI_INTERNAL_SUBSYSTEM_NOMINAL` with argument *id*.
ISF(*id*)	Implemented by internal hardware interrupt `Interrupt.HWI_INTERNAL_SUBSYSTEM_FAILURE` with argument *id*.
Stimuli received from UL	
UG	Message from uplink decoded through PacketParser and made available as software interrupt `IH.SWI_UG`.
DI(*id, p*)	Message from uplink decoded through PacketParser and made available as software interrupt `IH.SWI_DI` with arguments *id* and *p*.
TE	Message from uplink decoded through PacketParser and made available as software interrupt `IH.SWI_TE`.
UB	Message from uplink decoded through PacketParser and made available as software interrupt `IH.SWI_UB`.
Stimuli received from DL	
DG	Message from downlink decoded through PacketParser and made available as software interrupt `IH.SWI_DG`.
PB(*id*)	Message from downlink decoded through PacketParser and made available as software interrupt `IH.SWI_PB` with argument *id*.
DTE	Message from downlink decoded through PacketParser and made available as software interrupt `IH.SWI_DTE`.
DB	Message from downlink decoded through PacketParser and made available as software interrupt `IH.SWI_DB`.

15.4. Step 3: Select an Implementation for Response Generation

The list of SOS responses is provided in Table 15.3 along with a description of how each response will be generated by the running software.

Table 15.3 Responses and response generation

Response	Response Generation Mechanism
Responses to GCS	
INA	The INA message will be sent to the GCS via the `PacketScheduler.send(Transmit.GROUND, PacketScheduler.INA, null)` method.
HF	The HF message will be sent to the GCS via the `PacketScheduler.send(Transmit.GROUND, PacketScheduler.HF, l)` method, where `l` is a vector composed of the lists of subsystems reporting a successful health check and the list of subsystems reporting a failed health check.
HS	The HS message will be sent to the GCS via the `PacketScheduler.send(Transmit.GROUND, PacketScheduler.HS, null)` method.
FF	The FF message will be sent to the GCS via the `PacketScheduler.send(Transmit.GROUND, PacketScheduler.FF, null)` method.
FS	The FS message will be sent to the GCS via the `PacketScheduler.send(Transmit.GROUND, PacketScheduler.FS, null)` method.
TSCAN(n)	The TSCAN message will be sent to the GCS via the `PacketScheduler.send(Transmit.GROUND, PacketScheduler.TSCAN, n)` method, where `n` is a vector containing one of the values 1, 2, or 3.
TEFg	The TEF message will be sent to the GCS via the `PacketScheduler.send(Transmit.GROUND, PacketScheduler.TEF, null)` method.
ERR	The ERR message will be sent to the GCS via the `PacketScheduler.send(Transmit.GROUND, PacketScheduler.ERR, null)` method.
FEg	The FE message will be sent to the GCS via the `PacketScheduler.send(Transmit.GROUND, PacketScheduler.FE, null)` method.
Responses to on-board subsystems	
CDI(d)	The CDI message will be sent to the on-board countdown timer via invocation of the `Interrupt.scheduleTimer(caller, d)` method of the kernel IH, where d is the requested duration, and `caller` is the object requesting the countdown. The object `caller` must implement the `Interrupt.TimerObserver` interface.
HT	The HT command is sent to all subsystems by the `Message.send(Message.BROADCAST, Message.HEALTH_TEST)` kernel method.

Response	Response Generation Mechanism
Responses to on-board subsystems	
FRF(*p, y, r*)	The FRF command is sent to the impulse control hardware via the `ICS.arm()` and the `ICS.fire(p, y, r)` kernel methods.
Responses to UL	
TGFu	The TGF command is sent to the UL by the `PacketScheduler.send(Transmit.UPLINK, PacketScheduler.TGF, null)` method.
SDT	The SDT command is sent to the UL by the `PacketScheduler.send(Transmit.UPLINK, PacketScheduler.SDT, null)` method.
TCFu	The TCF command is sent to the UL by the `PacketScheduler.send(Transmit.UPLINK, PacketScheduler.TCF, null)` method.
TEFu	The TEF command is sent to the UL by the `PacketScheduler.send(Transmit.UPLINK, PacketScheduler.TEF, null)` method.
PBF(*id*)	The PBF command is sent to the UL by the `PacketScheduler.send(Transmit.UPLINK, PacketScheduler.PBF, id)` method, where `id` is a vector containing the packet identifier of the bad packet.
FEu	The FE message is sent to the UL by the `PacketScheduler.send(Transmit.UPLINK, PacketScheduler.FE, null)` method.
Responses to DL	
TGFd	The TGF command is sent to the DL by the `PacketScheduler.send(Transmit.DOWNLINK, PacketScheduler.TGF, null)` method.
TCFd	The TCF command is sent to the DL by the `PacketScheduler.send(Transmit.DOWNLINK, PacketScheduler.TCF, null)` method.
TEFd	The TEF command is sent to the DL by the `PacketScheduler.send(Transmit.DOWNLINK, PacketScheduler.TEF, null)` method.
DO(*id, p*)	The DO command is sent to the DL by the `PacketScheduler.send(Transmit.DOWNLINK, PacketScheduler.DO, x)` method, where `x` is a vector containing `id` and `p`.
FEd	The FE message is sent to the DL by the `PacketScheduler.send(Transmit.DOWNLINK, PacketScheduler.FE, null)` method.

15.5 Step 4: Select an Implementation for the State Data Items

15.5.1 Allocation of Data to Objects

The state data items may now be allocated to the objects (Table 15.4). All access to the encapsulated state will be through accessor and mutator methods (there are no public variables).

Table 15.4   State data allocation to objects

State Data Item	Owner
Mode	Mode class
Processing	HealthCheck object FiringControl object
HealthCheck	HealthCheck object
Connected	Connection object
B/L[n]	BLTable object
Good_Systems	HealthCheck object
Bad_Systems	HealthCheck object

15.5.2 State Tests and Updates

Every case of a test of state data or an update to state data must be accounted for (Table 15.5). State data items have been migrated to objects and, in some cases, completely hidden from the top level.

Table 15.5   State data access and modification

State Data Item	Testing	Updating
Mode	`Mode.getMode()`	`Mode.setMode()`
Processing	`HealthCheck.getStatus()` `ICS.getStatus()`	`HealthCheck.reset()` sets to pending; otherwise, maintained internally by the HealthCheck object. `FiringControl.reset()` sets to idle; otherwise, maintained internally by the ICS kernel class object.

State Data Item	Testing	Updating
HealthCheck	`HealthCheck.getStatus()`	`HealthCheck.reset()` sets to pending; otherwise, maintained internally by the HealthCheck object.
Connected	Maintained internally by the Connection object. No public access required.	Handled internally by the Connection object.
Good_Systems	Maintained internally by the HealthCheck object. No public access required.	Handled internally by the HealthCheck object.
Bad_Systems	Maintained internally by the HealthCheck object. No public access required.	Handled internally by the HealthCheck object.
B/L	`BLTable.get()`	Handled internally by the BLTable object.

15.6 Step 5: Select an Implementation for Each Entry in the State Box Table

Each of the state box tables can now be rewritten as Java code based on the chosen implementation. Each stimulus implementation has been chosen, and each state data item is encapsulated in an object. The behavior described by each state box table is now allocated to an object. Additional object constraints are indicated in a Notes section in Tables 15.6 through 15.25, as appropriate. Each cell of the table must be verified against the corresponding state box cell (which is the intended function) to ensure correctness.

Table 15.6 Current stimulus: IN Implemented in `Connection.notify()` with `irqid == SWI_IN`

Current State	Response	State Update

any	`// Initialize hardware.`
	`Message.capture();`
	`Message.initialize();`
	`Message.release();`
	
	`// Send INA.`
	`this.ps.send(Transmit.GROUND,`
	`    PacketScheduler.INA,null);`
		`// Set Mode to none.`
		`Mode.setMode(Mode.NONE);`
		
		`// Set Processing to idle,`
		`// and HealthCheck to`
		`// pending, and both`
		`//; Good_Systems and`
		`//; Bad_Systems to {}.`
		`this.fc.reset();`
		`this.hc.reset();`
		
		`//; Set Connected to none.`
		`this.conn = Connection.NONE;`

Notes: The PacketScheduler, FiringControl, and HealthCheck objects will be provided to the Connection object constructor, and will be maintained in private instance variables—*ps*, *fc*, and *hc* respectively.

The connection status will be maintained as a local variable, *conn*, with values equal to the class constants NONE, UPLINK, DOWNLINK, FULL, and HALF.

Table 15.7 Current stimulus: HR
Implemented by `HealthCheck.notify()` with `irqid == SWI_HR`

Current State	Response	State Update

`Mode.getMode() != Mode.MAINTENANCE ||`
`this.getStatus() == HealthCheck.PROCESSING ||`
`ICS.getStatus() == ICS.IN_PROGRESS`
	`// Send ERR to GCS.`
	`this.ps.send (`
	`    Transmit.GROUND,`
	`    PacketScheduler.ERR, null);`
		no change

`Mode.getMode() == Mode.MAINTENANCE &&`
`this.getStatus() != HealthCheck.PROCESSING &&`
`ICS.getStatus() != ICS.IN_PROGRESS`
	`// Send the health test.`
	`Message.send (`
	`    Message.BROADCAST,`
	`    Message.HEALTH_TEST);`
	
	`// Initialize the`
	`// countdown timer.`
	`Interrupt.scheduleTimer (`
	`    this,`
	`    HealthCheck.HCTIME);`
		`// Set the`
		`// HealthCheck to`
		`// pending and`
		`// Processing to`
		`// health.`
		`this.status =`
		`    HealthCheck.PROCESSING;`
		
		`// Set both`
		`// Good_Systems`
		`// and`
		`// Bad_Systems`
		`// to {}.`
		`this.good = new Vector();`
		`this.bad = new Vector();`

Notes: The PacketScheduler object will be provided to the HealthCheck object constructor and will be maintained in private instance variable *ps*.

HCTIME will be a class constant equal to the number of milliseconds allowed for a health test.

The HealthCheck object will maintain a private instance variable status that will hold the current health check status, and private instance variables *good* and *bad*, which will hold the list of subsystems reporting good health and bad health respectively.

Table 15.8 Current stimulus: MG
Implemented in `Connection.notify()` with `irqid == SWI_MG`

Current State	Response	State Update
`Mode.getMode() == Mode.NONE`	`null`	`Mode.setMode(Mode.MAINTENANCE);`

`Mode.getMode() != Mode.NONE`	`// Send ERR to GCS.`
	`this.ps.send(`
	`Transmit.GROUND, PacketScheduler.ERR null);`
		no change

Table 15.9 Current stimulus: BR(*n, s*)
Implemented in `BLTable.notify()` with `irqid == SWI_BR` and `args == (n, s)`

Current State	Response	State Update

`Mode.getMode() ==Mode.NONE ||`
`Mode.getMode() ==Mode.TRANSMIT`
	`// Send ERR to GCS`
	`this.ps.send(`
	`Transmit.GROUND, PacketScheduler.ERR, null);`
		no change

`Mode.getMode() == Mode.MAINTENANCE &&`
`(this.hc.getStatus() !=`
`HealthCheck.COMPLETE ||`
`ICS.getStatus() == ICS.IN_PROGRESS)`
	`// Send ERR to GCS`
	`this.ps.send(`
	`Transmit.GROUND,`
	`PacketScheduler.ERR, null);`
		no change

`Mode.getMode() ==Mode.MAINTENANCE &&`
`this.hc.getStatus() ==`
`HealthCheck.COMPLETE &&`
`ICS.getStatus() != ICS.IN_PROGRESS`
	`// Send BRA to GCS`
	`this.ps.send(`
	`Transmit.GROUND,`
	`PacketScheduler.BRA,`
	`null);`
		`// Save the data`
		`// in the B/L`
		`// table.`
		`NVMM.put(n,`
		`s.getName(), s);`
		
		`// The n and s are`
		`// obtained from`
		`// the argsVector.`

Notes: The PacketScheduler and HealthCheck objects will be provided to the BLTable object constructor and stored in private instance variables *ps* and *hc* respectively.

Table 15.10 Current stimulus: FR(*p, y, r*)
Implemented in `FiringControl.notify` with `irqid == SWI_FR` and `args == (`*p, y, r*`)`

Current State	Response	State Update

`Mode.getMode() == Mode.NONE ||`
`Mode.getMode() == Mode.TRANSMIT`
	`// Send ERR to GCS`
	`this.ps.send(`
	`Transmit.GROUND, PacketScheduler.ERR, null);`
		no change

`Mode.getMode() == Mode.MAINTENANCE &&`
`(this.hc.getStatus() !=`
`HealthCheck.COMPLETE ||`
`ICS.getStatus() == ICS.IN_PROGRESS)`
	`// Send ERR to GCS`
	`this.ps.send(`
	`Transmit.GROUND, PacketScheduler.ERR, null);`
		no change

`Mode.getMode() == Mode.MAINTENANCE &&`
`this.hc.getStatus() ==`
`HealthCheck.COMPLETE &&`
`ICS.getStatus() != ICS.IN_PROGRESS`
	`// Send FRF to ICS.`
	`ICS.arm();`
	`ICS.fire(p,y,r);`
	`// Initialize the`
	`// countdown timer.`
	`Interrupt.scheduleTimer(`
	`this, FiringControl.FRTIME);`
		no change
		
		(ICS will change status.)

Notes: The PacketScheduler and HealthCheck objects will be provided to the BLTable object constructor and stored in private instance variables *ps* and *hc* respectively.

FRTIME will be a class constant equal to the number of milliseconds allowed for a firing.

Table 15.11 Current stimulus: TG(*u, d*)
Implemented in `Connection.notify()` with `irqid == SWI_TG` and `args == (u, d)`

Current State	Response	State Update

`Mode.getMode() == Mode.NONE ||`
`Mode.getMode() == Mode.TRANSMIT`
	`// Send ERR to GCS`
	`this.ps.send(`
	  `Transmit.GROUND, PacketScheduler.ERR, null);`
		no change

`Mode.getMode() == Mode.MAINTENANCE &&`
`(this.hc.getStatus() !=`
  `HealthCheck.COMPLETE ||`
`ICS.getStatus() == ICS.IN_PROGRESS)`
	`// Send ERR to GCS`
	`this.ps.send(`
	  `Transmit.GROUND, PacketScheduler.ERR, null);`
		no change

`Mode.getMode() == Mode.MAINTENANCE &&`
`this.hc.getStatus() ==`
  `HealthCheck.COMPLETE &&`
`ICS.getStatus() != ICS.IN_PROGRESS &&`
`this.blt.findSite(u.getName()) == null &&`
`this.blt.findSite(d.getName()) == null`
	`// Send TSCAN(3) to GCS`
	`Vector v = new Vector();`
	`v.addElement(new Integer(3));`
	`this.ps.send(`
	  `Transmit.GROUND, PacketScheduler.TSCAN, v);`
		no change

`Mode.getMode() == Mode.MAINTENANCE &&`
`this.hc.getStatus() ==`
  `HealthCheck.COMPLETE &&`
`ICS.getStatus() != ICS.IN_PROGRESS &&`
`this.blt.findSite(u.getName()) != null &&`
`this.blt.findSite(d.getName()) == null`
	`// Send TSCAN(2) to GCS`
	`Vector v = new Vector();`
	`v.addElement(new Integer(2));`
	`this.ps.send(`
	  `Transmit.GROUND, PacketScheduler.TSCAN, v);`
		no change

Current State	Response	State Update

`Mode.getMode() == Mode.MAINTENANCE &&`
`this.hc.getStatus() ==`
`HealthCheck.COMPLETE &&`
`ICS.getStatus() != ICS.IN_PROGRESS &&`
`this.blt.findSite(u.getName()) == null &&`
`this.blt.findSite(d.getName()) != null`
	`// Send TSCAN(1) to GCS`
	`Vector v = new Vector();`
	`v.addElement(new Integer(1));`
	`this.ps.send(`
	`    Transmit.GROUND, PacketScheduler.TSCAN, v);`
		no change

`Mode.getMode() == Mode.MAINTENANCE &&`
`this.hc.getStatus() ==`
`HealthCheck.COMPLETE &&`
`ICS.getStatus() != ICS.IN_PROGRESS &&`
`this.blt.findSite(u.getName()) != null &&`
`this.blt.findSite(d.getName()) != null`
	`// Send TGF to both the`
	`// UL and the DL.`
	`this.ps.send(`
	`    Transmit.UPLINK, PacketScheduler.TGF, null);`
	`this.ps.send(`
	`    Transmit.DOWNLINK, PacketScheduler.TGF, null);`
	
	`// Initialize the`
	`// countdown timer.`
	`Interrupt.scheduleTimer(`
	`    this, Connection.CTIME);`
		`Mode.setMode`
		`(Mode.TRANSMIT);`

Notes: The BLTable object will be provided to the Connection object constructor and will be maintained in private instance variable *blt*.

CTIME will be a class constant equal to the number of milliseconds allowed for connection.

Table 15.12 Current stimulus: TC
Implemented in `Connection.notify()` with `irqid == SWI_TC`

Current State	Response	State Update

`Mode.getMode() != Mode.TRANSMIT`	`// Send ERR to GCS.`
	`this.ps.send(`
	`Transmit.GROUND, PacketScheduler.ERR, null);`
		no change

`Mode.getMode() == Mode.TRANSMIT`	`// Send TCF to the UL`
	`// and the DL, then send`
	`// TEF to the GCS.`
	`this.ps.send(`
	`Transmit.UPLINK, PacketScheduler.TCF, null);`
	`this.ps.send(`
	`Transmit.DOWNLINK, PacketScheduler.TCF, null);`
	`this.ps.send(`
	`Transmit.GROUND, PacketScheduler.TEF, null);`
	
	`// Reset the timer, if`
	`// waiting for OTE.`
	`if(this.conn != Connection.FULL && this.conn !=`
	`Connection.HALF)`
	`Interrupt.timerReset();`
		`// Set Connected`
		`// to none.`
		`this.conn = Connection.NONE;`
		
		`// Reset the`
		`// HealthCheck`
		`// and Mode.`
		`Mode.setMode(Mode.NONE);`
		`this.hc.reset();`

Table 15.13 Current stimulus: OTE

Implemented in `HealthCheck.timerNotify()`, in `FiringControl.timerNotify()`, and in `Connection.timerNotify()`

Current State	Response	State Update
`Mode.getMode() == Mode.NONE`	null	no change
`Mode.getMode() == Mode.MAINTENANCE &&` `ICS.getStatus() != ICS.IN_PROGRESS &&` `this.hc.getStatus() !=` `HealthCheck.PROCESSING`	null	no change
If in HealthCheck object and `Mode.getMode() == Mode.MAINTENANCE &&` `this.hc.getStatus() ==` `HealthCheck.PROCESSING`	`// Send HF to GCS.` `this.ps.send(` `Transmit.GROUND, PacketScheduler.HF, null);`	`// Set HealthCheck` `// to done.` `this.status =` `HealthCheck.COMPLETE;` `// Reset good and` `// bad systems` `// lists.` `this.good = new Vector();` `this.bad = new Vector();`
If in FiringControl object and `Mode.getMode() == Mode.MAINTENANCE &&` `this.hc.getStatus() ==` `HealthCheck.COMPLETE`	`// Send FF to GCS.` `this.ps.send(` `Transmit.GROUND, PacketScheduler.FF, null);`	no change (ICS has set status.)

continued

Table 15.13 *continued*

Current State	Response	State Update

If in Connection object and
 	
`Mode.getMode() == Mode.TRANSMIT &&`
`this.conn == Connection.NONE`
	`// Send TSCAN(3) to GCS`
	`Vector v = new Vector();`
	`v.addElement(new`
	`Integer(3));`
	`this.ps.send(`
	`  Transmit.GROUND, PacketScheduler.TSCAN, v);`
	
	`// Send TCF to UL and DL`
	`this.ps.send(`
	`  Transmit.UPLINK, PacketScheduler.TCF, null);`
	`this.ps.send(`
	`  Transmit.DOWNLINK, PacketScheduler.TCF, null);`
		`// Set Mode to`
		`// none and`
		`// HealthCheck`
		`// to pending.`
		`Mode.setMode(Mode.NONE);`
		`this.hc.reset();`

If in Connection object and
 	
`Mode.getMode() == Mode.TRANSMIT &&`
`this.conn == Connection.UPLINK`
	`// Send TSCAN(2) to GCS`
	`Vector v = new Vector();`
	`v.addElement(new`
	`Integer(2));`
	`this.ps.send(`
	`  Transmit.GROUND, PacketScheduler.TSCAN, v);`
	
	`// Send TCF to UL and DL`
	`this.ps.send(`
	`  Transmit.UPLINK, PacketScheduler.TCF, null);`
	`this.ps.send(`
	`  Transmit.DOWNLINK, PacketScheduler.TCF, null);`
		`// Set Mode to`
		`// none and`
		`// HealthCheck`
		`// to pending.`
		`Mode.setMode(Mode.NONE);`
		`this.hc.reset();`
		
		`// Reset`
		`// connection.`
		`this.conn =`
		`Connection.NONE;`

Current state	Response	State update

If in Connection object and
 	
`Mode.getMode() == Mode.TRANSMIT &&`
`this.conn == Connection.DOWNLINK`
	`// Send TSCAN(1) to GCS`
	`Vector v = new Vector();`
	`v.addElement(new`
	`Integer(1));`
	`this.ps.send(`
	`    Transmit.GROUND, PacketScheduler.TSCAN, v);`
	
	`// Send TCF to UL and DL`
	`this.ps.send(`
	`    Transmit.UPLINK, PacketScheduler.TCF, null);`
	`this.ps.send(`
	`    Transmit.DOWNLINK, PacketScheduler.TCF, null);`
		`// Set Mode to`
		`// none and`
		`// HealthCheck`
		`// to pending.`
		`Mode.setMode(Mode.NONE);`
		`this.hc.reset();`
		
		`// Reset`
		`// connection.`
		`this.conn =`
		`Connection.NONE;`

If in Connection object and
 	
`Mode.getMode() == Mode.TRANSMIT &&`
`(this.conn == Connection.FULL ||`
`this.conn == Connection.HALF)`
	null	no change

Note: For FF it does not make sense to check `ICS.getStatus == ICS.IN_PROGRESS` because the ICS class may reset the status prior to generating the interrupt. Because of the way the timer is handled, however, this does not cause any problems.

Table 15.14   Current stimulus: FSR
Implemented in `FiringControl.notify()` with `irqid == HWI_FIRING_COMPLETE` and `ICS.getStatus()` `== SUCCESS`

Current State	Response	State Update
`Mode.getMode() == Mode.NONE ||` `Mode.getMode() == Mode.TRANSMIT`	null	no change
`Mode.getMode() == Mode.MAINTENANCE`	`// Send FS to GCS.` `this.ps.send(` `Transmit.GROUND, PacketScheduler.FS, null);` `// Reset the timer.` `Interrupt.timerReset();`	no change (ICS has set status.)

Note: An ICS status of SUCCESS ensures that the firing is complete.

Processing is equal to firing, since execution is in firing control.

Table 15.15   Current stimulus: FFR
Implemented in `FiringControl.notify()` with `irqid == HWI_FIRING_COMPLETE` and `ICS.getStatus()` `== FAIL`

Current State	Response	State Update
`Mode.getMode() == Mode.NONE ||` `Mode.getMode() == Mode.TRANSMIT`	null	no change
`Mode.getMode() == Mode.MAINTENANCE`	`// Send FF to GCS.` `this.ps.send(` `Transmit.GROUND, PacketScheduler.FF, null);` `// Reset the timer.` `Interrupt.timerReset();`	no change (ICS has set status.)

Table 15.16 Current stimulus: ISN(x)

Implemented in `HealthCheck.notify()` with `irqid == HWI_INTERNAL_SUBSYSTEM_NOMINAL` and `args == (x)`

Current State	Response	State Update
`Mode.getMode() == Mode.NONE ||` `Mode.getMode() == Mode.TRANSMIT`	null	no change
`Mode.getMode() == Mode.MAINTENANCE &&` `this.getStatus() != PROCESSING`	null	no change

`Mode.getMode() == Mode.MAINTENANCE &&`
`this.getStatus() == PROCESSING &&`
`if(!this.good.contains(x)) this.good.addElement(x)`
`&& this.good.size() + this.bad.size()`
`< HealthCheck.NUMSYS`
	null	(good was modified
		in the condition.)

`Mode.getMode() == Mode.MAINTENANCE &&`
`this.getStatus() == PROCESSING &&`
`if(!this.good.contains(x)) this.good.addElement(x)`
`&& this.good.size() + this.bad.size() >=`
`HealthCheck.NUMSYS &&`
`this.bad.size() != 0`
	`// Send HF to GCS.`
	`Vector v = new Vector();`
	`v.addElement(this.good);`
	`v.addElement(this.bad);`
	`this.ps.send(`
	`Transmit.GROUND,`
	`PacketScheduler.HF, v);`
		`// Reset the`
		`// HealthCheck`
		`this.reset();`
		`// Reset good and`
		`// bad system`
		`// lists.`
		`this.good = new Vector();`
		`this.bad = new Vector();`

`Mode.getMode() == Mode.MAINTENANCE &&`
`this.getStatus() == PROCESSING &&`
`if(!this.good.contains(x)) this.good.addElement(x)`
`&&this.good.size() >= HealthCheck.NUMSYS &&`
`this.bad.size() == 0`
	`// Send HS to GCS.`
	`this.ps.send(`
	`Transmit.GROUND,`
	`PacketScheduler.HS,`
	`null);`
		`// Reset the`
		`// HealthCheck`
		`this.reset();`
		`// Reset good and`
		`// bad system`
		`// lists.`
		`this.good = new Vector();`
		`this.bad = new Vector();`

Notes: NUMSYS is a class constant that is equal to the number of subsystems participating in the health check.

Table 15.17 Current stimulus: ISF(x)

Implemented in `HealthCheck.notify()` with `irqid == HWI_INTERNAL_SUBSYSTEM_FAILURE` and `args == (x)`

Current State	Response	State Update
`Mode.getMode() == Mode.NONE ||` `Mode.getMode() == Mode.TRANSMIT`	null	no change
`Mode.getMode() == Mode.MAINTENANCE &&` `this.getStatus() != PROCESSING`	null	no change

`Mode.getMode() == Mode.MAINTENANCE &&`
`this.getStatus() == PROCESSING &&`
`if(!this.bad.contains(x)) this.bad.addElement(x) &&`
`this.bad.size() + this.good.size() < HealthCheck.NUMSYS`
	null	no change
		
		(bad **was modified** in the condition.)

`Mode.getMode() == Mode.MAINTENANCE &&`
`this.getStatus() == PROCESSING &&`
`if(!this.good.contains(x)) this.good.addElement(x) &&`
`this.good.size() + this.bad.size() >= HealthCheck.NUMSYS`
	`// Send HF to GCS.`
	`Vector v = new Vector();`
	`v.addElement(this.good);`
	`v.addElement(this.bad);`
	`this.ps.send(`
	`Transmit.GROUND,`
	`PacketScheduler.HF, v);`
		`// Reset the`
		`// HealthCheck`
		`this.reset();`
		
		`// Reset good and`
		`// bad system`
		`// lists.`
		`this.good = new Vector();`
		`this.bad = new Vector();`

Table 15.18 Current stimulus: UG
Implemented in `Connection.notify()` with `irqid == SWI_UG`

Current State	Response	State Update
`Mode.getMode() == Mode.NONE ||` `Mode.getMode() == Mode.MAINTENANCE`	`null`	no change
`Mode.getMode() == Mode.TRANSMIT &&` `this.conn == Connection.NONE`	`null`	`this.conn =` `Connection.UPLINK;`

`Mode.getMode() == Mode.TRANSMIT &&`
`this.conn != Connection.NONE &&`
`this.conn != Connection.DOWNLINK`
	`null`	no change

`Mode.getMode() == Mode.TRANSMIT &&`
`this.conn == Connection.DOWNLINK`
	`// Send SDT to UL.`
	`this.ps.send(`
	`  Transmit.UPLINK, PacketScheduler.SDT,`
	`  null);`
		`this.conn =`
		`Connection.FULL`

Table 15.19 Current stimulus: DI(*id, p*)
Implemented in `Connection.notify()` with `irqid == SWI_DI` and `args == (id, p)`

Current State	Response	State Update
`Mode.getMode() == Mode.NONE ||` `Mode.getMode() == Mode.MAINTENANCE`	`null`	no change

`Mode.getMode() == Mode.TRANSMIT &&`
`this.conn != Connection.FULL &&`
`this.conn != Connection.HALF`
	`// Send ERR to GCS.`
	`this.ps.send(`
	`  Transmit.GROUND, PacketScheduler.ERR,`
	`  null);`
		no change

`Mode.getMode() == Mode.TRANSMIT &&`
`(this.conn == Connection.FULL ||`
`this.conn == Connection.HALF)`
	`// Send DO to DL.`
	`this.ps.send(`
	`  Transmit.DOWNLINK, PacketScheduler.DO,`
	`  args);`
		no change

Note: The interrupt arguments (*args*) are exactly the required arguments for the DO message.

Table 15.20 Current stimulus: TE

Implemented in `Connection.notify()` with `irqid == SWI_TE`

Current State	Response	State Update
`Mode.getMode() == Mode.NONE ||` `Mode.getMode() == Mode.MAINTENANCE`	null	no change

`Mode.getMode() == Mode.TRANSMIT &&`
`this.conn == Connection.NONE`
	`// Send FE to GCS.`
	`this.ps.send(`
	`  Transmit.GROUND, PacketScheduler.FE,`
	`  null);`
		`// Reset mode.`
		`Mode.setMode(Mode.NONE);`
		
		`// Reset HealthCheck.`
		`this.hc.reset();`

`Mode.getMode() == Mode.TRANSMIT &&`
`this.conn == Connection.UPLINK`
	`// Send FE to GCS and UL.`
	`this.ps.send(`
	`  Transmit.GROUND, PacketScheduler.FE,`
	`  null);`
	`this.ps.send(`
	`  Transmit.UPLINK, PacketScheduler.FE,`
	`  null);`
		`// Reset mode.`
		`Mode.setMode(Mode.NONE);`
		
		`// Reset HealthCheck.`
		`this.hc.reset();`
		
		`// Reset`
		`// connection.`
		`this.conn = Connection.NONE;`

`Mode.getMode() == Mode.TRANSMIT &&`
`this.conn == Connection.DOWNLINK`
	`// Send FE to GCS and DL.`
	`this.ps.send(`
	`  Transmit.GROUND, PacketScheduler.FE,`
	`  null);`
	`this.ps.send(`
	`  Transmit.DOWNLINK, PacketScheduler.FE,`
	`  null);`
		`// Reset mode.`
		`Mode.setMode(Mode.NONE);`
		
		`// Reset HealthCheck.`
		`this.hc.reset();`
		
		`// Reset`
		`// connection.`
		`this.conn = Connection.NONE;`

Current State	Response	State Update

`Mode.getMode() == Mode.TRANSMIT &&`
`this.conn == Connection.FULL`
	`// Send TEF to DL.`
	`this.ps.send(`
	`    Transmit.DOWNLINK, PacketScheduler.TEF,`
	`    null);`
		`this.conn = Connection.HALF`

`Mode.getMode() == Mode.TRANSMIT &&`
`this.conn == Connection.HALF`
	`// Send TEF to DL.`
	`this.ps.send(`
	`    Transmit.DOWNLINK, PacketScheduler.TEF,`
	`    null);`
		no change

Table 15.21   Current stimulus: UB
Implemented in `Connection.notify()` with `irqid == SWI_UB`

Current State	Response	State Update
`Mode.getMode() == Mode.NONE ||` `Mode.getMode() == Mode.MAINTENANCE`	`null`	no change

`Mode.getMode() == Mode.TRANSMIT`	`// Send TSCAN(1) to GCS.`
	`Vector v = new Vector();`
	`v.addElement(new Integer(1));`
	`this.ps.send(`
	`    Transmit.GROUND, PacketScheduler.TSCAN, v);`
	`// Send TCF to UL and DL.`
	`this.ps.send(`
	`    Transmit.UPLINK, PacketScheduler.TCF, null);`
	`this.ps.send(`
	`    Transmit.DOWNLINK, PacketScheduler.TCF, null);`
		`// Reset mode.`
		`Mode.setMode(Mode.NONE);`
		`// Reset`
		`// HealthCheck.`
		`this.hc.reset();`
		`// Reset`
		`// connection.`
		`this.conn = Connection.NONE;`

Table 15.22 Current stimulus: DG
Implemented in `Connection.notify()` with `irqid == SWI_DG`

Current State	Response	State Update
`Mode.getMode() == Mode.NONE ||` `Mode.getMode() == Mode.MAINTENANCE`	null	no change
`Mode.getMode() == Mode.TRANSMIT &&` `this.conn == Connection.NONE`	null	`this.conn = Connection.DOWNLINK;`

`Mode.getMode() == Mode.TRANSMIT &&`
`this.conn != Connection.NONE &&`
`this.conn != Connection.UPLINK`
	null	no change

`Mode.getMode() == Mode.TRANSMIT &&`
`this.conn == Connection.UPLINK`
	`// Send SDT to UL.`
	`this.ps.send(`
	`    Transmit.UPLINK, PacketScheduler.SDT,`
	`    null);`
		`this.conn = Connection.FULL`

Table 15.23 Current stimulus: PB(*id*)
Implemented in `Connection.notify()` with `irqid == SWI_PB` and `args == (`*id*`)`

Current State	Response	State Update
`Mode.getMode() == Mode.NONE ||` `Mode.getMode() == Mode.MAINTENANCE`	null	no change

`Mode.getMode() == Mode.TRANSMIT &&`
`this.conn != Connection.FULL &&`
`this.conn != Connection.HALF`
	`// Send ERR to GCS.`
	`this.ps.send(`
	`    Transmit.GROUND, PacketScheduler.ERR, null);`
		no change

`Mode.getMode() == Mode.TRANSMIT &&`
`(this.conn == Connection.FULL ||`
`this.conn == Connection.HALF)`
	`// Send PBF to UL.`
	`this.ps.send(`
	`    Transmit.UPLINK, PacketScheduler.PBF, args);`
		no change

Note: The interrupt arguments (*args*) are exactly the required arguments for the PBF message.

Table 15.24 Current stimulus: DTE
Implemented in `Connection.notify()` with `irqid == SWI_DTE`

Current State	Response	State Update
`Mode.getMode() == Mode.NONE ||` `Mode.getMode() == Mode.MAINTENANCE`	null	no change

`Mode.getMode() == Mode.TRANSMIT &&`
`this.conn == Connection.NONE`
	`// Send FE to GCS.`
	`this.ps.send(`
	`  Transmit.GROUND, PacketScheduler.FE,`
	`  null);`
		`// Reset mode.`
		`Mode.setMode(Mode.NONE);`
		
		`// Reset HealthCheck.`
		`this.hc.reset();`

`Mode.getMode() == Mode.TRANSMIT &&`
`this.conn == Connection.UPLINK`
	`// Send FE to GCS and UL.`
	`this.ps.send(`
	`  Transmit.GROUND, PacketScheduler.FE,`
	`  null);`
	`this.ps.send(`
	`  Transmit.UPLINK, PacketScheduler.FE,`
	`  null);`
		`// Reset mode.`
		`Mode.setMode(Mode.NONE);`
		
		`// Reset HealthCheck.`
		`this.hc.reset();`
		
		`// connection.`
		`this.conn = Connection.NONE;`

`Mode.getMode() == Mode.TRANSMIT &&`
`this.conn == Connection.DOWNLINK`
	`// Send FE to GCS and DL.`
	`this.ps.send(`
	`  Transmit.GROUND, PacketScheduler.FE,`
	`  null);`
	`this.ps.send(`
	`  Transmit.DOWNLINK, PacketScheduler.FE,`
	`  null);`
		`// Reset mode.`
		`Mode.setMode(Mode.NONE);`
		
		`// Reset HealthCheck.`
		`this.hc.reset();`
		
		`// Reset`
		`// connection.`
		`this.conn = Connection.NONE;`

continued

Table 15.24 *continued*

Current State	Response	State Update

`Mode.getMode() == Mode.TRANSMIT &&`
`this.conn == Connection.FULL`
	`// Send FE to GCS, UL, DL.`
	`this.ps.send(`
	`    Transmit.GROUND, PacketScheduler.FE,`
	`    null);`
	`this.ps.send(`
	`    Transmit.UPLINK, PacketScheduler.FE,`
	`    null);`
	`this.ps.send(`
	`    Transmit.DOWNLINK, PacketScheduler.FE,`
	`    null);`
		`// Reset mode.`
		`Mode.setMode(Mode.NONE);`
		
		`// Reset HealthCheck.`
		`this.hc.reset();`
		
		`// Reset`
		`// connection.`
		`this.conn = Connection.NONE;`

`Mode.getMode() == Mode.TRANSMIT &&`
`this.conn == Connection.HALF`
	`// Send TEF to UL and DL.`
	`this.ps.send(`
	`    Transmit.UPLINK, PacketScheduler.TEF,`
	`    null);`
	`this.ps.send(`
	`    Transmit.DOWNLINK, PacketScheduler.TEF,`
	`    null);`
		`// Reset mode.`
		`Mode.setMode(Mode.NONE);`
		
		`// Reset HealthCheck.`
		`this.hc.reset();`
		
		`// Reset`
		`// connection.`
		`this.conn = Connection.NONE;`

Table 15.25 Current stimulus: DB
Implemented in `Connection.notify()` with `irqid == SWI_DB`

Current State	Response	State Update
`Mode.getMode() == Mode.NONE ||` `Mode.getMode() == Mode.MAINTENANCE`	null	no change

`Mode.getMode() == Mode.TRANSMIT`	`// Send TSCAN(2) to GCS.`
	`Vector v = new Vector();`
	`v.addElement(new Integer(2));`
	`this.ps.send(`
	`  Transmit.GROUND, PacketScheduler.TSCAN, v);`
	
	`// Send TCF to UL and DL.`
	`this.ps.send(`
	`  Transmit.UPLINK, PacketScheduler.TCF,`
	`  null);`
	`this.ps.send(`
	`  Transmit.DOWNLINK, PacketScheduler.TCF,`
	`  null);`
		`// Reset mode.`
		`Mode.setMode(Mode.NONE);`
		
		`// Reset`
		`HealthCheck.this.hc.reset();`
		
		`// Reset`
		`// connection.`
		`this.conn = Connection.NONE;`

15.7 Step 6: Reorganize the Implementations into Executable Code

When the implemented state box tables are complete, they may be transformed to executable code. In this step the architecture is merged with the behavioral specification of the state box. The resulting code may be reorganized to meet efficiency, performance, or other goals.

The transformation of Connection class to code is shown in the following pages. The stimuli with tables that have functionality allocated to Connection are IN, MG, TG(*u, d*), OTE, UG, DI(*id, p*), TE, UB, DG, PB(*id*), DTE, and DB. Collecting the information from these tables leads to the following final expansion of the Connection class.

Class: scs.sos.Connection

```
// Manage the connection.

package scs.sos;

import scs.kernel.ICS;
import scs.kernel.Message;
import scs.kernel.Transmit;
import scs.kernel.Interrupt;
import java.util.Vector;

/** This class manages the connection. */
public final class Connection
    implements IH.InterruptObserver, Interrupt.TimerObserver {
    /** Constructor for the connection object.
        @param hc A health check object.
        @param ps A packet scheduler object.
        @param fc A firing control object.
        @param blt A b/l table object. */
    public Connection(HealthCheck hc, PacketScheduler ps,
                    FiringControl fc, BLTable blt) {
        // Save the objects passed in.
        this.hc = hc;
        this.ps = ps;
        this.fc = fc;
        this.blt = blt;

        // Initially not connected.
```

```
            this.conn = Connection.NONE;
}


/** Interrupt notification arrives here. Interrupts indicate that
    the most recent request to the transmit hardware has completed.
    @param irqid The interrupt id.
    @param args Any arguments associated with the interrupt. */
public void notify(int irqid, Vector args) {
    // The following implements table 15.6.
    if(irqid == IH.SWI_IN) {
        // Initialize hardware.
        Message.capture();
        Message.initialize();
        Message.release();

        // Send INA.
        this.ps.send(Transmit.GROUND, PacketScheduler.INA, null);

        // Set mode to none.
        Mode.setMode(Mode.NONE);

        // Reset HealthCheck and FiringControl.
        this.fc.reset();
        this.hc.reset();

        // Set the connection to none.
        this.conn = Connection.NONE;
        return;
    }
    // The following implements table 15.8.
    else if(irqid == IH.SWI_MG) {
        if(Mode.getMode() == Mode.NONE) Mode.setMode(Mode.MAINTENANCE);
        else this.ps.send(Transmit.GROUND, PacketScheduler.ERR, null);
        return;
    }
    // The following implements table 15.11.
    else if(irqid == IH.SWI_TG) {
        Transmit.SiteInfo u = null;
        Transmit.SiteInfo d = null;
        try {
            // Get the arguments.
            u = this.blt.findSite((String)args.elementAt(0));
            d = this.blt.findSite((String)args.elementAt(1));
        }
```

```
catch(Exception e) {
    // Do nothing.
    return;

}

// Make sure the command is allowable here.
if(Mode.getMode() == Mode.NONE ||
   Mode.getMode() == Mode.TRANSMIT ||
   (Mode.getMode() == Mode.MAINTENANCE &&
    (this.hc.getStatus() != HealthCheck.COMPLETE ||
     ICS.getStatus() == ICS.IN_PROGRESS))) {
    // Send ERR to GCS.
    this.ps.send(Transmit.GROUND, PacketScheduler.ERR, null);
    return;

}
else {
    if(u == null && d == null) {
        // Send TSCAN(3) to GCS.
        Vector v = new Vector();
        v.addElement(new Integer(3));
        this.ps.send(Transmit.GROUND,
                     PacketScheduler.TSCAN, v);
        return;
    }
    else if(d == null) {
        // Send TSCAN(2) to GCS.
        Vector v = new Vector();
        v.addElement(new Integer(2));
        this.ps.send(Transmit.GROUND,
                     PacketScheduler.TSCAN, v);
        return;
    }
    else if(u == null) {
        // Send TSCAN(1) to GCS.
        Vector v = new Vector();
        v.addElement(new Integer(1));
        this.ps.send(Transmit.GROUND,
                     PacketScheduler.TSCAN, v);
        return;
    }
    else {
        // Send TGF to both the UL and the DL.
```

```
                    this.ps.send(Transmit.UPLINK,
                                 PacketScheduler.TGF, null);
                    this.ps.send(Transmit.DOWNLINK,
                                 PacketScheduler.TGF, null);

                    // Initialize the countdown timer.
                    Interrupt.scheduleTimer(this, Connection.CTIME);

                    // Set mode to transmit.
                    Mode.setMode(Mode.TRANSMIT);
                    return;
                }
            }
        } // IH.SWI_TG case
        // The following implements table 15.12.
        else if(irqid == IH.SWI_TC) {
            // See if the command is valid now.
            if(Mode.getMode() != Mode.TRANSMIT) {
                // Send ERR to the GCS.
                this.ps.send(Transmit.GROUND,
                             PacketScheduler.ERR, null);
                return;
            }
            else {
                // Send TCF to the UL and the DL, then send TEF to
                //   the GCS.
                this.ps.send(Transmit.UPLINK,
                             PacketScheduler.TCF, null);
                this.ps.send(Transmit.DOWNLINK,
                             PacketScheduler.TCF, null);
                this.ps.send(Transmit.GROUND,
                             PacketScheduler.TEF, null);

                // Reset the timer, if waiting for OTE.
                if(this.conn != Connection.FULL &&
                   this.conn != Connection.HALF) {
                    Interrupt.resetTimer();
                }

                // Set connected to none.
                this.conn = Connection.NONE;

                // Reset HealthCheck and Mode.
                Mode.setMode(Mode.NONE);
```

```
                this.hc.reset();
        }
    } // IH.SWI_TC case
    // The following implements table 15.18.
    else if(irqid == IH.SWI_UG) {
        // See if the command is valid now.
        if(Mode.getMode() != Mode.TRANSMIT) return;

        // If the downlink has connected, the connection is complete.
        if(this.conn == Connection.DOWNLINK) {
            // Send SDT to the UL.
            this.ps.send(Transmit.UPLINK,
                        PacketScheduler.SDT, null);
            this.conn = Connection.FULL;
        }
        else if (this.conn == Connection.NONE)
          this.conn = Connection.UPLINK;
        return;
    } // IH.SWI_UG case
    // The following implements table 15.19.
    else if(irqid == IH.SWI_DI) {
        // See if the command is valid now.
        if(Mode.getMode() != Mode.TRANSMIT) return;

        // If not fully connected, generate an error.
        if(this.conn != Connection.FULL ||
           this.conn != Connection.HALF) {
            // Send ERR to GCS.
            this.ps.send(Transmit.GROUND,
                        PacketScheduler.ERR, null);
            return;
        }
        else {
            // Send DO to the DL.
            this.ps.send(Transmit.DOWNLINK,
                        PacketScheduler.DO, args);
            return;
        }
    } // IH.SWI_DI case
    // The following implements table 15.20.
    else if(irqid == IH.SWI_TE) {
        // See if the command is valid now.
        if(Mode.getMode() != Mode.TRANSMIT) return;

        // If connection is full or half, forward the message.
```

```
    if(this.conn == Connection.FULL ||
       this.conn == Connection.HALF) {
        // Send TEF to the DL.
        this.ps.send(Transmit.DOWNLINK,
                     PacketScheduler.TEF, null);

        // The connection is now half open.
        this.conn = Connection.HALF;
        return;
    }
    else {
        // Send FE to GCS.
        this.ps.send(Transmit.GROUND,
                     PacketScheduler.FE, null);

        // Send FE to a connected site.
        if(this.conn == Connection.UPLINK) {
            this.ps.send(Transmit.UPLINK,
                         PacketScheduler.FE, null);
        }
        if(this.conn == Connection.DOWNLINK) {
            this.ps.send(Transmit.DOWNLINK,
                         PacketScheduler.FE, null);
        }

        // Reset mode.
        Mode.setMode(Mode.NONE);

        // Reset HealthCheck.
        this.hc.reset();

        // Reset the connection.
        this.conn = Connection.NONE;
        return;
    }
} // IH.SWI_TE case
// The following implements table 15.21.
else if(irqid == IH.SWI_UB) {
    // See if the command is valid now.
    if(Mode.getMode() != Mode.TRANSMIT) return;
    // Send TSCAN(1) to GCS.
    Vector v = new Vector();
    v.addElement(new Integer(1));
    this.ps.send(Transmit.GROUND,
```

```
                              PacketScheduler.TSCAN, v);

        // Send TCF to the UL and the DL.
        this.ps.send(Transmit.UPLINK,
                     PacketScheduler.TCF, null);
        this.ps.send(Transmit.DOWNLINK,
                     PacketScheduler.TCF, null);

        // Reset mode.
        Mode.setMode(Mode.NONE);

        // Reset HealthCheck.
        this.hc.reset();

        // Reset the connection.
        this.conn = Connection.NONE;
        return;
    } // IH.SWI_UB case
    // The following implements table 15.22.
    else if(irqid == IH.SWI_DG) {
        // See if the command is valid now.
        if(Mode.getMode() != Mode.TRANSMIT) return;

        // If the uplink has connected, the connection is complete.
        if(this.conn == Connection.UPLINK) {
            // Send SDT to the UL.
            this.ps.send(Transmit.UPLINK,
                         PacketScheduler.SDT, null);
            this.conn = Connection.FULL;
        }
        else if (this.conn == Connection.NONE)
          this.conn = Connection.DOWNLINK;
        return;
    } // IH.SWI_DG case
    // The following implements table 15.23.
    else if(irqid == IH.SWI_PB) {
        // See if the command is valid now.
        if(Mode.getMode() != Mode.TRANSMIT) return;

        // If not fully connected, generate an error.
        if(this.conn != Connection.FULL ||
          this.conn != Connection.HALF) {
          // Send ERR to GCS.
          this.ps.send(Transmit.DOWNLINK,
                       PacketScheduler.ERR, null);
```

```
            return;
        }
        else {
            // Send PBF to UL.
            this.ps.send(Transmit.UPLINK,
                        PacketScheduler.PBF, args);
            return;
        }
    } // IH.SWI_PB case
    // The following implements table 15.24.
    else if(irqid == IH.SWI_DTE) {
        // See if the command is valid now.
        if(Mode.getMode() != Mode.TRANSMIT) return;

        // If connection is half, close the connection.
        if(this.conn == Connection.HALF) {
            // Send TEF to the UL and the DL.
            this.ps.send(Transmit.UPLINK,
                        PacketScheduler.TEF, null);
            this.ps.send(Transmit.DOWNLINK,
                        PacketScheduler.TEF, null);

            // Reset mode.
            Mode.setMode(Mode.NONE);

            // Reset HealthCheck.
            this.hc.reset();

            // The connection is now closed.
            this.conn = Connection.NONE;
            return;
        }
        else {
            // Send FE to GCS.
            this.ps.send(Transmit.GROUND,
                        PacketScheduler.FE, null);

            // Send FE to any connected sites.
            if(this.conn == Connection.UPLINK ||
               this.conn == Connection.FULL) {
                this.ps.send(Transmit.UPLINK,
                            PacketScheduler.FE, null);
            }
```

```
                if(this.conn == Connection.DOWNLINK ||
                    this.conn == Connection.FULL) {
                    this.ps.send(Transmit.DOWNLINK,
                                 PacketScheduler.FE, null);
                }

                // Reset mode.
                Mode.setMode(Mode.NONE);

                // Reset HealthCheck.
                this.hc.reset();

                // Reset the connection.
                this.conn = Connection.NONE;
                return;
            }
    } // IH.SWI_DTE case
    // The following implements table 15.25.
    else if(irqid == IH.SWI_DB) {
        // See if the command is valid now.
        if(Mode.getMode() != Mode.TRANSMIT) return;

        // Send TSCAN(2) to GCS.
        Vector v = new Vector();
        v.addElement(new Integer(2));
        this.ps.send(Transmit.GROUND, PacketScheduler.TSCAN, v);

        // Send TCF to the UL and the DL.
        this.ps.send(Transmit.UPLINK, PacketScheduler.TCF, null);
        this.ps.send(Transmit.DOWNLINK, PacketScheduler.TCF, null);

        // Reset mode.
        Mode.setMode(Mode.NONE);

        // Reset HealthCheck.
        this.hc.reset();

        // Reset the connection.
        this.conn = Connection.NONE;
        return;
    } // IH.SWI_DB case
}
```

```
/** On-board timer interrupts arrive here to be processed.
    This implements parts of table 15.13. */
public void timerNotify() {
    // If mode is not transmit, ignore this.
    if(Mode.getMode() != Mode.TRANSMIT) return;

    // Take action depending on who has connected.
    if(this.conn == Connection.FULL ||
       this.conn == Connection.HALF)
        return;

    Vector v = new Vector();
    if(this.conn == Connection.NONE) {
        // Send TSCAN(3) to GCS.
        v.addElement(new Integer(3));
    }
    else if(this.conn == Connection.UPLINK) {
        // Send TSCAN(2) to GCS.
        v.addElement(new Integer(2));
    }
    else if(this.conn == Connection.DOWNLINK) {
        // Send TSCAN(1) to GCS.
        v.addElement(new Integer(1));
    }
    this.ps.send(Transmit.GROUND, PacketScheduler.TSCAN, v);

    // Send TCF to the UL and the DL.
    this.ps.send(Transmit.UPLINK, PacketScheduler.TCF, null);
    this.ps.send(Transmit.DOWNLINK, PacketScheduler.TCF, null);

    // Set mode to none and reset HealthCheck.
    Mode.setMode(Mode.NONE);
    this.hc.reset();

    // Reset the connection.
    this.conn = Connection.NONE;
}

// The following are public class constants that correspond
// to the various connection statuses.
public static final int NONE = 0;
public static final int UPLINK = 1;
public static final int DOWNLINK = 2;
```

```
public static final int FULL = 3;
public static final int HALF = 4;

// Private instance variables.
private HealthCheck hc = null;
private PacketScheduler ps = null;
private FiringControl fc = null;
private BLTable blt = null;
private int conn = Connection.NONE;

// The following is a private class constant for the number
// of milliseconds to wait for a connection.
private static final long CTIME = 30000;
}
```

Production of final code follows the process just shown. All code should be verified to confirm that the Java implementation of the state box is correct. The verified code would then be tested as described in Chapter 16.

16

Satellite Control System Testing and Certification

16.1 Statistical Testing

The fundamentals of statistical testing based on usage models were provided in Chapter 5. The work flow for testing and certifying the SOS is summarized in the following list:

Step 1: Define certification plan.

1. Set goals.
2. Define users, uses, and environments.

Step 2: Build model structure.

1. Determine the states of use.
2. Determine allowable state transitions.

Step 3: Determine state transition probabilities.

1. Establish constraints on arc probabilities.
2. Generate probabilities.

Step 4: Validate the usage model.

1. Validate with respect to known or anticipated usage.
2. Validate with respect to test plans.

Step 5: Generate test cases, and execute and evaluate results.

1. Perform nonrandom testing.
2. Perform random testing.

16.2 Step 1: Define Certification Plan

16.2.1   Goals

The goals for the statistical testing of the SOS software are the following:

- To visit every state of use and experience every transition at least one time
- To demonstrate that the SOS correctly processes every canonical sequence
- To test every requirement
- To demonstrate that the software reliability exceeds 0.999 with at least 95% confidence in expected general field operations
- To demonstrate that the software reliability exceeds 0.95 with at least 95% confidence for each error situation
- To acknowledge that the SOS will not be accepted with a known error, even if the reliability goals are met

16.2.2   Users, Uses, and Environments

The test boundary determines the system under test. All interfaces that are cut by the boundary must be "driven" by the test in the following sense: All inputs should be controllable by the testers, and all outputs must be observable by the testers. If inputs cannot be controlled, the software will not be in a well-defined state of use, and results cannot be predicted. If outputs cannot be observed, then software success or failure on a test case cannot be determined.

For the SOS, the test boundary will cut the following external interfaces:

- The interface between the receiver hardware and the packet parser
- All interfaces to the transmit hardware

A "use" of the SOS will be either a completion (all events beginning with initialization of the SOS through to completion of a successful transmission by exiting transmit mode) or a failure (all events from initialization of the SOS to a fatal error or reset). Thus, the initial and final states for a use will be software initialized prior to entering maintenance mode. A use shall be a nonempty sequence of events beginning in the initial state and ending in the final state.

There are three classes of users: GCS, UL, and DL. These user classes are further subdivided and defined as shown in Table 16.1.

Table 16.1 Classes of SOS user

User Class	Description
GCS normal	Normal GCS user; initiates valid communications, allows transmissions to complete
GCS error	Error-prone GCS user; initiates communications with out-of-sequence commands (such as transmit mode commands during maintenance mode), invalid sites, and transmission interrupts
UL good	Good uplink site; sends correct sequence of packets with correct information, no out-of-sequence messages or transmission interrupts
UL bad	Bad uplink site; sends packets out of sequence or with incorrect checksums, sends transmission interrupts and out-of-sequence messages (such as UG during DI packet sequence)
DL good	Good downlink site; all packets received, no out-of-sequence messages, only requests resending valid packets, no transmission interrupts
DL bad	Bad downlink site; some packets dropped, PB sent for nonexistent packets, transmission interrupts

For certification testing purposes there is only a single environment of use for the SOS. Operations under adverse environmental circumstances (e.g., poor atmospheric conditions) will be represented through the "bad" user classes.

General field operations, for which the reliability must be shown to exceed 0.999, include all eight of the following strata:

1. GCS normal, UL good, DL good
2. GCS normal, UL good, DL bad
3. GCS normal, UL bad, DL good
4. GCS normal, UL bad, DL bad
5. GCS error, UL good, DL good
6. GCS error, UL good, DL bad
7. GCS error, UL bad, DL good
8. GCS error, UL bad, DL bad

The error situations, each of which must be certified separately to have a reliability exceeding 0.95, are strata 2 through 8. Statistical sampling will be used for all strata to meet testing goals. As will be seen in the following pages, the testing goals imply that error situations must be tested far in excess of their expected frequency in general operations. The general field operations reliability and confidence calculations will include the testing performed for the individual error strata but will discount each to its correct proportions. One usage model will be developed to guide testing and generate test cases for all strata, and will be built with special "bookkeeping" states to facilitate correct sampling.

16.3 Step 2: Build Model Structure

The most likely scenario is given at the start of Chapter 12. Based on this scenario, Figure 16.1 is a high-level view of the SOS use.

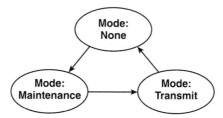

Figure 16.1   Initial usage model

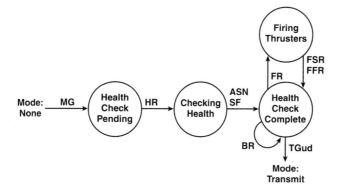

Figure 16.2   Expansion of Mode: Maintenance

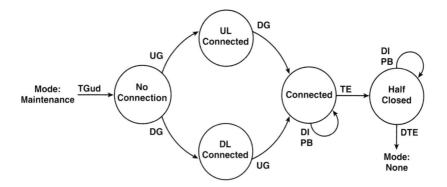

Figure 16.3   Expansion of Mode: Transmit

The high-level model will be refined to the necessary level of detail by successively refining states and transitions. The state designated [Mode: Maintenance] can be expanded as shown in Figure 16.2, and the state designated [Mode: Transmit] can be expanded as shown in Figure 16.3.

Many arcs were excluded from these figures so that the essential structure of the model would not be obscured. The complete usage model consists of 68 states and 1,071 arcs. The model was designed to facilitate sampling control by strata, and this required that the basic model be replicated. The replication is described, but details are omitted because of space limitations.

The model is presented in a usage modeling notation. Comments are indicated by //, state names are enclosed in square brackets, arc names are enclosed in quotation marks, and probability values or relative frequencies are enclosed in parentheses. The general pattern is

[from state]

(probability) "arc name" [to state]

. . .

(probability) "arc name" [to state]

Each state has a probability distribution over its exit arcs, and when probability or frequency values are omitted from exit arcs of a state, a default value set by the "assume" command in the modeling notation is used. Probabilities are always normalized so that the exit arcs have a legitimate probability distribution.

The model presented reads as follows. Begin in state [Software Not Invoked]. There is only one exit arc "IN," therefore it has probability 1.0 of being taken (defaulted to 0.0005 and then normalized to 1.0), which will lead to state [Mode: None]. There are 21 exit arcs from [Mode: None]. Arc "MG" will be taken with probability 0.99 and the remaining 0.01 probability mass will be distributed equally across the remaining 20 arcs. The arcs are classified and identified by the comment lines.

The very last section of the model is a set of bookkeeping states that will be used for stratification of sampling. They are named according to the following conventions:

- Axxx means GCS aborts
- xBxx means GCS causes an error
- xxBx means UL causes an error
- xxxB means DL causes an error

Stratum 1 is represented by [GGG] and [AGGG], stratum 2 by [GGB] and [AGGB], and so forth. Many state names throughout the model include a suffix that indicates the bookkeeping states through which the model will ultimately pass. Usage model analysis shows for each state its probability of appearing in a random walk through the model, in the long run. This reveals, for example, the percentage of test cases that will result in [BBB] in the long run, given the probabilities in the model.

The model as presented is compiled into a format that is accepted by analysis and script generation tools. Usage models are treated as directed graphs for some purposes and as stochastic matrices for other purposes. As directed graphs, multiple arcs from one state to another are permitted (see, for example, the eight arcs from [Mode: None] to [Mode: None, BGG]). However, when the model is represented as a stochastic matrix, only one arc is permitted from one state to another and the probability mass on that single arc is the sum of the masses on the individual arcs.

Notice that just above the bookkeeping states, comments indicate that half the model has been omitted because of space limitations. The omitted section is a replication of the upper half of the model for the case in which the GCS has caused a protocol error (i.e., all the states of the form [. . . ,BGG], [. . . ,BGB], [. . . ,BBG], and [. . . ,BBB]).

```
// Usage model for Satellite Operations Software (SOS)
assume (.0005)
[Software Not Invoked]
        "IN"    [Mode:None]


// IN
[Mode:None]
        // Reinitialization ends the use.
        "IN"    [AGGG]


        // Moves to maintenance mode. A health check is required.
(.99)   "MG"    [Health Check Pending]


        // The following commands from the GCS generate protocol errors.
        "HR"    [Mode:None,BGG]
        "BR"    [Mode:None,BGG]
        "FR"    [Mode:None,BGG]
        "TG"    [Mode:None,BGG]
        "TGu"   [Mode:None,BGG]
        "TGd"   [Mode:None,BGG]
        "TGud"  [Mode:None,BGG]
        "TC"    [Mode:None,BGG]


        // The following signals are ignored.
        "OTE"   [Mode:None]
        "FSR"   [Mode:None]
        "FFR"   [Mode:None]
```

```
            // The following commands are ignored if not in transmit mode.
            "UG"     [Mode:None]
            "DI"     [Mode:None]
            "TE"     [Mode:None]
            "UB"     [Mode:None]
            "DG"     [Mode:None]
            "PB"     [Mode:None]
            "DTE"    [Mode:None]
            "DB"     [Mode:None]

// IN MG
[Health Check Pending]
            "IN"     [AGGG]

            // The health check is expected.
(.99)     "HR"     [Checking Health]

            // The following commands from the GCS generate protocol errors.
            "MG"     [Health Check Pending,BGG]
            "BR"     [Health Check Pending,BGG]
            "FR"     [Health Check Pending,BGG]
            "TG"     [Health Check Pending,BGG]
            "TGu"    [Health Check Pending,BGG]
            "TGd"    [Health Check Pending,BGG]
            "TGud"   [Health Check Pending,BGG]
            "TC"     [Health Check Pending,BGG]

        // The following signals are ignored.
            "OTE"    [Health Check Pending]
            "FSR"    [Health Check Pending]
            "FFR"    [Health Check Pending]

        // The following commands are ignored if not in transmit mode.
            "UG"     [Health Check Pending]
            "DI"     [Health Check Pending]
            "TE"     [Health Check Pending]
            "UB"     [Health Check Pending]
            "DG"     [Health Check Pending]
            "PB"     [Health Check Pending]
            "DTE"    [Health Check Pending]
            "DB"     [Health Check Pending]

// IN MG HR
[Checking Health]
            "IN"     [AGGG]
```

```
         // The health check completion signals.
(.495)   "ASN"   [Health Check Complete]
(.495)   "SF"    [Health Check Complete]

         // The following commands from the GCS generate protocol errors.
         "HR"    [Checking Health,BGG]
         "MG"    [Checking Health,BGG]
         "BR"    [Checking Health,BGG]
         "FR"    [Checking Health,BGG]
         "TG"    [Checking Health,BGG]
         "TGu"   [Checking Health,BGG]
         "TGd"   [Checking Health,BGG]
         "TGud"  [Checking Health,BGG]
         "TC"    [Checking Health,BGG]

         // The following signals are ignored.
         "OTE"   [Checking Health]
         "FSR"   [Checking Health]
         "FFR"   [Checking Health]

         // The following commands are ignored if not in transmit mode.
         "UG"    [Checking Health]
         "DI"    [Checking Health]
         "TE"    [Checking Health]
         "UB"    [Checking Health]
         "DG"    [Checking Health]
         "PB"    [Checking Health]
         "DTE"   [Checking Health]
         "DB"    [Checking Health]

// IN MG HR ASN
[Health Check Complete]
         "IN"    [AGGG]

         // Another health request is valid.
         "HR"    [Checking Health]

         // B/L table update requests are valid.
         "BR"    [Health Check Complete]

         // Thruster firing requests are valid.
         "FR"    [Firing Thrusters]

         // The following commands from the GCS generate protocol errors.
         "MG"    [Health Check Complete,BGG]
         "TC"    [Health Check Complete,BGG]
```

```
           // The GCS can signal a switch to transmit mode.
           "TG"    [Health Check Complete,BGG]
           "TGu"   [Health Check Complete,BGG]
           "TGd"   [Health Check Complete,BGG]
(.99)      "TGud"  [No Connection]

           // The following signals are ignored.
           "OTE"   [Health Check Complete]
           "FSR"   [Health Check Complete]
           "FFR"   [Health Check Complete]

           // The following commands are ignored if not in transmit mode.
           "UG"    [Health Check Complete]
           "DI"    [Health Check Complete]
           "TE"    [Health Check Complete]
           "UB"    [Health Check Complete]
           "DG"    [Health Check Complete]
           "PB"    [Health Check Complete]
           "DTE"   [Health Check Complete]
           "DB"    [Health Check Complete]

// IN MG HR ASN FR
[Firing Thrusters]
           "IN"    [AGGG]

           // Thruster firings can succeed or fail.
(.33)      "OTE"   [Health Check Complete]
(.33)      "FSR"   [Health Check Complete]
(.33)      "FFR"   [Health Check Complete]

           // The following commands from the GCS generate protocol errors.
           "MG"    [Firing Thrusters,BGG]
           "TC"    [Firing Thrusters,BGG]
           "HR"    [Firing Thrusters,BGG]
           "BR"    [Firing Thrusters,BGG]
           "FR"    [Firing Thrusters,BGG]
           "TG"    [Firing Thrusters,BGG]
           "TGu"   [Firing Thrusters,BGG]
           "TGd"   [Firing Thrusters,BGG]
           "TGud"  [Firing Thrusters,BGG]

           // The following commands are ignored if not in transmit mode.
           "UG"    [Firing Thrusters]
           "DI"    [Firing Thrusters]
```

```
        "TE"    [Firing Thrusters]
        "UB"    [Firing Thrusters]
        "DG"    [Firing Thrusters]
        "PB"    [Firing Thrusters]
        "DTE"   [Firing Thrusters]
        "DB"    [Firing Thrusters]

// IN MG HR ASN TGud
[No Connection]
        "IN"    [AGGG]

        // The GCS can cancel the transmission at any time.
        "TC"    [AGGG]

        // If the connection experiences a time-out, both sites fail.
        "OTE"   [GBB]

        // Either site can connect now.
(.495)  "UG"    [UL Connected]
(.495)  "DG"    [DL Connected]

        // Either site can fail.
        "UB"    [GBG]
        "DB"    [GGB]

        // The following commands from the GCS generate protocol errors.
        "HR"    [No Connection,BGG]
        "MG"    [No Connection,BGG]
        "BR"    [No Connection,BGG]
        "FR"    [No Connection,BGG]
        "TG"    [No Connection,BGG]
        "TGu"   [No Connection,BGG]
        "TGd"   [No Connection,BGG]
        "TGud"  [No Connection,BGG]

        // The following signals are ignored.
        "FSR"   [No Connection]
        "FFR"   [No Connection]

        // The following commands generate an error if not fully connected.
        "DI"    [No Connection,GBG]
        "TE"    [GBG]
        "PB"    [No Connection,GGB]
        "DTE"   [GGB]
```

```
// IN MG HR ASN TGud UG
[UL Connected]
        "IN"    [AGGG]

        // The GCS can cancel the transmission at any time.
        "TC"    [AGGG]

        // If the connection experiences a time-out now, DL fails.
        "OTE"   [GGB]

        // Either site can connect now.
        "UG"    [UL Connected]
(.99)   "DG"    [Connected]

        // Either site can fail.
        "UB"    [GBG]
        "DB"    [GGB]

        // The following commands from the GCS generate protocol errors.
        "HR"    [UL Connected,BGG]
        "MG"    [UL Connected,BGG]
        "BR"    [UL Connected,BGG]
        "FR"    [UL Connected,BGG]
        "TG"    [UL Connected,BGG]
        "TGu"   [UL Connected,BGG]
        "TGd"   [UL Connected,BGG]
        "TGud"  [UL Connected,BGG]

        // The following signals are ignored.
        "FSR"   [UL Connected]
        "FFR"   [UL Connected]

        // The following commands generate an error if not fully connected.
        "DI"    [UL Connected,GBG]
        "TE"    [GBG]
        "PB"    [UL Connected,GGB]
        "DTE"   [GGB]

// IN MG HR ASN TGud DG
[DL Connected]
        "IN"    [AGGG]

        // The GCS can cancel the transmission at any time.
        "TC"    [AGGG]
```

```
        // If the connection experiences a time-out now, UL fails.
        "OTE"   [GBG]

        // Either site can connect now.
(.99)   "UG"    [Connected]
        "DG"    [DL Connected]

        // Either site can fail.
        "UB"    [GBG]
        "DB"    [GGB]

        // The following commands from the GCS generate protocol errors.
        "HR"    [DL Connected,BGG]
        "MG"    [DL Connected,BGG]
        "BR"    [DL Connected,BGG]
        "FR"    [DL Connected,BGG]
        "TG"    [DL Connected,BGG]
        "TGu"   [DL Connected,BGG]
        "TGd"   [DL Connected,BGG]
        "TGud"  [DL Connected,BGG]

        // The following signals are ignored.
        "FSR"   [DL Connected]
        "FFR"   [DL Connected]

        // The following commands generate an error if not fully connected.
        "DI"    [DL Connected,GBG]
        "TE"    [GBG]
        "PB"    [DL Connected,GGB]
        "DTE"   [GGB]

// IN MG HR ASN TGud UG DG
[Connected]
        "IN"    [AGGG]

        // The GCS can cancel the transmission at any time.
(.09)   "TC"    [AGGG]

        // Either site can send good status.
        "UG"    [Connected]
        "DG"    [Connected]

        // Either site can fail.
        "UB"    [GBG]
        "DB"    [GGB]
```

```
            // Data can be transferred now.
(.5)    "DI"    [Connected]
(.2)    "PB"    [Connected]


            // The UL can signal end of data.
(.2)    "TE"    [Half-Closed]


            // The following commands from the GCS generate protocol errors.
        "HR"    [Connected,BGG]
        "MG"    [Connected,BGG]
        "BR"    [Connected,BGG]
        "FR"    [Connected,BGG]
        "TG"    [Connected,BGG]
        "TGu"   [Connected,BGG]
        "TGd"   [Connected,BGG]
        "TGud"  [Connected,BGG]


            // The following signals are ignored.
        "FSR"   [Connected]
        "FFR"   [Connected]
        "OTE"   [Connected]


            // The following commands generate an error if not fully connected.
        "DTE"   [GGB]

// IN MG HR ASN TGud UG DG TE
[Half-Closed]
        "IN"    [AGGG]


            // The GCS can cancel the transmission at any time.
        "TC"    [AGGG]


            // Either site can send good status.
        "UG"    [Half-Closed]
        "DG"    [Half-Closed]


            // Either site can fail.
        "UB"    [GBG]
        "DB"    [GGB]


            // Data can be transferred now.
(.245)  "DI"    [Half-Closed]
(.245)  "PB"    [Half-Closed]
```

```
        // The UL can signal end of data.
        "TE"    [Half-Closed]

        // The DL can signal end of data.
(.5)    "DTE"   [GGG]

        // The following commands from the GCS generate protocol errors.
        "HR"    [Half-Closed,BGG]
        "MG"    [Half-Closed,BGG]
        "BR"    [Half-Closed,BGG]
        "FR"    [Half-Closed,BGG]
        "TG"    [Half-Closed,BGG]
        "TGu"   [Half-Closed,BGG]
        "TGd"   [Half-Closed,BGG]
        "TGud"  [Half-Closed,BGG]

        // The following signals are ignored.
        "FSR"   [Half-Closed]
        "FFR"   [Half-Closed]
        "OTE"   [Half-Closed]

// IN MG HR ASN TGud (with UL error)
[No Connection,GBG]
        "IN"    [AGBG]

        // The GCS can cancel the transmission at any time.
        "TC"    [AGBG]

        // If the connection experiences a time-out, both sites fail.
        "OTE"   [GBB]

        // Either site can connect now.
(.495)  "UG"    [UL Connected,GBG]
(.495)  "DG"    [DL Connected,GBG]

        // Either site can fail.
        "UB"    [GBG]
        "DB"    [GBB]

        // The following commands from the GCS generate protocol errors.
        "HR"    [No Connection,BBG]
        "MG"    [No Connection,BBG]
        "BR"    [No Connection,BBG]
        "FR"    [No Connection,BBG]
        "TG"    [No Connection,BBG]
        "TGu"   [No Connection,BBG]
```

```
        "TGd"   [No Connection,BBG]
        "TGud"  [No Connection,BBG]


        // The following signals are ignored.
        "FSR"   [No Connection,GBG]
        "FFR"   [No Connection,GBG]


        // The following commands generate an error if not fully connected.
        "DI"    [No Connection,GBG]
        "TE"    [GBG]
        "PB"    [No Connection,GBB]
        "DTE"   [GBB]

// IN MG HR ASN TGud UG (with UL error)
[UL Connected,GBG]
        "IN"    [AGBG]


        // The GCS can cancel the transmission at any time.
        "TC"    [AGBG]


        // If the connection experiences a time-out now, DL fails.
        "OTE"   [GBB]


        // Either site can connect now.
        "UG"    [UL Connected,GBG]
(.99)   "DG"    [Connected,GBG]


        // Either site can fail.
        "UB"    [GBG]
        "DB"    [GBB]


        // The following commands from the GCS generate protocol errors.
        "HR"    [UL Connected,BBG]
        "MG"    [UL Connected,BBG]
        "BR"    [UL Connected,BBG]
        "FR"    [UL Connected,BBG]
        "TG"    [UL Connected,BBG]
        "TGu"   [UL Connected,BBG]
        "TGd"   [UL Connected,BBG]
        "TGud"  [UL Connected,BBG]


        // The following signals are ignored.
        "FSR"   [UL Connected,GBG]
        "FFR"   [UL Connected,GBG]
```

```
         // The following commands generate an error if not fully connected.
         "DI"    [UL Connected,GBG]
         "TE"    [GBG]
         "PB"    [UL Connected,GBB]
         "DTE"   [GBB]


// IN MG HR ASN TGud DG (with UL error)
[DL Connected,GBG]
         "IN"    [AGBG]

         // The GCS can cancel the transmission at any time.
         "TC"    [AGBG]

         // If the connection experiences a time-out now, UL fails.
         "OTE"   [GBG]

         // Either site can connect now.
(.99)    "UG"    [Connected,GBG]
         "DG"    [DL Connected,GBG]

         // Either site can fail.
         "UB"    [GBG]
         "DB"    [GBB]

         // The following commands from the GCS generate protocol errors.
         "HR"    [DL Connected,BBG]
         "MG"    [DL Connected,BBG]
         "BR"    [DL Connected,BBG]
         "FR"    [DL Connected,BBG]
         "TG"    [DL Connected,BBG]
         "TGu"   [DL Connected,BBG]
         "TGd"   [DL Connected,BBG]
         "TGud"  [DL Connected,BBG]

         // The following signals are ignored.
         "FSR"   [DL Connected,BBG]
         "FFR"   [DL Connected,BBG]

         // The following commands generate an error if not fully connected.
         "DI"    [DL Connected,GBG]
         "TE"    [GBG]
         "PB"    [DL Connected,GBB]
         "DTE"   [GBB]
```

```
// IN MG HR ASN TGud UG DG (with UL error)
[Connected,GBG]
        "IN"   [AGBG]

        // The GCS can cancel the transmission at any time.
(.09)   "TC"   [AGBG]

        // Either site can send good status.
        "UG"   [Connected,GBG]
        "DG"   [Connected,GBG]

        // Either site can fail.
        "UB"   [GBG]
        "DB"   [GBB]

        // Data can be transferred now.
(.5)    "DI"   [Connected,GBG]
(.2)    "PB"   [Connected,GBG]

        // The UL can signal end of data.
(.2)    "TE"   [Half-Closed,GBG]

        // The following commands from the GCS generate protocol errors.
        "HR"   [Connected,BBG]
        "MG"   [Connected,BBG]
        "BR"   [Connected,BBG]
        "FR"   [Connected,BBG]
        "TG"   [Connected,BBG]
        "TGu"  [Connected,BBG]
        "TGd"  [Connected,BBG]
        "TGud" [Connected,BBG]

        // The following signals are ignored.
        "FSR"  [Connected,GBG]
        "FFR"  [Connected,GBG]
        "OTE"  [Connected,GBG]

        // The following commands generate an error if not fully connected.
        "DTE"  [GBB]

// IN MG HR ASN TGud UG DG TE (with UL error)
[Half-Closed,GBG]
        "IN"   [AGBG]
```

```
            // The GCS can cancel the transmission at any time.
            "TC"    [AGBG]

            // Either site can send good status.
            "UG"    [Half-Closed,GBG]
            "DG"    [Half-Closed,GBG]

            // Either site can fail.
            "UB"    [GBG]
            "DB"    [GBB]

            // Data can be transferred now.
(.245)  "DI"    [Half-Closed,GBG]
(.245)  "PB"    [Half-Closed,GBG]

            // The UL can signal end of data.
            "TE"    [Half-Closed,GBG]

            // The DL can signal end of data.
(.5)    "DTE"   [GBG]

            // The following commands from the GCS generate protocol errors.
            "HR"    [Half-Closed,BBG]
            "MG"    [Half-Closed,BBG]
            "BR"    [Half-Closed,BBG]
            "FR"    [Half-Closed,BBG]
            "TG"    [Half-Closed,BBG]
            "TGu"   [Half-Closed,BBG]
            "TGd"   [Half-Closed,BBG]
            "TGud"  [Half-Closed,BBG]

            // The following signals are ignored.
            "FSR"   [Half-Closed,GBG]
            "FFR"   [Half-Closed,GBG]
            "OTE"   [Half-Closed,GBG]

// IN MG HR ASN TGud (with DL error)
[No Connection,GGB]
            "IN"    [AGGB]

            // The GCS can cancel the transmission at any time.
            "TC"    [AGGB]

            // If the connection experiences a time-out, both sites fail.
            "OTE"   [GBB]
```

```
          // Either site can connect now.
(.495)   "UG"     [UL Connected,GGB]
(.495)   "DG"     [DL Connected,GGB]

          // Either site can fail.
          "UB"     [GBB]
          "DB"     [GGB]

          // The following commands from the GCS generate protocol errors.
          "HR"     [No Connection,BGB]
          "MG"     [No Connection,BGB]
          "BR"     [No Connection,BGB]
          "FR"     [No Connection,BGB]
          "TG"     [No Connection,BGB]
          "TGu"    [No Connection,BGB]
          "TGd"    [No Connection,BGB]
          "TGud"   [No Connection,BCB]

          // The following signals are ignored.
          "FSR"    [No Connection,GGB]
          "FFR"    [No Connection,GGB]

          // The following commands generate an error if not fully connected.
          "DI"     [No Connection,GGB]
          "TE"     [GBB]
          "PB"     [No Connection,GGB]
          "DTE"    [GGB]

// IN MG HR ASN TGud UG (with DL error)
[UL Connected,GGB]
          "IN"     [AGGB]

          // The GCS can cancel the transmission at any time.
          "TC"     [AGGB]

          // If the connection experiences a time-out now, DL fails.
          "OTE"    [GGB]

          // Either site can connect now.
          "UG"     [UL Connected,GGB]
(.99)    "DG"     [Connected,GGB]

          // Either site can fail.
          "UB"     [GBB]
          "DB"     [GGB]
```

```
        // The following commands from the GCS generate protocol errors.
        "HR"    [UL Connected,BGB]
        "MG"    [UL Connected,BGB]
        "BR"    [UL Connected,BGB]
        "FR"    [UL Connected,BGB]
        "TG"    [UL Connected,BGB]
        "TGu"   [UL Connected,BGB]
        "TGd"   [UL Connected,BGB]
        "TGud"  [UL Connected,BGB]

        // The following signals are ignored.
        "FSR"   [UL Connected,GGB]
        "FFR"   [UL Connected,GGB]

        // The following commands generate an error if not fully connected.
        "DI"    [UL Connected,GBB]
        "TE"    [GBB]
        "PB"    [UL Connected,GGB]
        "DTE"   [GGB]

// IN MG HR ASN TGud DG (with DL error)
[DL Connected,GGB]
        "IN"    [AGGB]

        // The GCS can cancel the transmission at any time.
        "TC"    [AGGB]

        // If the connection experiences a time-out now, UL fails.
        "OTE"   [GBB]

        // Either site can connect now.
        "UG"    [Connected,GGB]
(.99)   "DG"    [DL Connected,GGB]

        // Either site can fail.
        "UB"    [GBB]
        "DB"    [GGB]

        // The following commands from the GCS generate protocol errors.
        "HR"    [DL Connected,BGB]
        "MG"    [DL Connected,BGB]
        "BR"    [DL Connected,BGB]
        "FR"    [DL Connected,BGB]
        "TG"    [DL Connected,BGB]
```

```
        "TGu"    [DL Connected,BGB]
        "TGd"    [DL Connected,BGB]
        "TGud"   [DL Connected,BGB]

        // The following signals are ignored.
        "FSR"    [DL Connected,GGB]
        "FFR"    [DL Connected,GGB]

        // The following commands generate an error if not fully connected.
        "DI"     [DL Connected,GBB]
        "TE"     [GBB]
        "PB"     [DL Connected,GGB]
        "DTE"    [GGB]

// IN MG HR ASN TGud UG DG (with DL error)
[Connected,GGB]
        "IN"     [AGGB]

        // The GCS can cancel the transmission at any time.
(.09)   "TC"     [AGGB]

        // Either site can send good status.
        "UG"     [Connected,GGB]
        "DG"     [Connected,GGB]

        // Either site can fail.
        "UB"     [GBB]
        "DB"     [GGB]

        // Data can be transferred now.
(.5)    "DI"     [Connected,GGB]
(.2)    "PB"     [Connected,GGB]

        // The UL can signal end of data.
(.2)    "TE"     [Half-Closed,GGB]

        // The following commands from the GCS generate protocol errors.
        "HR"     [Connected,BGB]
        "MG"     [Connected,BGB]
        "BR"     [Connected,BGB]
        "FR"     [Connected,BGB]
        "TG"     [Connected,BGB]
        "TGu"    [Connected,BGB]
```

```
        "TGd"    [Connected,BGB]
        "TGud"   [Connected,BGB]

        // The following signals are ignored.
        "FSR"    [Connected,GGB]
        "FFR"    [Connected,GGB]
        "OTE"    [Connected,GGB]

        // The following commands generate an error if not fully connected.
        "DTE"    [GGB]

// IN MG HR ASN TGud UG DG TE (with DL error)
[Half-Closed,GGB]
        "IN"     [AGGB]

        // The GCS can cancel the transmission at any time.
        "TC"     [AGGB]

        // Either site can send good status.
        "UG"     [Half-Closed,GGB]
        "DG"     [Half-Closed,GGB]

        // Either site can fail.
        "UB"     [GBB]
        "DB"     [GGB]

        // Data can be transferred now.
(.245)  "DI"     [Half-Closed,GGB]
(.245)  "PB"     [Half-Closed,GGB]

        // The UL can signal end of data.
        "TE"     [Half-Closed,GGB]

        // The DL can signal end of data.
(.5)    "DTE"    [GGB]

        // The following commands from the GCS generate protocol errors.
        "HR"     [Half-Closed,BGB]
        "MG"     [Half-Closed,BGB]
        "BR"     [Half-Closed,BGB]
        "FR"     [Half-Closed,BGB]
        "TG"     [Half-Closed,BGB]
        "TGu"    [Half-Closed,BGB]
```

```
      "TGd"   [Half-Closed,BGB]
      "TGud"  [Half-Closed,BGB]

      // The following signals are ignored.
      "FSR"   [Half-Closed,GGB]
      "FFR"   [Half-Closed,GGB]
      "OTE"   [Half-Closed,GGB]

// IN MG HR ASN TGud (with UL and DL error)
[No Connection,GBB]
      "IN"    [AGBB]

      // The GCS can cancel the transmission at any time.
      "TC"    [AGBB]

      // If the connection experiences a time-out, both sites fail.
      "OTE"   [GBB]

      // Either site can connect now.
(.495) "UG"    [UL Connected,GBB]
(.495) "DG"    [DL Connected,GBB]

      // Either site can fail.
      "UB"    [GBB]
      "DB"    [GBB]

      // The following commands from the GCS generate protocol errors.
      "HR"    [No Connection,BBB]
      "MG"    [No Connection,BBB]
      "BR"    [No Connection,BBB]
      "FR"    [No Connection,BBB]
      "TG"    [No Connection,BBB]
      "TGu"   [No Connection,BBB]
      "TGd"   [No Connection,BBB]
      "TGud"  [No Connection,BBB]

      // The following signals are ignored.
      "FSR"   [No Connection,GBB]
      "FFR"   [No Connection,GBB]

      // The following commands generate an error if not fully connected.
      "DI"    [No Connection,GBB]
      "TE"    [GBB]
```

```
        "PB"     [No Connection,GBB]
        "DTE"    [GBB]

// IN MG HR ASN TGud UG (with UL and DL error)
[UL Connected,GBB]
        "IN"     [AGBB]

        // The GCS can cancel the transmission at any time.
        "TC"     [AGBB]

        // If the connection experiences a time-out now, DL fails.
        "OTE"    [GBB]

        // Either site can connect now.
        "UG"     [UL Connected,GBB]
(.99)   "DG"     [Connected,GBB]

        // Either site can fail.
        "UB"     [GBB]
        "DB"     [GBB]

        // The following commands from the GCS generate protocol errors.
        "HR"     [UL Connected,BBB]
        "MG"     [UL Connected,BBB]
        "BR"     [UL Connected,BBB]
        "FR"     [UL Connected,BBB]
        "TG"     [UL Connected,BBB]
        "TGu"    [UL Connected,BBB]
        "TGd"    [UL Connected,BBB]
        "TGud"   [UL Connected,BBB]

        // The following signals are ignored.
        "FSR"    [UL Connected,GBB]
        "FFR"    [UL Connected,GBB]

        // The following commands generate an error if not fully connected.
        "DI"     [UL Connected,GBB]
        "TE"     [GBB]
        "PB"     [UL Connected,GBB]
        "DTE"    [GBB]

// IN MG HR ASN TGud DG (with UL and DL error)
[DL Connected,GBB]
        "IN"     [AGBB]
```

```
        // The GCS can cancel the transmission at any time.
        "TC"    [AGBB]

        // If the connection experiences a time-out now, UL fails.
        "OTE"   [GBB]

        // Either site can connect now.
(.99)   "UG"    [Connected,GBB]
        "DG"    [DL Connected,GBB]

        // Either site can fail.
        "UB"    [GBB]
        "DB"    [GBB]

        // The following commands from the GCS generate protocol errors.
        "HR"    [DL Connected,BBB]
        "MG"    [DL Connected,BBB]
        "BR"    [DL Connected,BBB]
        "FR"    [DL Connected,BBB]
        "TG"    [DL Connected,BBB]
        "TGu"   [DL Connected,BBB]
        "TGd"   [DL Connected,BBB]
        "TGud"  [DL Connected,BBB]

        // The following signals are ignored.
        "FSR"   [DL Connected,BBB]
        "FFR"   [DL Connected,BBB]

        // The following commands generate an error if not fully connected.
        "DI"    [DL Connected,GBB]
        "TE"    [GBB]
        "PB"    [DL Connected,GBB]
        "DTE"   [GBB]

// IN MG HR ASN TGud UG DG (with UL and DL error)
[Connected,GBB]
        "IN"    [AGBB]

        // The GCS can cancel the transmission at any time.
(.09)   "TC"    [AGBB]

        // Either site can send good status.
        "UG"    [Connected,GBB]
        "DG"    [Connected,GBB]
```

```
          // Either site can fail.
          "UB"    [GBB]
          "DB"    [GBB]

          // Data can be transferred now.
(.5)      "DI"    [Connected,GBB]
(.2)      "PB"    [Connected,GBB]


          // The UL can signal end of data.
(.2)      "TE"    [Half-Closed,GBB]

          // The following commands from the GCS generate protocol errors.
          "HR"    [Connected,BBB]
          "MG"    [Connected,BBB]
          "BR"    [Connected,BBB]
          "FR"    [Connected,BBB]
          "TG"    [Connected,BBB]
          "TGu"   [Connected,BBB]
          "TGd"   [Connected,BBB]
          "TGud"  [Connected,BBB]

          // The following signals are ignored.
          "FSR"   [Connected,GBB]
          "FFR"   [Connected,GBB]
          "OTE"   [Connected,GBB]

          // The following commands generate an error if not fully connected.
          "DTE"   [GBB]

// IN MG HR ASN TGud UG DG TE (with UL and DL error)
[Half-Closed,GBB]
          "IN"    [AGBB]

          // The GCS can cancel the transmission at any time.
          "TC"    [AGBB]

          // Either site can send good status.
          "UG"    [Half-Closed,GBB]
          "DG"    [Half-Closed,GBB]

          // Either site can fail.
          "UB"    [GBB]
          "DB"    [GBB]
```

```
            // Data can be transferred now.
(.245)  "DI"    [Half-Closed,GBB]
(.245)  "PB"    [Half-Closed,GBB]

            // The UL can signal end of data.
        "TE"    [Half-Closed,GBB]

            // The DL can signal end of data.
(.5)    "DTE"   [GBB]

            // The following commands from the GCS generate protocol errors.
        "HR"    [Half-Closed,BBB]
        "MG"    [Half-Closed,BBB]
        "BR"    [Half-Closed,BBB]
        "FR"    [Half-Closed,BBB]
        "TG"    [Half-Closed,BBB]
        "TGu"   [Half-Closed,BBB]
        "TGd"   [Half-Closed,BBB]
        "TGud"  [Half-Closed,BBB]

            // The following signals are ignored.
        "FSR"   [Half-Closed,GBB]
        "FFR"   [Half-Closed,GBB]
        "OTE"   [Half-Closed,GBB]

// SECOND HALF OF MODEL GOES HERE
// Structure of second half is identical to that of first half, and
   consists of the following states:
// [Mode:None,BGG], [Health Check Pending,BGG], [Checking Health,BGG],
// [Health Check Complete,BGG], [Firing Thrusters,BGG],
// [No Connection,BGG], [UL Connected,BGG], [DL Connected,BGG],
// [Connected,BGG], [Half-Closed,BGG],
// [No Connection,BBG], [UL Connected,BBG], [DL Connected,BBG],
// [Connected,BBG], [Half-Closed,BBG],
// [No Connection,BGB], [UL Connected,BGB], [DL Connected,BGB],
// [Connected,BGB], [Half-Closed,BGB],
// [No Connection,BBB], [UL Connected,BBB], [DL Connected,BBB],
// [Connected,BBB], [Half-Closed,BBB],

// Bookkeeping states.

[GGG]
        "End of Use"    [Software Terminated]

[GBG]
        "End of Use"    [Software Terminated]
```

```
[GGB]
        "End of Use"    [Software Terminated]

[GBB]
        "End of Use"    [Software Terminated]

[BGG]
        "End of Use"    [Software Terminated]

[BBG]
        "End of Use"    [Software Terminated]

[BGB]
        "End of Use"    [Software Terminated]

[BBB]
        "End of Use"    [Software Terminated]

[AGGG]
        "End of Use"    [Software Terminated]

[AGBG]
        "End of Use"    [Software Terminated]

[AGGB]
        "End of Use"    [Software Terminated]

[AGBB]
        "End of Use"    [Software Terminated]

[ABGG]
        "End of Use"    [Software Terminated]

[ABBG]
        "End of Use"    [Software Terminated]

[ABGB]
        "End of Use"    [Software Terminated]

[ABBB]
        "End of Use"    [Software Terminated]
```

16.4 Step 3: Determine State Transition Probabilities

Transition probabilities must be assigned to every arc in the usage model. The model structure can be used with different sets of transition probabilities to make different models. Multiple models will be needed to plan and to conduct testing according to the certification criteria.

The usage model notation shows assigned probabilities in parentheses. The arcs with no probabilities shown have been defaulted to 0.0005. In other words, the model explicitly accounts for 99% of the probability mass of the exit arcs for each state. The controlling probabilities use the following pattern:

```
[No Connection]
(0.495)         "UG"
(0.495)         "DG"

[UL Connected]
(0.990)         "DG"

[DL Connected]
(0.990)         "UG"

[Connected]
(0.010)         "TC"
(0.900)         "DI"
(0.070)         "PB"
(0.010)         "TE"

[Half-Closed]
(0.245)         "DI"
(0.245)         "PB"
(0.500)         "DTE"
```

The probability values shown in the usage model represent the expected use of the system in general field operations. These values were determined by instrumentation of a similar predecessor system.

Different usage models can be generated with this same structure but with different probability values. The directed graph would remain the same but the stochastic matrix would be different. A usage model can also be represented as a system of equations (constraints). A solution to the system of constraints yields the stochastic matrix of the Markov chain.

16.5 Step 4: Validate the Usage Model

The first step in model validation is to examine all the states of use and allowable transitions in terms of tagged requirements for the system. Next, examine requirements in terms of scenarios of use (paths through the model). Then, consider various paths through the model in terms of operational implications for the system.

Analytical calculations on the Markov chain can help to validate the model. All such results describe long-run behavior (i.e., what to expect on average in the long run). For example, the expected sequence length for the model presented above is 55 events. Does this make sense in terms of the application? If not, then the controlling probabilities must be changed. One could set a constraint to determine the expected sequence length and then generate a set of model probabilities that will necessarily satisfy the constraint.

The expected number of test cases (uses) required to cover the least likely state is almost 74 million, and, of course, far more will be required to cover all states in strictly random testing, and even far more will be required to cover all arcs. In this instance, the requirement to visit every state and to experience every transition will not be met through random testing. An efficient way to satisfy the requirements is presented next.

Analytical results for the 12 mainstream states and the 16 bookkeeping states are presented in Table 16.2. Not all states of the model are included in the table. All those not included have a long-run occupancy of less than 0.0001.

Validation of the model should proceed by checking the reasonableness of these long-run results. The bookkeeping states consume 3.64% of the long-run occupancy, which is not enough to distort the picture. More than 94% of the time the system will be in one of the mainstream states: Does this agree with experience? Should the system be in the Connected state 68% of the time? All values should be checked for reasonableness in the application. If they disagree with experience and reason, then the model must be changed.

The bookkeeping states are mutually exclusive, and every test case runs through exactly one of them. A successful test case (no errors of any kind in operation) passes through GGG (36.7% of them) or AGGG (39.5% of them), thus 76.2% of the test cases in long-run random sampling will represent error-free operations. The percentages of uses that will occur in the various strata during general field operations are represented in Table 16.3.

Using the binomial model 2,995 test cases must pass for certification of general field operation, and 60 are needed to certify an error stratum. Thus any stratum getting more than 2% of the traffic should be certified as a consequence of certification for general field operations. It would appear safe to assume that strata 2, 3, and 5 will be so certified. The other error strata will require prior, additional testing.

Table 16.2 Analysis of the SOS usage model

State	Long-run Occupancy	Expected Transitions Until State First Occurs	Probability of Occurrence in a Test Case
Software Not Invoked	0.018195	55	1.000000
Mode: None	0.018295	2	1.000000
Health Check Pending	0.018212	3	0.995475
Checking Health	0.018139	4	0.990971
Health Check Complete	0.018066	5	0.985991
Firing Thrusters	0.000009	110,710	0.000496
No Connection	0.017903	6	0.983007
UL Connected	0.008880	64	0.487319
DL Connected	0.008880	64	0.487319
Connected, BGG	0.141452	273	0.171296
Connected	0.675212	9	0.966342
Half-Closed, BGG	0.002926	677	0.080800
Half-Closed	0.013351	144	0.371669
GGG	0.006682	148	0.367262
GGB	0.000728	1,372	0.040015
GBG	0.000392	2,550	0.021544
GBB	0.000012	85,564	0.000642
BGG	0.001464	681	0.080478
BGB	0.000147	6,799	0.008082
BBG	0.000075	13,378	0.004108
BBB	0.000001	1,936,574	0.000028
AGGG	0.007186	138	0.394946
AGGB	0.000005	206,648	0.000266
AGBG	0.000007	139,800	0.000393
AGBB	<0.000001	4,564,512	0.000012
ABGG	0.001492	669	0.081978
ABGB	0.000003	345,155	0.000159
ABBG	0.000002	652,418	0.000084
ABBB	<0.000001	23,595,426	0.000002
Software Terminated	0.018194	54	1.000000

Table 16.3   Expected use versus strata

Stratum	Bookkeeping States		Percent Use
1	GGG	AGGG	76.22%
2	GGB	AGGB	4.03%
3	GBG	AGBG	2.19%
4	GBB	AGBB	0.07%
5	BGG	ABGG	16.28%
6	BGB	ABGB	0.82%
7	BBG	ABBG	0.42%
8	BBB	ABBB	0.003%

16.6 Step 5: Generate Test Cases, and Execute and Evaluate Results

Because of the certification requirement that the product will not be accepted with a known error, and because of the high degree of reliability required, the cost of a failure (in terms of additional testing) after random testing has begun will be very expensive. Consequently, a testing protocol will be followed that will minimize this possibility. Under less stringent certification requirements, a different protocol might be followed.

16.6.1 Model Coverage

A graph algorithm was used to generate the "least cost" set of scripts to experience each transition at least one time. Performing this test will ensure that the testers know how to recognize and to evaluate each state of use, and to experience and to evaluate each transition. Because this is a graph algorithm, multiple arcs between two states are recognized and all will be covered.

Because arc coverage is achieved by "walking the graph," each state and arc is reached in a legitimate scenario of use of the system. This means that some states and arcs will be visited many times before every arc has been visited at least once. If the cost of conducting and evaluating each arc test differs from arc to arc, this cost can be taken into account so that arc coverage will be achieved at the least cost of testing. Using unit costs on the arcs, the least cost coverage test consists of 332 test cases with a total of 3,679 transitions and state visitations. (These are obviously atypical because the long-run average random test case length is about 55 transitions, which would imply more than 18,000 transitions.) A copy of the usage model structure can be marked to show exactly the paths taken.

If failures are seen during model coverage testing, the test engineers will have to decide when to stop testing and when to order engineering changes to the code. Find-one-fix-one is the safest policy, but is often too time-consuming and expensive to be followed. Ideally, the model coverage scripts should be repeated until they are run without failure.

16.6.2 Requirements Coverage

Each canonical sequence is a use case that should be run. These sequences will exercise the mathematically essential control state, regardless of how the system is implemented. It is likely that the model coverage scripts will have actually covered some of the canonical sequences and, if so, they need not be run again. If any failures occur, engineering changes should be made and testing repeated until the canonical sequences run failure free.

Each requirement can now be checked against testing already done. If a test case for a requirement has not already been run, a suitable test case can be traced on the model, produced, and executed on the system.

Any additional testing that results from requirements coverage should be recorded on the usage model to update the testing record and to show the paths taken and the number of times each state and arc have been visited.

16.6.3 SOS Error Strata

Four of the seven error strata must be tested using test cases generated randomly from the model to satisfy the certification criteria. To demonstrate a reliability in excess of 0.95 with 95% confidence, 60 randomly generated test scripts must be run without failure. (This is using the binomial model; other models are possible. The purpose of the case study is to illustrate general technique, rather than advocate any particular models.) If a failure occurs, then additional analysis is necessary.

A model to generate test cases for stratum 8, [BBB] and [GBBB], could be realized in two ways. One could alter the structure of the SOS usage model by working backward from the bookkeeping states and deleting arcs and states that cannot lead to these two to produce a new model. Alternatively, one could add a new constraint, that bookkeeping state [BBB] appears in 100% of the test cases, to all other constraints on arc probabilities, and solve the system of equations. The solution variables would be the cells in the stochastic matrix of a Markov chain usage model suitable for this test. This will be a submodel of the full usage model.

There will be four such submodels, one for each error stratum requiring additional testing. Testing of the error strata should be done in the following order: stratum 8, run 60 test cases; stratum 4, run 58 test cases; stratum 7, run 48 test cases; and stratum 6, run 36 test cases. This plan is based on expected, average results from sampling. As mentioned, if a failure is seen, additional analysis will be necessary, and generally more tests must be run (successfully) to wash out the bad news of the failure.

16.6.4   General Field Operations

This is the final phase of testing and is based on the full usage model. Using the binomial model to demonstrate that the system exceeds a reliability of 0.999 with 95% confidence, it will be necessary to run 2,995 randomly generated sequences without failure. This amount of testing, following the error strata testing, is expected to satisfy both certification goals regarding reliability and confidence. If the sampling does not conform to the expectations, supplemental sampling in the error strata will be necessary. Again, all testing experience should be recorded on the model. The cumulative test history can be seen in terms of paths taken, and the number of times each state is visited and each arc is taken. The cumulative testing history can be compared with the usage model using the discriminant as testing progresses to measure the degree to which the testing experience differs from expected general field operations.

Index